Creativity Fourteen

14

A Photographic Review Edited By Don Barron

ART DIRECTION BOOK COMPANY New York, N.Y. 10016

Advertising Directions, Volume 18

Designed by Al Lichtenberg

Copyright © 1985 Art Direction Book Company
10 East 39th Street, New York, N.Y. 10016
All rights reserved

ISBN: 0-88108-022-5
ISBN for Creativity Annuals Standing Orders: 0-910158-10-X
Library of Congress Catalog Card #74-168254

Printed in Japan

Distributors:
USA and Canada: Art Direction Book Company
Foreign Distributor: Fleetbooks c/o Feffer & Simons, Inc.
                         100 Park Avenue, New York, N.Y. 10017

Contents

Publisher's Statement

A Cross Section of Creativity 14 in Color

PRINT

TELEVISION / FILM

SPECIAL CREATIVE ACHIEVEMENT

Creativity Fourteen

. . .The Art Director is the genre artist of our time. His talent is the eye and mind for the contemporary scene and his skill the ability to depict his client's product in terms of the immediate moment.

FROM THE ANNOUNCEMENT FOR THE FIRST CREATIVITY SHOW, 1970

In a sense, Creativity 14 was like its predecessor, a fusion of opposites that was both perplexing and exhilarating. It reflected yet another year of the "parade of one," in which nearly everybody was free to art-direct in virtually any style they chose. But it also mirrored a number of signs that anything-goes art-directing may have finally reached its zenith. An emerging set of vague standards — admittedly subtle and unspoken — continues to exert a quiet influence on the entire field of advertising design. And though it's easy enough to debunk any notion of standards as nothing more than one critic's particular fantasy, careful study of the following pages might convince you otherwise. For you'll see a quality of professionalism that's been absent from award shows for many years.

•　　　•　　　•

Note, however, how the standards vary. Annual Reports, Letterheads, and Brochures & Booklets continue to be the most demanding categories, and the latter deserve particular mention. Brochures & Booklets have improved measurably year after year, often so much it was hard to believe further strides were possible. But this year's entries were once again a marvel of design and execution. Concept, choice of type, paper and color were just plain superb.

•　　•　　•

Record Album Covers made a beautiful about-face and most certainly reflected better business conditions in this field. The entries displayed vast improvement; they were innovative, thoughtfully conceived and well done.

•　　•　　•

Book Jackets was another category that showed decided improvement. Art Directors here used type, illustration and photography with style and taste to come up with a large number of award winning entries.

•　　•　　•

The ups and downs of packaging design over the years makes this category work worth discussing in some detail. It was a great category to judge when the Creativity Show started in the early 1970s. The entries were imaginative and good work was evident for an extremely wide range of products. Then something happened; it seemed to fall apart. The entries began to imitate each other; color diminished to black and everything looked like it had been "created" (?) on a production line. The decline continued year after year until one wondered if there would ever be a turnaround. Still, the judges felt clients would one day be forced to invest a little extra money to get something special. In this show, that something happened. Without any advance notice, the number of good entries jumped and it was great to do this category again. It is a mystery why and howcome the switches take place, but they do turn judging a Creativity Show into one large window looking out on the entire field of advertising design.

•　　•　　•

This was another good year for Posters. They are now strong, positively motivated. However, Editorial Design and Magazine Covers fell back. Trade-paper advertising, which had been maintaining an edge over Consumer Advertising, also declined. Type treatments of both headline and body text just didn't have the zing of past years.

•　　•　　•

This was a good year for Consumer Advertising. The use of a complete page or spread halftone with the type dropped out has declined. We are now seeing innovative uses of white space and borders. Body copy and headlines are being intelligently placed to good effect. Photo work seems stronger, clearer, sharper. Art and illustration are now definitely part of the scene, although there is no clear support for one art style over another.

· · ·

More than half the Television Commercials selected used the "real people" approach and most of those were amusing rather than straight hard-sell. The photography continues to improve. Color is more subtle and actors have shed their theatrical makeup. Naturalness is the operative word. Another, smaller, group went with the New Wave approach-more fantasy, wilder imagination were their means of getting viewers' attention. In total, the TVCs were engrossing to watch and when our audiences saw them, they reacted the way the advertisers would wish.

· · ·

Radio turned to comedy for some of its strongest spots this year. There were well produced musical numbers and a few 'straight' pitches, but the standouts were knee-slappers, often in the form of dialogues. What passes for humor in TV and Print could take a page from some of the fresh concepts heard here.

· · ·

Unlike many past Creativity Shows in which the various design categories seemingly marched off rather independently of each other, this Show appeared to present a much more coherent body of work. Agency, Editorial and Collateral Art Directors and Designers seemed to be more aware of each other's work than has been true for a good many years.

· · ·

Perhaps this is what persuaded the judges to guess that "parade of one" art directing just may be nearing its end. But there was no agreement whatsoever whether this development, should it continue, bodes good or bad.

· · ·

As noted earlier, it was the high quality of professionalism throughout the Show that seemed to be the unifying influence. Art Directors created more work more to sell products and services than to sell themselves.

· · ·

S HOT, IT'S HERE, IT'S FIERO!

w away those old maps. Pontiac just paved a
 road to driving excitement.
ero is an all-new kind of car. Designed and
 to be exhilarating to drive, yet easy to own.
id-engine design and balanced weight
ribution give Fiero an amazing command
e road. And its innovative high-strength
ce frame chassis is wrapped with a beautifully
rodynamic Enduraflex™ body that resists
or dents and will never rust.
ero's standard equipment makes serious
dwork a distinct pleasure: A fully independent
suspension that keeps it glued to the road.
4-wheel disc brakes that pull it down from speed
quickly. Rack and pinion steering that delivers
precise road feel and directional control. A
quick-shifting manual transmission. Bolstered,
body-contoured bucket seats. Full instrumen-
tation. And an electronically fuel injected 2.5 liter
engine that gives instant throttle response and
outstanding mileage.*

The totally new Fiero, America's first and only
mid-engine production car.

Only at your Pontiac dealer.

PONTIAC ▼ WE BUILD EXCITEMENT

EXCITEMENT AHEAD

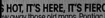

*Pontiac Fiero Sport Coupe with available automatic transmission offers an EPA EST MPG of 27 and a highway estimate of 40.
Use estimated MPG for comparisons. Your mileage may differ depending on speed, distance, weather. Actual highway
mileage lower. Some Pontiacs are equipped with engines produced by other GM divisions, subsidiaries, or affiliated
companies worldwide. See your Pontiac dealer for details.

31
David Bence, Greg Moy, David Carnegie Art Directors
Noel Nauber Creative Director
Ron Strong Photographer
Walt Trussell, Les Hardy Illustrators
McNamara & Associates Studio
D'Arcy MacManus Masius Agency
Pontiac Motor Division Client

Dine on England's most beautiful border.

Never has a pattern captured more of England's country splendor, more of the charm that enhances any meal, from the simple to the sophisticated. It's Lancaster, the setting never out of place. Suggested retail prices: 5-piece place setting, $50; crystal, $33.75 to $46.25 a set of four; accessories and giftware, $7.25 to $116. Wedgwood, 41 Madison Avenue, New York 10010.

Fine English Ironstone by Adams® for
Wedgwood

MEETINGS & CONVENTIONS

SECTION 2

Arizona Brazil Cocktails Duty-free shops Entertainment France Germany Hawaii Ireland Japan Kenya Las Vegas Mexico Nice Oslo Puerto Rico Queen Elizabeth II (Cruise Ship) Resorts Incentive Travel from A to Z Safari Tahiti United Kingdom Venice Wind Surfing Xianzen (China) Yugoslavia Zanzibar

129

Debra Johnston Art Director
Connie Hansen Photographer
Candace Whitman Copywriter
J. Walter Thompson Agency
Wedgwood Client
New York NY

1001

Lee Ann Jaffee Art Director
Tim Girvin Illustrator
MEETINGS & CONVENTIONS Magazine
    Ziff-Davis Publishing Company Client
New York NY

982

Alain Evrard Photographer
Kan Tai-keung, Freeman Lau Siu-hong Designers
SS Design & Production Agency
The Mandarin International Hotels Limited Client
Hong Kong

791

Barbara Solowan Art Director/Designer
Nigel Dickson Photographer
Shirley Gregory Fashion Editor
CITY WOMAN Magazine—
        Comac Communications Ltd. Client
Toronto, Canada

917

Matthew Imperiale Illustrator
Bruce Crocker Art Director/Designer
Altman+Manley Agency
Sweet Micro Systems Client
Cambridge MA

REVEL WITHOUT A PAUSE

Ah, champagne…the eternal lubricant that washes over all sorts of differences, including peculiar friends of varying income, sexuality, height, age, occupation and pretence. Under the tent, all are equal: The Mafioso feasts chockablock with the occasional member of the horsey set; the dissipated writer chats up the hired help; the social columnist writes up the movie star; and the matron looks through her lorgnette onto a table groaning with the weight of so much of the bride's dowry and so little of the groom's. Yes, something's fishy here. No matter, our young husband and older but wiser bride will soon be off on a second honeymoon filled with great, though not necessarily similar, expectations.

The bride looks elegant in a cream silk lace and sequin gown with cape collar, by Rina di Montella. The bridesmaids are stunning in strapless red-silk taffeta gowns by Winston; both are extravagantly flounced—one has a ring of ruffles around the chandliers, the other, triangular petals to the waist. The society columnist interviewing the movie star has chosen a three-piece Alfred Sung ensemble: the navy-and-cream print blouse and shirt are silk; the short boxy jacket is a cream silk blend to set off by a matching silk scarf threaded through epaulettes. The hostess wears Wayne Clark's white chiffon dress with a long satin woven scarf. Great Aunt Peg looks regal in Edith Strauss's royal blue crepe de chine tiered dress trimmed with bugle beads. Young Samantha's cream lace dress by Elen Henderson has a pretty pink hip sash. The groom sports a three-piece tuxedo by Giorgio Armani from Alan Cherry. Bow tie, Turnbull & Asser. Flamboyant Stan, the movie star, makes a bold statement in a yellow, navy and white outfit from Classics Ewans. The bearded director wears a jacket and shirt from Brown's Shoe Man, riding breeches, boots and long from Ehrlich's Harness & Saddlery, and a silk ascot from Turnbull & Asser. The gangster and his young son are immaculate in matching pinstripe suits by Halpern's Boys' and Men's Clothiers. The Truman Capote clone wears a cream suit by Dior and accessories from Brown's Street Man. The gigolo's outfit is from Classy Formal Wear. The rock star adds a dash of color to his Classics Ewans tuxedo with a red silk tie and cummerbund from Harry Rosen.

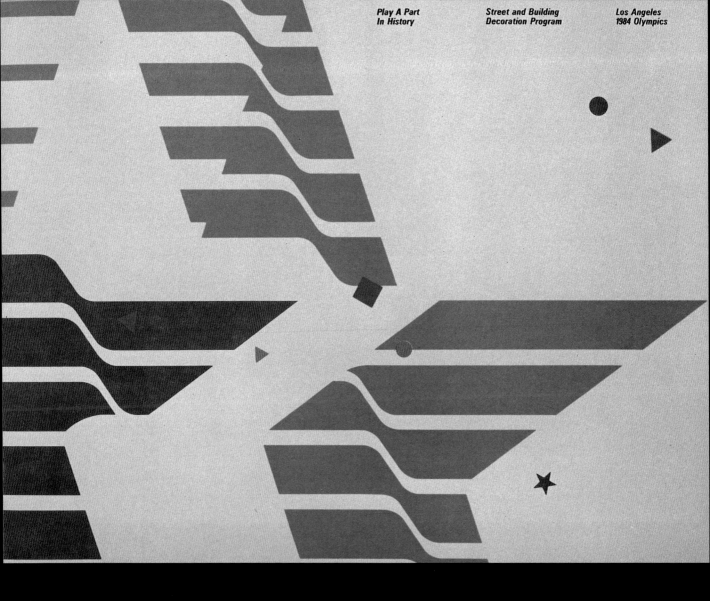

Play A Part
In History

Street and Building
Decoration Program

Los Angeles
1984 Olympics

665
Hinsche + Associates Design/Illustration
Hinsche + Associates Studio
Los Angeles Olympic Committee Client
Santa Monica CA

YOU CAN'T BE IN FASHION IF YOUR SHOES AIN'T SMASHIN'.

HipOppo'Tamus®
by Internor Trade Inc.

It pays to be in his shoes.
Suede moccasin softies
for only $36.

Hipoppotamus® by Internor Trade Inc., 1230 Avenue of the Americas, N.Y. 10020.
Shown: "Robin Hood II" in ombre multi, bright multi, plum, forest green, navy, camel.

Bob McGrath Art Director/Designer
Derik Murray Photographer
Diane Lund Copywriter
Simons Advertising Ltd. Agency
Slicko Studio Studio
Canada Safeway Ltd. Client
Vancouver, Canada

Allen Weinberg Art Director/Designer
CBS Records Client
New York NY

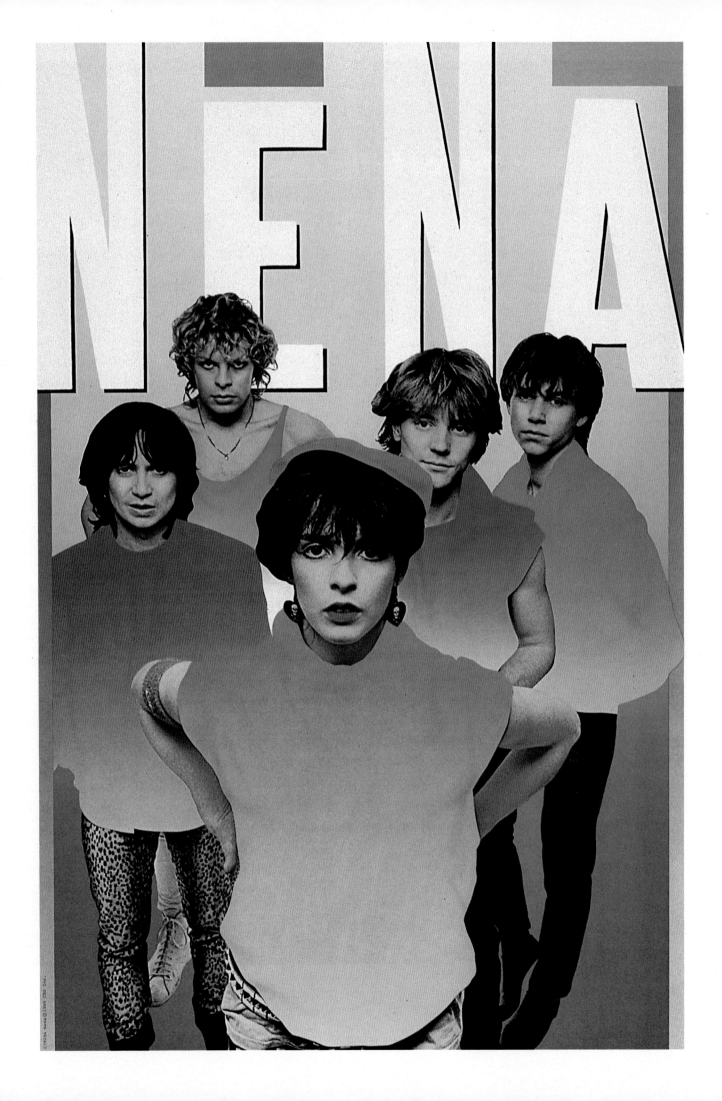

Take the red to the green.

AVIS

The House Love Built.

Ronald McDonald House

A "home away from home" for parents of children hospitalized at Toledo area hospitals. For further information call 419-472-1120 or write the Ronald McDonald House of Northwest Ohio, 3883 Monroe Street, Toledo, Ohio 43606.

967
Gregory Thorp Photographer
Thomas E. Hawley Art Director/Designer
OHIO Magazine Client
Columbus OH

"The suspension bridge seems eternal like the hills that ring the central city or the Ohio River itself."

BEN ROSENTHAL

722
Cheryl Lewin Art Director/Designer
Ben Rosenthal Photographer
Cheryl Lewin Design Studio
Graphique de France Client
New York NY

The Exceptional Child

A FUNCTIONAL APPROACH

ROBERT M. SMITH
JOHN T. NEISWORTH
FRANCES M. HUNT

235
Nicholas Krenitsky Art Director/Designer
Annette Shaw Photographer
McGraw-Hill Book Company Client
New York NY

MAKEUP

with staying power

Whether you're heading to work or a night out, playing sports or sunbathing, you want makeup that'll stay put, that won't let you down. Here, tips and tricks for makeup you can count on—hour after beautiful hour

986
Laurie Simmons Photographer
Paula Greif Art Director
Julia Gorton Designer
MADEMOISELLE Magazine—Conde Nast Client
New York NY

HAMMERMILL
PRESENTS THE EXTRAORDINARY...

57
David Zahner Photographer
Lisandro Sarasola Client
New York NY

61
Bryan Forman Art Director
Eric Meola Photographer
Charlie Breen Copywriter
Backer & Spielvogel, Inc. Agency
The Paddington Corporation Client
New York NY

141
D. Hovhannesian, R. Richert Art Directors
Terry Scullin Copywriter
F. Robert Fuller Account Supervisor
Hammerhill Papers Group Client
New York NY

Recycling Illinois Paper Resources

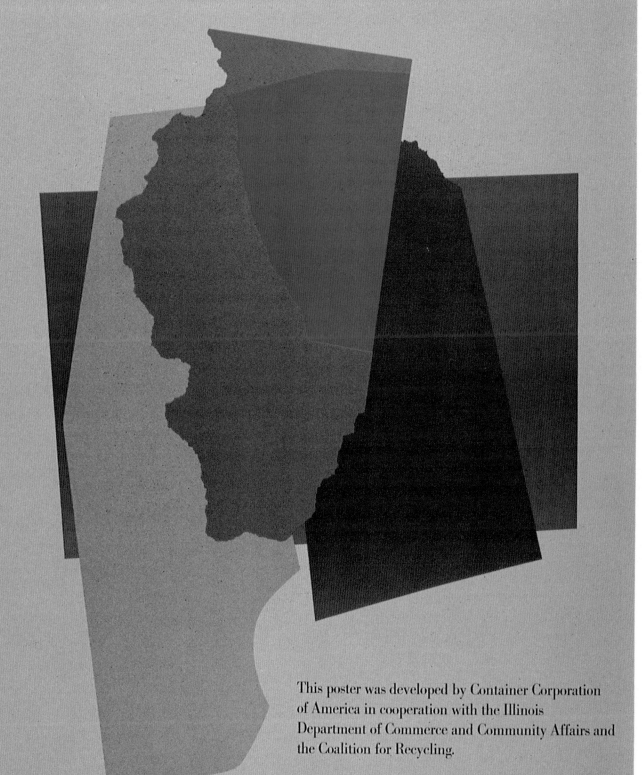

This poster was developed by Container Corporation of America in cooperation with the Illinois Department of Commerce and Community Affairs and the Coalition for Recycling.

Illinois

For more information, call 217 785-2264.

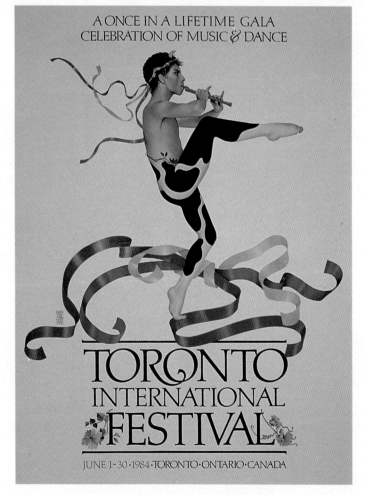

A ONCE IN A LIFETIME GALA
CELEBRATION OF MUSIC & DANCE

TORONTO
INTERNATIONAL
FESTIVAL

JUNE 1-30·1984·TORONTO·ONTARIO·CANADA

966
Roger Lantaff Photographer/Client
Langley WA

302
Heather Cooper Designer/Illustrator
Burns, Cooper, Hynes Ltd. Studio
Herzig-Sommerville Ltd. Printer
Toronto International Festival Client
Toronto, Canada

SERVUS BOOTS. MORE VALUE IN THE LINE OF FIRE.

Sitting around the station, things can get, well, pretty relaxed. But when the bell sounds and you grab your bunker pants, being a firefighter becomes a different matter. That's why you need Servus boots. Recognized for years as the finest boot manufacturer in the fire industry, we strive to live up to that reputation. We use only the highest quality materials to insure strength and durability. And we're just as concerned with comfort. That's why we design our boots with extra thick layers of foam and cork,

for insulation and shock absorption. And only in Servus boots can you find "protekshin", a patented built-in shin guard to absorb and distribute damaging blows and ladder lock pressures. But all these extras don't cost extra. Check our price. You'll see that it is possible to get quality and value in the line of fire. Then get a pair of Servus boots. And relax. Servus Rubber Company, Inc., 1136 2nd Street, Box 36, 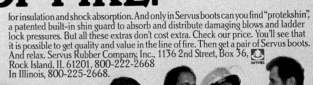 Rock Island, IL 61201, 800-222-2668 In Illinois, 800-225-2668.

143

Billy Wilkins Art Director/Designer
Bill Barley Photographer
Cathy Rigg Copywriter
Wilkins and Associates Agency
Servus Rubber Company Client
Columbia SC

500

David Coven Art Director/Illustrator
Don Snyder Photographer
Leadworks, In-House Studio
Leadworks, Inc. Client
Beachwood OH

Straw Hat Spring/Summer 1984 Advertising: Appearing in

The promise of an endless summer. Straw Hat

Cologne by Fabergé.

985
Barbara Bordnick Photographer
Irwin Goldberg Art Director/Designer
Nadler & Larimer, Inc. Agency
Faberge Client
New York NY

, Cosmopolitan, Good Housekeeping and Woman's Day.

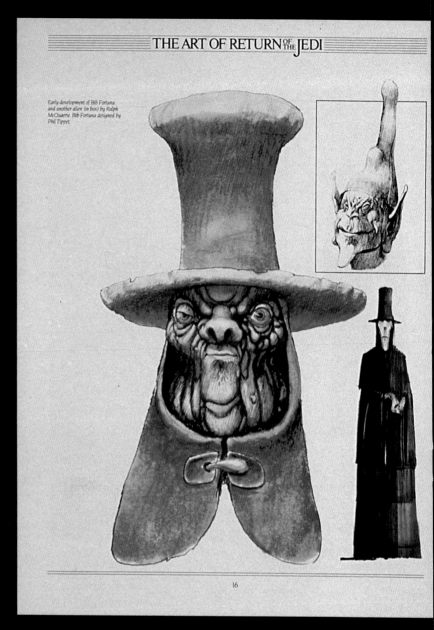

Early development of Bib Fortuna
and another alien (in box) by Ralph
McQuarrie. Bib Fortuna designed by
Phil Tippet.

16

804
Sylvain Michaelis Art Director/Designer
Michaelis/Carpelis Design Assoc. Studio
Fred Dodnick Production
Ballantyne Books Client
New York NY

948
Steven Guarnaccia Illustrator
Robert Manley Art Director
Altman + Manley Agency
Multigroup Health Plan Client
Cambridge MA

Bib costumes designed by Aage Gurand Rodgers and Nilo Rodis-Jamero. Drawn by Nilo Rodis-Jamero

17

465
Millie Falcaro, Mary Tiegreen Designers
Falcaro & Tiegreen Ltd. Studio/Client
New York NY

SQUIBBLINE

Winter 1904

868
Jim Greenwood Art Director
Joey Reiman, B.A. Albert Creative Directors
David Marinaccio Copywriter
D'Arcy MacManus Masius, Atlanta Agency
CHARLEX, New York Production
Dairmen, Inc. Client
Atlanta GA

290
Anthony Russell Art Director
Kevin McPhee Designer
Eric Sauter Editor
Squibb Corporation Client
New York NY

383
Larry Jennings Art Director/Designer
Charles Collum, Albert Watson Photographers
Vivien Flesher Illustrator
Macy's New York Client
New York NY

Some of us have more finely developed nesting instincts than others.

Karastan Rug Mills, a Division of Fieldcrest Mills, Inc.

INVEST IN *Karastan*

The truck stops here.

BOAR'S HEAD BRAND

PROVISIONS

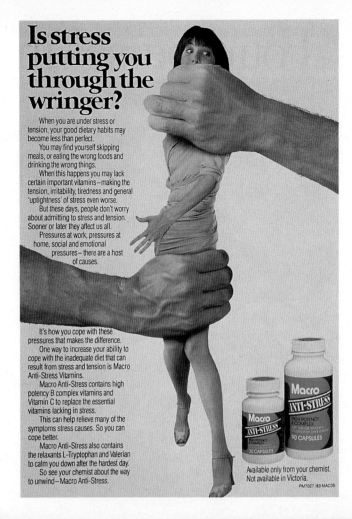

404
Milton Glaser Art Director
Karen Skelton Designer
Jim McMullan Illustrator
Seth McCormack, Jean Claude Comert Copywriters
Milton Glaser, Inc. Studio
Schlumberger Limited Client
New York NY

PRINT

Consumer

SINGLE UNIT

1

Charles Guarino Art Director/Designer
Andrew Unangst Photographer
Diana Kramer Copywriter
Warwick Advertising Inc. Agency
Calvert Distillers Client
New York NY

2

Mike Rizzo Art Director/Designer
Jim Hyman Creative Director
Paul Giovanopoulos Illustrator
Chuck Rudnick Copywriter
Marsteller Inc. Agency
Dow Corning Client
Chicago IL

The new QT range of portable stereo radio and cassette players from about £40 to £180. Just the sounds you've been praying for **SHARP**

Wasabrød er rikt på fiber fordi det er bakt av hele kornet waša

*W*hen Moses Phillips came to America
and started selling shirts to coal miners,
he never dreamed how far he would go.

Moses Phillips
Annual Sales, 1881 . . . . *About $250.*

Phillips-Van Heusen Corporation
Annual Sales, 1983 . . . *Over $505,000,000.*

3
Lyn Cushing Art Director
Roy Botterell Photographer
Katy Pollitt Copywriter
Ayer Barker Ltd. Agency
Square 1 Studio
Sharp Electronics Client
London. England

4
Jack Hagbru Art Director
Christina Wigren Illustrator
Frode Karlberg Copywriter
ide reklame & marketing/AB Bates Agency
Wasa Crispbread Client
Oslo. Norway

5
Irwin Goldberg Art Director/Designer
Evan Stark Copywriter
Nadler & Larimer, Inc. Agency
Phillips-Van Heusen Corp. Client
New York NY

6
Frederick H. Myers Art Director/Designer
John Vallini Photographer
Grey Advertising Inc. Agency
ABC Movies for Television Client
New York NY

ANN-MARGRET And TREAT WILLIAMS Star In The TENNESSEE WILLIAMS Masterpiece
A STREETCAR NAMED DESIRE Starring BEVERLY D'ANGELO And RANDY QUAID
Teleplay by TENNESSEE WILLIAMS Adaptation by OSCAR SAUL Directed by JOHN ERMAN
An ABC Theater Presentation Sunday March 4   ABC Television Network ⓐⓑⓒ

Dress Lori Haggis, Tuxedo Piero D'Mtn for D'Mtn Couture Ltd.

If you've ever left a concert dressed up and dignified, then found yourself night-crawling the naughty side of town, there's a new experience awaiting. JAZ Paris. French design with so much style even one is a wardrobe.

JAZ PARIS *The watch that turned quartz into fashion.*

7
Bruce Bloch Art Director/Designer
Chris Callis, Doug Fraser Photographers
Carol Tudor Copywriter
A C & R Advertising Agency
JAZ Paris Client
New York NY

8
Noel Frankel Art Director/Designer
Steve Steigman Photographer
Beber Silverstein & Partners Agency
Empire State Observatory Client
New York NY

9
Harlen Fleming Art Director/Copywriter
William Paul Creative Director
Howard Bjornson Photographer
Menaker & Wright Agency
Medley Distilling Co. Client
Chicago IL

10
John Garbarini Art Director/Photographer
Norman Ferber Copywriter
Designers Furniture Center Client
New York NY

11
Stephen Megargee Art Director/Designer
Scott Griswold, Jr. Photographer
Wild Oats Client
Ocean City NJ

12
Mike Soper Art Director/Designer
Mike Phillips Creative Director
Bob Ebel Photographer
Mike Marn Copywriter
Marsteller Inc. Agency
Beatrice Companies, Inc. Client
Chicago IL

5 states on $2.75 a day.

The Empire State Observatory offers more than the sights of New York. For the price of admission, you get four neighboring states in the bargain. On a clear day, see the Jersey shore, the Pennsylvania Poconos, and the lakes of Connecticut and Massachusetts, shimmering in the noonday sun. For $2.75 a day, you'll tour the countryside. And never set foot out of Manhattan.

Empire State Observatory

In the heart of midtown Manhattan at Fifth Avenue & 34th Street.
Open daily from 9:30 AM to midnight. To check visibility call, 736-3100.

Good Old Ezra.

Our Chairs are really straight...

from Italy...

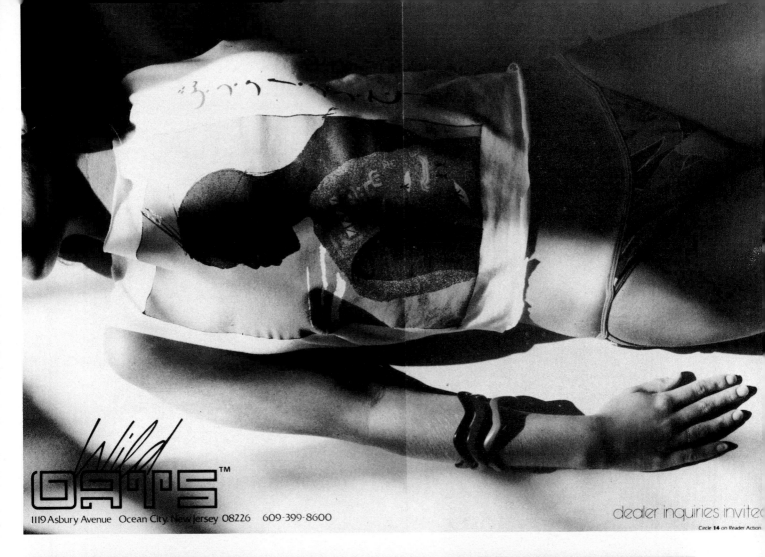

CELEBRATING FIFTY YEARS OF BRIDES AT CARSONS! The 1984 bride knows her wedding will flow smoothly if it's put in the capable hands of Carsons Wedding Services. For fifty years, ever since 1934, Carsons has had a Joan Adair Wedding Consultant to attend to the bride's every wish, from selecting her gown and those of her attendants, to every last detail of flowers and wedding etiquette. (She'll even go to the ceremony with you.) To let everyone know what you want and need, and to make life easier for your wedding guests, register at Carsons Wedding Gift Service as soon as you announce your engagement. You'll live happier ever after. Carson Pirie Scott & Co., Chicago; Edens, Evergreen, Lakehurst, Lincoln Mall, Marquette Mall, North Riverside, Orland Square, Randhurst, Southlake Mall, Stratford Square, Woodmar, Yorktown.

13
Valerie Hacias Alessi Art Director
Shirley Ross, Valerie Alessi Designers
David Puffer Photographer
Joan Carney Copywriter
Carson Pirie Scott Agency/Client
Chicago IL

14
Hilton Gottschall Art Director/Designer
Rick Strauss Photographer
Joe Alexander Copywriter
Dayton's In-House Production
Dayton's Client
Minneapolis MN

15
Bruno Brugnatelli Art Director/Designer
Dick Frank Photographer
Hy Abady Copywriter
Sullivan & Brugnatelli Agency
Reader's Digest Software Client
New York NY

READER'S DIGEST INTRODUCES SOFTWARE GOOD ENOUGH TO GO OUT AND BUY A COMPUTER FOR.

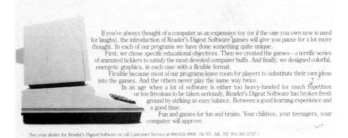

If you've always thought of a computer as an expensive toy (or if the one you own now is used for laughs), the introduction of Reader's Digest Software games will give you pause for a lot more thought. In each of our programs we have done something quite unique.

First, we chose specific educational objectives. Then we created the games – a terrific series of animated ticklers to satisfy the most devoted computer buffs. And finally, we designed colorful, energetic graphics, in each case with a flexible format.

Flexible because most of our programs leave room for players to substitute their own ideas into the games. And the others never play the same way twice.

In an age when a lot of software is either too heavy-handed for much repetition or too frivolous to be taken seriously, Reader's Digest Software has broken fresh ground by striking an easy balance. Between a good learning experience and a good time.

Fun and games for fun and brains. Your children, your teenagers, your computer will approve.

See your dealer for Reader's Digest Software or call Customer Service at 800/431-8800. (In NY, AK, HI: 914/241-5727.)

THE WRIGHT BROTHERS WEREN'T THE FIRST TO FLY.
THEY WERE JUST THE FIRST NOT TO CRASH.

20
John Buckley Art Director
Greg Karraker Creative Director
Friend, Denny Photographers
Steve Goldstein Copywriter
D'Arcy MacManus Masius—San Francisco Agency
Priam Corporation Client
San Francisco CA

Nöjesresan kan bli en god affär.

21
Ann Bodlund Art Director/Designer
Lars-Gunnar Nilsson Copywriter
HLR/BBDO Agency
Globetrotter Client
Stockholm, Sweden

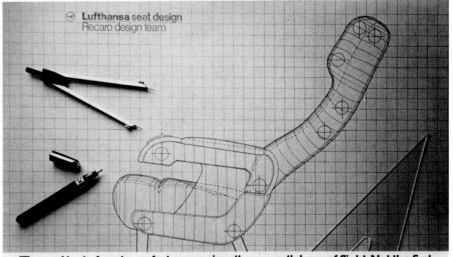

The real test of seat comfort comes in   the seventh hour of flight. Not the first.

22
Peter Barba Art Director
Gary Perweiler Photographer
McCann Ericson Agency
Perweiler Studio
Lufthansa Client
New York NY

The BMW Anti-lock Braking System. The difference between life and death.

Speed: 100 km/h. Road surface: lethal. Instinctive response: hard braking into a tight corner. Result: in any other car you'd be totally out of control.

Deep beneath the bonnet of the BMW 7-Series range is a computer controlled electronic brain which could spell the difference between life and death in what would normally be an uncontrollable situation.

This is the BMW Anti-lock Braking System (ABS). A masterpiece of technology controlled by sensors on each of the car's wheels, pulsing the brakes for a fraction of a second to prevent the wheels from locking and the car from skidding under emergency braking.

The car, furthermore, remains fully controllable. Even to the extent of manoeuvering it around obstacles whilst braking hard whether on a wet highway or a dirt road.

Geoff Dalglish of Star Motoring writes: "Braking as hard as possible, I was able to steer the car without any loss of control" and adds "again and again I tried to defeat the system in the wet and dry to no avail".

The BMW 7-Series. The only South African cars with ABS.

BMW's revolutionary ABS is now standard equipment on the new 7-Series range, from the 745i through to the 728i Executive. It's the ABS together with other of the world's most technologically advanced safety features, that make the 7-Series the safest range of cars on the road. And in a country with one of the highest accident rates in the world, the safest place on the road is inside a BMW.

If you'd like to discover more about the Anti-lock Braking System, test stop a BMW 7-Series at your nearest BMW dealer.

BMW 745i, 735i, 733i, 728i.

Sheer driving pleasure

GREY PHILLIPS, BUNTON, MUNDEL & BLAKE 72962

INTRODUCING *Mufich Designs*
Each pair individually hand painted.
Available at fine stores.

Mufich Designs
Hand painted Originals

Mufich Designs P.O. Box 2568   Shawnee Mission, Kansas 66201   913-677-2836

The ultimate satisfaction.
Dunhill. The finest cigarette in the world.
London · Paris · New York

DUNHILL
KING SIZE
The name Dunhill is the registered trade mark
of Alfred Dunhill Ltd. London
25
London·Paris·New York

25

Beth Schack Art Director/Designer
Herb Gorgoglione Photographer
Joanne Palmer Copywriter
SEVENTEEN Magazine Promotion Agency
Mufich Designs™ Client
New York NY

26

Ron Cockcroft, Bruce McBain
     Art Directors/Creative Directors
Will Davies Illustrator
Doug Moen Copywriter
Hayhurst Advertising Ltd. Agency
Rothmans of Pall Mall Canada Ltd. Client
Toronto, Canada

27

Rebecca Wong Young Creative Director
Charles Tracy Photographer
Phyllis Kutz Copy Chief
Saks Fifth Avenue (In-House) Agency
Saks Fifth Avenue Client
New York NY

23

Julie L. Greenfield Art Director
Irving Penn Photographer
Clinique Labs Inc. (In-House) Agency
Clinique Labs Inc. Client
New York NY

24

Johann Hoekstra Art Director/Designer
Georgina Karvellas Photographer
Jonathan Harries Copywriter
Grey Phillips, Bunton, Mundel/Blake Agency
BMW S.A. (Pty) Ltd. Client
Johannesburg, RSA

Saks Fifth Avenue today sees Jag as the commanding officer on duty in the world of rigorous modern fashion...for they've designed some khaki cottons that are class A uniforms for Spring/Summer 1984. The twill pants, sizes 4 to 12; $40. The zip-front jacket that snaps and buckles at the waist. Sizes S,M,L; $74. And the short-sleeved cadet shirt with tie; sizes S,M,L; $36. Everything—from the tie of the shirt to the taping running down the sides of the 5-pocket pants—is 100% khaki; 100% cotton. Find them now in 'SFAntastic Sportswear Collections, Fifth Floor. At ease! Dismissed?

SSAToday

Carats for Christmas

TIFFANY & CO.

"Close Relationships" by Ron Chereskin, February 1984
One in a series by Ron Chereskin, the American artist/designer who brings a fresh new meaning to words like color, texture and pattern in clothes for the American woman.   Collect Chereskins at fine stores everywhere.

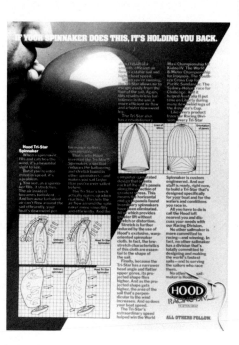

32
Valerie Hacias Alessi Art Director
Mary Rakovic, Valerie Alessi Designers
Joan Carney Copywriter
Carson Pirie Scott Agency/Client
Chicago IL

33
Paul Tanck Art Director/Designer
Nancy Andrews Photographer
Britt Ehringer Illustrator
Paul Tanck Design Studio
FLIP of Hollywood Client
Venice CA

34
Bob Kasper Art Director/Designer
Myron Photographer
John Burgoyne Illustrator
Tom Pedulla Copywriter
HBM/MacDonald Agency
Hood Sailmakers Client
Boston MA

35
Tborjorn Lindgren Art Director
Stefan Anderson, Guide Hildebrand, Andre Rau, Gilles Tapie, Michelle Wirth Photographers
Mats Gustavsson Illustrator
HLR/BBDO Agency
AB Nordiska Kompaniet Client
Stockholm. Sweden

36
Darrell Wilks Art Director/Designer
Bernard Owett Creative Director
Georg I. Parrish, Jr. Illustrator
Larry Volpi Copywriter
J. Walter THompson Agency
Samsonite Client
New York NY

37
Dale Calvert Art Director/Designer
Jerry Comann Creative Director
Graham French Photographer
Loretta Schurr Copywriter
Muller, Joran, Weiss Agency
Monsanto Client
New York NY

38
Barbara L. Borejko Art Director/Designer
Serge Nivelle Photographer
Magna Marketing Services Production
The Wool Bureau Inc. Client
New York NY

39
Josiane Ohana Art Director/Designer
David Haggerty Photographer
Rumrill-Hoyt Advertising Agency
UNISA Client
New York NY

40
Don Barnard Art Director/Designer
Iain Campbell Photographer
Grey Phillips, Bunton, Mundel/Blake Agency
S. Wainstein & Co. Client
Johannesburg. RSA

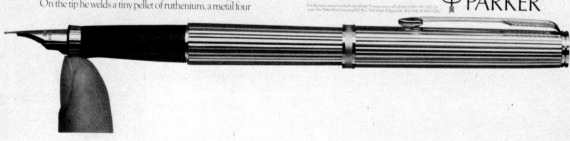

41
Manfred Enickl Art Director
D. Bowes-Taylor, F. Esposito Photographers
Nigel Fox Copywriter
Jonssons Johannesburg Agency
Pagan International Client
Johannesburg, RSA

42
Richard Kimmel, Garry Horner Art Directors
Dave Jordano, Stak Photographers
Ron Hawkins, Indra Sinha Copywriters
Ogilvy & Mather Agency
The Parker Pen Company Client
Chicago IL

43
Miks Schell Art Director/Designer
Ken Stidwell Photographer
Mark Fenske Copywriter
Young & Rubicam NY Agency
Lincoln-Mercury Client
New York NY

44
Tom Wolsey Art Director/Designer
Henry Wolf Photographer
Helayne Spivak Copywriter
Ally & Gargano Agency
Henry Wolf Productions Studio
Karastan Client
New York NY

45
Robert H. Petrocelli Art Director/Designer
Ryszard Horowitz Photographer
Andrze Dudzinski Illustrator
Mark Schwatka Copywriter
Ted Bates Agency
Joseph Garneau Co. Client
New York NY

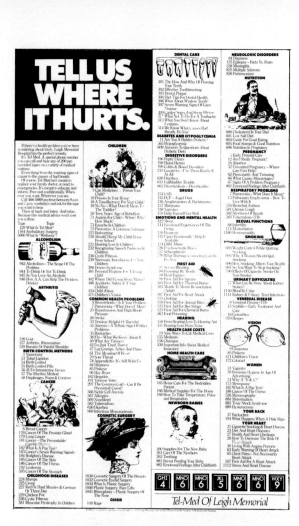
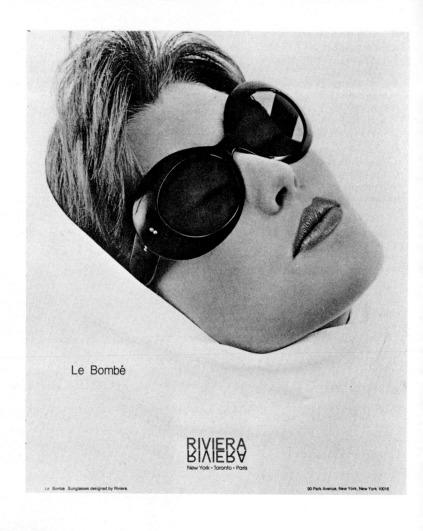

46

Mike McMahon Art Director/Designer
Ken Hines Copywriter
Leigh Memorial Hospital Client
Virginia Beach VA

47

Ed Nagler Art Director/Designer
Bill Stettner Photographer
Four-Color Photo Lab Retouching
P.C. Fiore & Assoc. Inc. Agency
Riviera Trading Corp. Client
Montclair NJ

48

Bob Wolowich Art Director
Bil Petro Photographer
Mary-Jane Palmer Copywriter
MacLaren Advertising Agency
Burma Castrol Client
Toronto, Canada

Thursday... The Day Before

Friday... The Day Of

Saturday...

This is what it would be like, if you were there that day, and...

THE DAY AFTER

Beyond Imagining

Starring
JASON ROBARDS **JOBETH WILLIAMS** **STEVE GUTTENBERG** **JOHN CULLUM** **JOHN LITHGOW** Directed by **NICHOLAS MEYER** Written by **EDWARD HUME**

An ABC Theatre Presentation **Sunday, November 20,** **8:00 PM, 7:00 Central** **ABC Television Network** abc
May Not Be Suitable For Younger Viewers.   Parental Discretion Is Advised.

49
Frederick H. Myers Art Director/Designer
John Vallini Photographer
David Ames Copywriter
Grey Advertising Inc. Agency
ABC Movies for Television Client
New York NY

50
Jeff Vogt Art Director
Jere Cockrell Photographer
David Tessler Copywriter
Ammirati & Puris, Inc. Agency
BMW of North America Client
New York NY

THE CAR THAT TURNED INFORMATION INTO AN ALTERNATE SOURCE OF ENERGY.

There's a finite amount of fossil fuel in the world. And an infinite amount of information.

No car makes more of the infinite than the BMW 528e.

Its engine, for example, owes its superior responsiveness to microprocessors, not massive displacements. Because a data processing system called Digital Motor Electronics (DME) masterminds the myriad intricacies of internal combustion.

DME is the basis for the system used in the BMW-powered race car that captured the 1983 Grand Prix Formula One World Championship. It monitors an endless stream of facts revealed by the engine—such as air/fuel mixtures, throttle openings and idling speeds—

then calculates the optimum timing for fuel ignition.

The result is a car that makes superior use of conventional energy sources. It delivers an EPA-estimated [25] mpg, 32 highway.*

But information doesn't only help the BMW 528e run. It also helps keep it running.

The BMW Service Indicator evaluates how the car is driven, then determines when routine service is needed—based on such hard facts as engine speeds and the number of cold starts, not the arbitrary dictates of a maintenance schedule.

The 528e assumes that information is equally vital to the driver. That's why other systems provide such valu-

able insights as accurate fuel-mileage figures and 7 different readings on the car's operational readiness.

So for those who are sensitive to the ever-increasing importance of information in this world, the BMW 528e qualifies as a well-informed choice.

After all, it's a car built with the same sensitivity.

THE ULTIMATE DRIVING MACHINE.

*Fuel-efficiency figures are for comparison only. Your actual mileage may vary, depending on speed, weather and trip length; actual highway mileage will most likely be lower. ©1984 BMW of North America, Inc. The BMW trademark and logo are registered. European Delivery can be arranged through your authorized U.S. BMW dealer.

51
Kaarl Hllis Art Director
Jem Grischotti Photographer
Trevor Beattie Copywriter
Ayer Barker Ltd. Agency
Square 1 Studio
Sharp Electronics Client
London. England

52
Steve Feldman Art Director/Designer
Gary Feinstein Photographer
Tom Nathan Copywriter
TBWA Advertising Agency
Art Rivera Studio
Mohawk Data Sciences Client
New York NY

53
Barry Lund Art Director
Dennis Wiand Photographer
Bill Ludwig, Jerry Burton Copywriters
Campbell-Ewald Company Agency
Chevrolet Motor Division Client
Warren MI

Today's Chevrolet
Grab hold of the future.

Camaro Berlinetta. Above, the night sky is black, punctuated by the flickering of stars and planets. Below, the white lines of the roadway snake deep into the unknown. Ahead, the blue-green glow of your instrument cluster advises you all systems are go on board Starship Camaro. This is not science fiction. This is Berlinetta.

Starship control central. Climb in. Buckle up. Adjust the retractable push-button instrument pods so your hands never have to leave the wheel in controlling vital functions. Turn the key and watch the system monitor perform seven preflight tests as the engine sparks to life. Blip the throttle and watch the vacuum-fluorescent tach dance to

the rhythm of your right foot.
To orchestrate your voyage, dial up a symphony on the pivoting. Delco stereo and optional graphic equalizer (Radio may be deleted for credit.) Now, put it in gear, give it some gas and watch the digital speedometer numbers multiply. Set the available electronic speed control at your desired

cruising speed. Your journey has begun.
Enter a new realm. Camaro Berlinetta is a higher form of terrestrial transportation. So climb on board and grab hold of the future.
Today's Chevrolet. Bringing you the cars and trucks you want and need. That's what Taking Charge is all about.

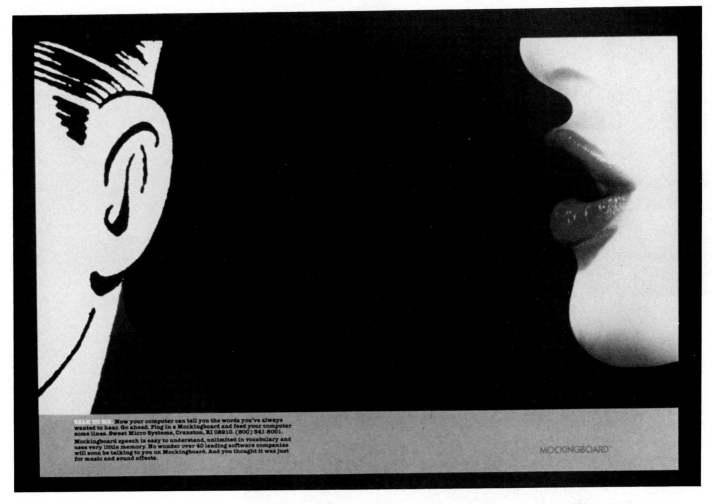

54
Bob Manley Art Director
Rob Van Petten Photographer
Mark Fisher Illustrator
Dan Altman Copywriter
Altman & Manley Agency
Sweet Micro Systems Inc. Client
Cambridge MA

55
Jurgen Dahlen, Hans Peter Weiss Art Directors
Tod Watts Photographer
Pete Peabody Copywriter
GGK New York Agency
Carrier Corporation Client
New York NY

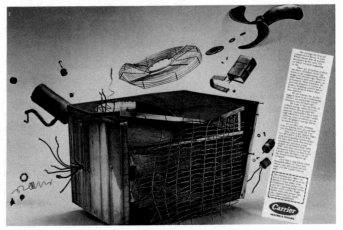

Express yourself softly . . . Kathryn Conover.

"A man's fragrance projects his power of pure style."

Oscar de la Renta

59
David Buck Art Director
Stephen Green-Armytage Photographer
Bernie Schmidt Copywriter
Rumrill-Hoyt Inc. Agency
Eastman Koday Company Client
Rochester NY

56
David Wenman Art Director/Designer
Deborah Turbeville Photographer
Carol Wenman Copywriter
David Wenman Associates, Inc. Agency
Kathryn Conover Client
New York NY

57
David Zahner Photographer
Lisandro Sarasola Client
New York NY

58
Marvin Berk Art Director/Designer
Bob Stern Photographer
K.E. Ladd & Co., Inc. Copywriter
Creative Images in Inc. Agency
Parfums Stern, Inc. Client
New York NY

BOW

WOW

When it comes to photographs, bigger is often better. That's why you should ask for Magnaprint35™ service from Kodak.

magnaprint service

Have your next roll of 35 mm Kodak color print film, or your favorite negatives, done up big.

You'll get 4" x 6" glossy, borderless prints that are 37% larger than standard prints, so they show off your work in all its beauty.

Look for the Processing by Kodak emblem—the sign of quality worth asking for.

Ask for

Introducing the eyes
you wish you had been
born with.

New SOFTCOLORS™ are one of the most advanced, most comfortable soft contact lenses yet. But their real beauty is in the eye of the beholder.

SOFTCOLORS not only correct your vision, they make your eyes look more beautiful...brighter, more colorful. Depending on your natural eye color, SOFTCOLORS can even change the color of your eyes. From light grey to blue for instance. Or light blue to dramatic green. All in the wink of an eye.

SOFTCOLORS are from Ciba...one of the most respected names in vision care. SOFTCOLORS come in four natural tints and everything you see is crisp and clear. And from a practical point of view, the natural tints of SOFTCOLORS make them easy to find and easy to handle.

So go see for yourself. Call your eye care professional and ask about SOFTCOLORS. They may be just right for you.

SOFTCOLORS™
by Ciba (tefilcon)

60
Jim Condit, Kim Youngblood Art Directors
Linda Kelley Designer
Klaus Lucka Photographer

Linda Morse Copywriter
Bowes/Hanlon Advertising Agency
Ciba Vision Care Client
Atlanta GA

61
Bryan Forman Art Director
Eric Meola Photographer
Charlie Breen Copywriter
Backer & Spielvogel, Inc. Agency
The Paddington Corporation Client
New York NY

62
Bob McGrath Art Director/Designer
Derik Murray Photographer
Diane Lund Copywriter
Simons Advertising Ltd. Agency
Slicko Studio Studio
Canada Safeway Ltd. Client
Vancouver. Canada

63
Beverly R. McCombs Art Director
Aili E. Buchanan Designer
Robert Fagen Illustrator
Anne Buhl Copywriter
Dillards Department Stores Client
Ft. Worth TX

Det våre konsulenter ikke har i hodet har de på skjermen.

A Tale of Two TVs.

Panasonic

Escreva um texto de 20 linhas dizendo
tudo que você espera de um carro.

VOLKSWAGEN DO BRASIL S.A.

64
Asmund Sand·Art Director
Sigurd Eidsoren Photographer
Frode Karlberg Copywriter
ide reklame & marketing/AB Bates Agency
Bennett Business Client
Oslo, Norway

65
Tomoo Sekine Art Director/Designer
Hisashi Kawaguchi Photographer
Douglas Biro Copywriter
CDP Japan Ltd. Advertising Agency
Matsushita Electric Trading Co. Client
Tokyo, Japan

66
Enido Angelo Michelini Art Director
Peter Michael Photographer
Enio Basilio Rodrigues Copywriter
Alcantara Machado, Periscinoto Com. Ltda. Agency
Volkswagen do Brasil S.A. Client
Sao Paulo, Brazil

67
Bob Manley, Dick Davis Art Directors
Al Fisher Photographer
Dan Altman, Rich Binell Copywriters
Altman & Manley Agency
Greenleaf Associates Production
Jaclar Client
Cambridge MA

Consumer
SMALL SPACE

68
Douglas Boyd, Scott A. Mednick Art Directors
Scott A. Mednick, Randy Momii Designers
Randy Momii Illustrator
Douglas Boyd Design & Marketing Agency
CBS-TV Client
Los Angeles CA

69
John Alexander Art Director
Richard Barre Copywriter
Linda Graphics Typography
Barre Advertising Inc. Agency
The Mandalay Restaurant Client
Santa Barbara CA

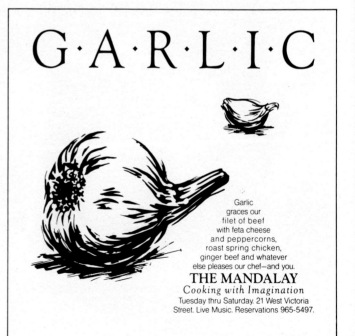

Serve an ace every time. Play to win.

Imported from England. Slowly, gently distilled from 100% pure grain spirits. The court favorite; mixed, doubles or singles.

©Carillon Importers, Ltd., N.Y. 86 Proof, 100% grain neutral spirits.

Best round of the day. Play to win.

Imported from England. Slowly, gently distilled from 100% pure grain spirits. Way above par at the 19th Hole.

©Carillon Importers, Ltd., N.Y. 86 Proof, 100% grain neutral spirits.

A hit in any league. Play to win.

Imported From England. Slowly, gently distilled from 100% pure grain spirits. Why sacrifice? Pick the major league gin.

© Carillon Importers, Ltd., N.Y. 86 Proof, 100% grain neutral spirits.

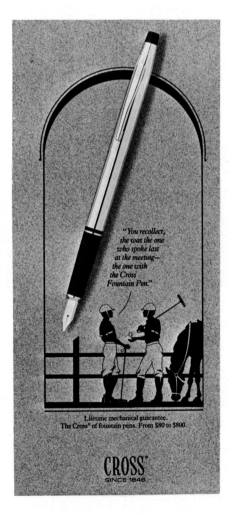

70
Geoff Hayes Art Director/Designer
Whistl'n Dixie Illustrator
Tom Nathan Copywriter
TBWA Advertising Agency
Carillon Importers, Ltd. Client
New York NY

71
Amy Perron Art Director
Chris Roe Designer
Bruno Joachim Photographer
Bobbye Cochran Illustrator
Potter Hazlehurst, Inc. Agency
A.T. Cross Client
East Greenwich RI

72
Clare Taylor Designer/Copywriter
Karen Coshoff, S. Dumouchel, Barry O'Rourke,
 Fred Maroon Photographers
Moscovitz & Taylor Agency
The Sheraton Towers Client
Montreal Canada

73
G. Maniates Art Director
Lionel Kalish Illustrator
Bernadette Doran Copywriter
J. Walter Thompson Agency
Kraft Client
Chicago IL

74
Jane Rubini Art Director/Designer
Tom Nathan Copywriter
TBWA Advertising Agency
Art Rivera Studio
Mohawk Data Sciences Client
New York NY

75
David Freeman Art Director
Clark Mishler Creative Director
Jim Hayes, Mark Hoffman Illustrator
Ken Flynn and Associates Agency
Clark Mishler & Associates Studio
Cellar Master of Anchorage Client
Anchorage AK

BURGUNDY

Burgundy, as the saying goes, produces the King of Wines. Out of this radiant district, with its billowing wooded hills, come round, full, extravagant, even flamboyant wines. Regal qualities, certainly.

The eminent C.E. Montague said that Burgundy is "the soul and greatest common measure of all the kindly wines of the earth." A bit extravagant? Maybe. Until you've savored a glass of fine Burgundy. Then the description becomes . . . adequate.

The Cellar Master's love of Burgundy wines has led him to acquire some of the rarest and finest Burgundies available. You'll want to see his gallery of old and recent vintages. Or ask about his Beaujolais that delightful, high-spirited young wine. And the investor will want to consider the wines of the Cote D'Or. They are scarce and expensive, and with an ever-increasing demand, can only become more so.

If you're taking your first tentative steps toward Burgundy, consider a handful of California wine producers are having excellent success with Burgundys great grape, the Pinot Noir and the resultant wines are attractively priced. If you don't know or can't decide on which vineyard or vintage, what is incomparable or merely very good, ask the Cellar Master. He has dedicated himself to seeking out the true bargains and values.

Burgundy, the King of Wines. Distributed (democratically) by the Cellar Master.

PRODUCT OF FRANCE
VOSNE-ROMANEE
APPELLATION CONTROLÉE
Jean GROS
Propriétaire-Viticulteur à Vosne-Romanée (Côte-d'Or)

CELLAR ❖ MASTER
FINE WINE, BEER & SPIRITS
IN THE GREATLAND MALL, 360 WEST BENSON BLVD. (WEST OF C STREET) 561-5434

Champagne

The 17th-Century Monk, Dom Perignon, is credited with having discovered, accidentally, the secondary fermentation process which produces Champagne. The rest, if you will, is celebration.

True Champagne comes only from the district of the same name north-east of Paris, the most important villages of which are Reims, Ay (pronounced Ah-ee) and Epernay.

You might well wonder if you really need to know this. Well, the French say that the finest pleasures are those that are learned. The suggestion is that the more you know about Champagne, the more fun it is. And that's true.

The finest Champagnes are a blend of the juice from Chardonnay grapes, which give the wine freshness and finesse, and the juice of the black grape, Pinot Noir, which lends body and character.

The Cellar Master will show you his extraordinary rare vintage Champagnes, if you like. And if you're just learning about the finer pleasures he'll introduce you to some excellent Champagne values, at prices that are very comfortable.

From the day of its discovery Champagne has worked its spell on the world as has no other wine. It's something you'll want to know more about. Who knows? You might even be moved to say, as was that serendipitous Monk upon tasting the first frothing gulp of his new creation, "I am drinking stars."

Champagne epitomizes celebration. Come celebrate with us at Cellar Master. The suggestion is that after a chat with him, your next bottle of Champagne will be more fun.

And that's true.

CELLAR ❖ MASTER
FINE WINE, BEER & SPIRITS
IN THE GREATLAND MALL, 360 WEST BENSON BLVD. (WEST OF C STREET), 276-5434

BEER

The Ancient Egyptians drank beer. Now everyone drinks it. Such is progress.

Although the Germans are reputed to have perfected it, very nearly, other cultures have experimented with it, socially and otherwise: The Kofyar of Northern Nigeria spend almost every waking moment making, drinking, talking, and thinking about beer. (There is much to be said for the Kofyar, although they hardly ever appear in the news.)

Americans' interests used to lie solely in lager types: Pilseners, California steam beers, and Muenchners, for example. But our tastes have grown to include the sharper, more strongly-flavored imports from Great Britain: ales, porters, and stouts. (We have much in common with our English cousin: Criticize his Brand and he will stare floridly and unremittingly at you, much as if you had said something ungenerous about his tie.)

All of which means you ought to come to the Cellar Master, where we have Your Brand, whether it be the exquisite Paulaner Ur-Bock or Wies'n-Marzen (the original Munich Oktoberfest beer) or the Grand Old Domestics (grudgingly admired by some Germans, even).

Buy your favorite by the attractively-priced case, or taste your way through the vast spectrum of international flavors.

Come to the Cellar Master. Not just an extraordinary wine store, but the home of extraordinary beers and spirits, too. (One final note: The Ancient Babylonians drank beer too, although it probably was not very good, since there are no longer any Babylonians.)

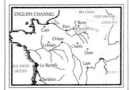

CELLAR ❖ MASTER
FINE WINE, BEER & SPIRITS
IN THE GREATLAND MALL, 360 WEST BENSON BLVD. (WEST OF C STREET), 276-5434

REAL MAYONNAISE IN ONE HOUR

For real mayonnaise, take a few fresh egg yolks, add some mustard, a pinch of salt and mix in the finest white vinegar. Then, to get that smooth, creamy texture, blend in the very best vegetable oil you can find, drop by drop by drop. For the next hour or so...

REAL MAYONNAISE IN ONE SECOND

For real mayonnaise, open up a jar of smooth and creamy Hellmann's. In one second, your salads, sandwiches, chicken and cold meat dishes will change for the better. Because Hellmann's unique taste doesn't mask the flavour of your food. It just brings out the best.

76

Robin French Art Director/Designer
Iain Campbell Photographer
Yvonne van Onselen Copywriter
Grey Phillips, Bunton, Mundel/Blake Agency
Robertsons (PTY) Ltd. Client
Johannesburg. RSA

77

Melissa Burtner Art Director
Vicki Wehrman Illustrator
Karla Merrifield Copywriter
Hutchins Y&R Agency
Lincoln First Bank Client
Rochester NY

IT TAKES A LITTLE SEED MONEY HERE AND THERE TO GROW THE FLOWER CITY.

A new business takes root. Rows of shops sprout up. A major manufacturer breaks ground for another factory.

Year in, year out, Rochester prospers.

At Lincoln First we've helped others cultivate that success over the years. Planting a little here. A little there. And then some.

Today, as then, we continue to support local business and industry, laying the groundwork for tomorrow.

And as the city grows through the years ahead, so can you. With Lincoln First Bank. We've got what you need to succeed.

 Lincoln First Bank, N.A.

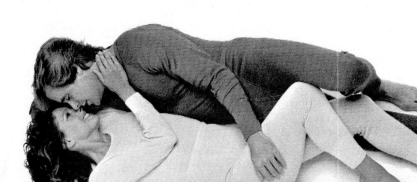

These are the ones.
The lightest, comfiest, snuggliest Stanfield's® ever knit.
Because we use 100% polypropylene.
A miracle fibre that wicks away moisture, but locks
in precious heat.
To keep active people toasty, while skiing, skating, working
— or doing anything else in the cold.
Stanfield's® polypropylene underwear. They're not the only
way to stay warm this winter. Just the best.

POLAR-THERM AND
STANFIELD'S POLYPROPYLENE

Look for Stanfield's® polypropylene
underwear at leading department stores, and
Polar-therm® at your favourite sports shop.

YOU CAN'T GET MUCH WARMER THAN
STANFIELD'S® POLYPROPYLENE UNDERWEAR.

78
Raymond Lee Art Director/Designer
Powey Chang Photographer
Graziano Palumbo Copywriter
Peter Baker Artist
Raymond Lee + Associates Agency
Stanfields' Limited Client
Toronto. Canada

79
Graham de Lacy Art Director/Designer
Athol Lewis Photographer
Wyn Crane Copywriter
Preller Sharpe Rice (Pty) Ltd. Agency
Budget Foto Client
Johannesburg. RSA

1904 Restaurant/Bar 4th & Stewart 682 4142

LOOK DICK. SEE FOOD!

80
Warren Wilkins, Tommer Peterson Art Directors/
  Designers/Agency
KiKi Foster Illustrator
1904 Restaurant/Bar Client
Seattle WA

81
David Gauger Art Director/Copywriter
Jan Milstead Designer
David Seligman Photographer
Gauger Sparks Silva, Inc. Agency
El Greco Client
San Francisco. CA

NO TACOS

A misconception held by
some is that Spanish and
Mexican food are the same.
At El Greco, we want to
dispel that myth. There is
nothing to compare with the
grand cuisine of Barcelona,
Madrid and Granada. The
classic dining of Spain is
unique in every way. From

succulent seafood prepared
with delicate sauces to fla-
vorful gazpacho and paella.
  Old World tradition at
El Greco in the Cannery. Delight your palate for lunch,
11:00-3:00, or dinner, 5:00-
12:00. 2801 Leavenworth,
San Francisco (415)771-0410.

El Greco

WE CATER TO PENNY PINCHERS

At Warehouse Imports, we sell the best quality contemporary furniture money can buy at prices even a miser would love.

The way we see it, times are tough, you work hard for your money, and if we can give you more value for your dollar, well, why shouldn't we?

After all, to be a penny pincher (and who isn't these days?), you have to follow certain rules. And rule #1 is that you spend your money where you get the most value in return.

Here, for example. At Warehouse Imports. It's one of the very few places you'll ever find that makes being a penny pincher one of life's more rewarding pleasures.

WAREHOUSE imports

Route 70 & Lexington Ave.
Pennsauken, N.J.
665-1441
Open 7 days a week.

OUR SHIP COMES IN EVERY WEEK

The whole wide world sends its best to us. And we mean that quite literally.

Beautiful teak home furnishings from Denmark. The latest designs from Milan. Solid maple butcher block from Vermont, USA. Precision-engineered wall systems from Germany. Hand-painted screens and cabinets from China.

We could go on, and on, and on, but by now you've gotten our drift: wherever in the world great design is to be found, we find it. And ship it home to New Jersey just for you.

WAREHOUSE imports

Route 70 & Lexington Ave.
Pennsauken, N.J.
665-1441
Open 7 days a week.

82

Marci Mansfield Art Director/Designer
Marci Mansfield, Lorraine Guttormsen Illustrator
Caroline Henderson Copywriter
Perceptive Marketers Agency, Ltd. Agency
Warehouse Imports Client
Philadelphia PA

83

Gene Trivell Art Director
Louis Jurado Photographer
Elizabeth Plate Copywriter
COMSPEC Agency
Jean Couzon Client
New York NY

84

Robert Manley Art Director
Steven Guarniccia Illustrator
Daniel Altman Copywriter
Altman + Manley Agency
MultiGroup Health Plan Client
Cambridge MA

Made in France, the rich warmth of sterling serving pieces with a design elegance that, at once, reaches back into three centuries of French history and is comfortable with the most contemporary.

And yet it isn't sterling. The museum-quality collection is wholly stainless steel, brought to a finish that retains everything you want in the silver look, forever, without polishing, with dishwasher and oven qualities. Write for illustrative folio and where to find JEAN COUZON 509 Madison Avenue, NY NY 10022. In Canada 68 Carnforth Road, Toronto, Ontario M4A 2K7.

Now at Bloomingdale's, Marshall Field, I Magnin

Sterling without tears

Jean Couzon

85
Robin Batina-Wessel Art Director/Designer
Jill Spear Copywriter
Nansee Nielsen Advertising Director
Pointe Communications Agency
The Pointe Client
Phoenix AZ

87
Ellie Malavis Art Director/Designer
Charles Hively Creative Director
Swain Eden Photographer
Harvey Marks Copywriter
The Metzdorf-Marschalk Company Agency
Hotel InterContinental San Antonio Client
Houston TX

86
Roger Sherman II Art Director/Designer
aka, Santa Cruz Publishing Tyesetters
Roger Sherman Advertising Agency
Pasatiempo Inn Client
Santa Cruz CA

Consumer
CAMPAIGN

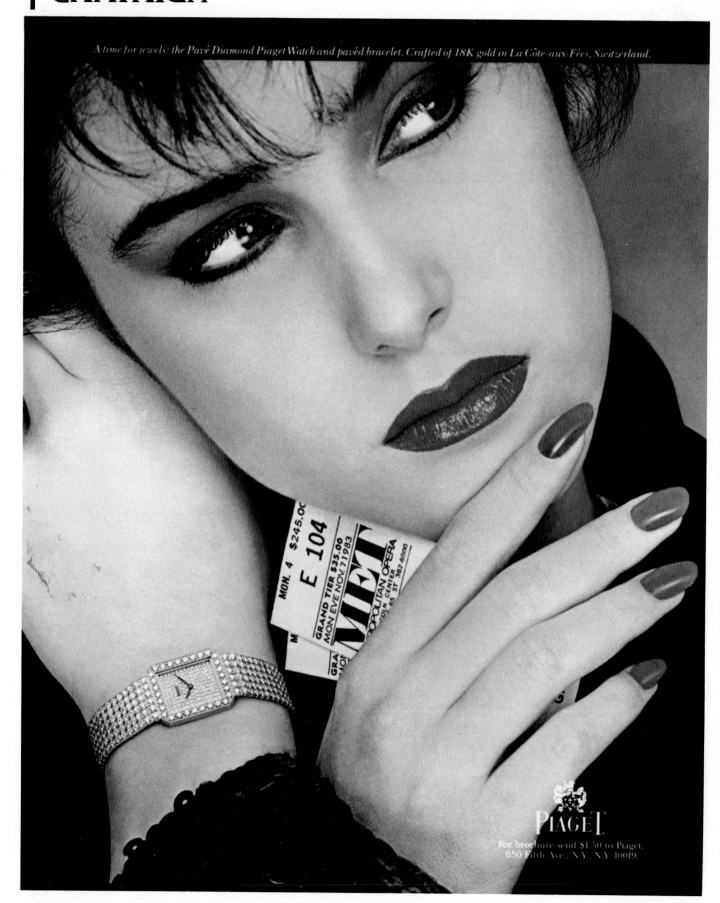

A time for jewels: the Pavé Diamond Piaget Watch and pavéd bracelet. Crafted of 18K gold in La Côte-aux-Fées, Switzerland.

PIAGET

For brochure send $1.50 to Piaget, 650 Fifth Ave., N.Y., N.Y. 10019.

88

Chuck Davidson Art Director/Designer
Albert Watson Photographer
Deanne Trobert Dunning Copywriter
Harry Viola Advertising Agency
Piaget Watch Corporation Client
New York NY

89

Johann Hoekstra Art Director
Jonathan Harries Designer/Copywriter
David Bergen Illustrator
Grey Phillips, Bunton, Mundel & Blake Agency
African Oxygen Ltd. Client
Johannesburg. RSA

There's one more sandwich in there somewhere.

A sandwich just isn't a sandwich without the tangy zip of
Miracle Whip salad dressing from Kraft. **"THE BREAD SPREAD"**

There's one more sandwich in there somewhere.

A sandwich just isn't a sandwich without the tangy zip of
Miracle Whip salad dressing from Kraft. **"THE BREAD SPREAD"**

There's one more sandwich in there somewhere.

A sandwich just isn't a sandwich without the tangy zip of
Miracle Whip salad dressing from Kraft. **"THE BREAD SPREAD"**

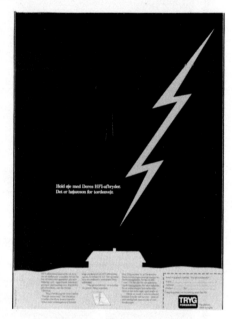

90
David DeVary Art Director/Designer
John Scott Creative Director
Dennis Manarchy Photographer
Sandy Stern Copywriter
J. Walter Thompson Agency
Kraft Client
Chicago IL

91
Dorte Zangenberg Art Director/Illustrator
Claus Lembourn Copywriter
Zangenberg & Lembourn Agency
Tryg Forsikring Client
Copenhagen K. Denmark

92
Janet K. Leadholm Art Director/Designer
Dennis Manarchy, Jerry Brimacombe Photographer
Laurie Casagrande Copywriter
Campbell-Mithun, Inc. Agency
Raphaele, Inc. Retouching
Land O'Lakes, Inc. Client
Minneapolis MN

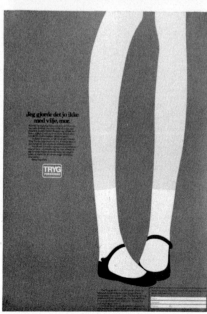

Discover the taste
that captured the country.

Land O Lakes® Butter is here.

Discover the taste that captured the country.
Land O Lakes Butter is here.

SHATTERED DREAMS

Baccarat

CHRISTMAS

IN VICTORIA COURT

Warm smiles. Friendly greetings. Cheerful help
in selecting the perfect gift.
That's what makes Victoria Court special. And that's
what makes Victoria Court your place to shop for Christmas.
You'll find everything from imports to Christmas
cards. Handmade clothes and sportswear. Toys and jewelry
and candy. And more. Plus restaurants to brighten your spirits.
Come to Victoria Court. We have your gift because we
have your Christmas. For You. And your tree.

93

John Martinez Art Director
Andrew Unangst Photographer
Palmer Davis Copywriter
Cato Johnson/Y&R, Inc. Agency
Baccarat, Inc. Client
New York NY

94

Mark Oliver Art Director/Designer
Carolyn Tyler Illustrator
Doris O'Leske Copywriter
Mark Oliver Inc. Agency
Victoria Court Client
Santa Barbara CA

Go farther...faster.

Marines

Earn a degree in leadership.

Marines

97

Barbara DiLorenzo Art Director
John Margeotes, John Weiss Creative Directors
Will Ryan Photographer
Leticia Hernandez Copywriter
Margeotes Fertitta & Weiss, Inc. Agency
Remy Martin Amerique Client
New York NY

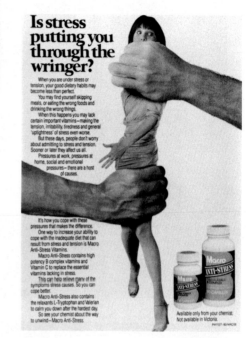

Is stress putting you through the wringer?

When you are under stress or tension, your good dietary habits may become less than perfect.

You may find yourself skipping meals, or eating the wrong foods and drinking the wrong things.

When this happens you may lack certain important vitamins—making the tension, irritability, tiredness and general 'uptightness' of stress even worse.

But these days, people don't worry about admitting to stress and tension. Sooner or later they affect us all.

Pressures at work, pressures at home, social and emotional pressures—there are a host of causes.

It's how you cope with these pressures that makes the difference.

One way to increase your ability to cope with the inadequate diet that can result from stress and tension is Macro Anti-Stress Vitamins.

Macro Anti-Stress contains high potency B complex vitamins and Vitamin C to replace the essential vitamins lacking in stress.

This can help relieve many of the symptoms stress causes. So you can cope better.

Macro Anti-Stress also contains the relaxants L-Tryptophan and Valerian to calm you down after the hardest day.

So see your chemist about the way to unwind—Macro Anti-Stress.

Available only from your chemist. Not available in Victoria.

95

Pedro S. Gonzales Art Director
Dennis Brack Photographer
Daniel M. Hanover Copywriter
J. Walter Thompson USA Agency
United States Marine Corps Client
Washington DC

96

Robert Rogers Art Director
Greg Slater Photographer
Stephen Dodds Copywriter
Robert Dean Retoucher
Sudler & Hennessey, Sydney Agency
Macro Vitamin Distributors Client
North Sydney, Australia

Pride runs in the family.

A parent's pride in a son runs deep. From the day he's born, through learning how to walk and talk, through graduating from high school and beyond, your pride grows. But with each step of maturing there also comes concern, it's part of the blood bond that comes with family. Because parents worry about the person their son will develop into. Will he be able to look out for himself, be productive and happy? We want you to share your concern. Our Drill Instructors have a mission. To help each young man develop to his full potential. They teach him that pride in himself, his family, his country and Corps go hand in hand. And that with it, a man's potential is unlimited.

Above: Boot camp will bring out the best in your son. *Right.* Experience and travel help him discover the world. *Far Right.* The pride of being a Marine carries into everything he does.

Maybe he can be one of us.
The Few. The Proud. The Marines.

Marines

Savor the sense of Rémy.

REMY MARTIN V.S.O.P. COGNAC. SINCE 1724.

Arouse
your sense of Rémy.

REMY MARTIN V.S.O.P. COGNAC. SINCE 1724.
Imported by Rémy Martin Amerique, Inc. N.Y. N.Y. 80 Proof

Arouse
your sense of Rémy.

REMY MARTIN V.S.O.P. COGNAC. SINCE 1724.
Imported by Rémy Martin Amerique, Inc. N.Y. N.Y. 80 Proof

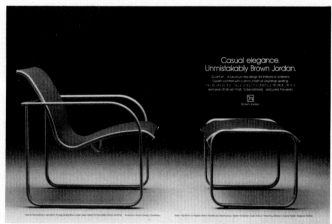

98
Carl Moore Art Director/Designer
Jay Silverman Photographer
Marion Sternbach Copywriter
Brown, Keefe, Marine/Bowes Agency
Brown Jordan Client
Los Angeles CA

99
Mark Oliver, Marty Neumeier Art Director
Marty Neumeier, Sandra Higashi Designer
Barrie Schwortz and various stock Photographer
Sandra Higashi Illustrator
Mark Oliver, Inc. Agency
Stubbies Client
Santa Barbara CA

100
Jim Fitts Art Director
Jean Michel Folon Illustrator
Jon Goward Copywriter
ClarkeGowardFitts Agency
The Boston Company Client
Boston MA

Do you know where you're going? **Are you already there?** **Boston Safe Deposit and Trust Company**

Do you know where you're going? **Are you already there?** **Boston Safe Deposit and Trust Company**

Do you know where you're going? **Are you already there?** **Boston Safe Deposit and Trust Company**

Do you know where you're going? **Are you already there?** **Boston Safe Deposit and Trust Company**

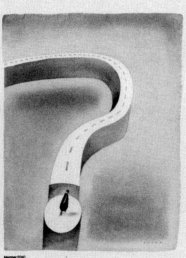

Member FDIC

SOON FOUR NEW DOORS
WILL OPEN UNDER ONE NEW ROOF.

A Hotel Unmatched In Its Class

NOW, STEPPING OUT ON THE TOWN
MEANS STEPPING INTO FOUR NEW PLACES.

A Hotel Unmatched In Its Class

IN JANUARY, WINING AND DINING
WILL BE FOUR TIMES AS INVITING.

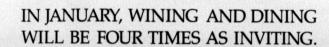

A Hotel Unmatched In Its Class   2201 Stemmons Frwy., Dallas, Texas 75207

101

Jill Hawkins Art Director
Jill Hawkins, Monique Davis, Macirj Pinno,
  Designers
Andy Vracin Photographer
Carroll St. George Copywriter
Jill Hawkins Design Studio
Loews Anatole Hotel Client
Dallas TX

John Alexander Art Director
Robert Peak Photographer
Richard Barre Copywriter
Barre Advertising Inc. Agency
Bryant & Sons, Ltd. Client
Santa Barbara CA

*Bryant's world
is your world.*

Bryant & Sons, Ltd.
MASTER JEWELERS/DESIGNERS/GEMOLOGISTS
812 State Street in El Paseo
Santa Barbara, 966-9187

Some of us have more finely developed nesting instincts than others.

Some of us have more finely developed nesting   instincts than others.

Tom Wolsey Art Director/Designer
Henry Wolf Photographer
Helayne Spivak Copywriter
Ally & Gargano Agency
Henry Wolf Productions Studio
Karastan Client
New York NY

Jorma Kosunen Art Director
Lasse Larsson, Ralf Turander Photographer
Fred Ekermann Copywriter
MK, Marknadskommunikation AB Agency
AB Pripps Bryggerier Client
Stockholm, Sweden

105
Hans-Joachim Timm, D. von Salzen Art Directors
Hans-Joachim Timm Creative Director
Detlef Trefz Photographer
Intermarco-Farner, Dusseldorf Agency
Sopexa, Dusseldorf Client
Frankfurt. West Germany

106
Jorma Kosunen Art Director
Ingvar Eriksson Photographer
Jen Wahlberg Copywriter
MK, Marknadskommunikation AB Agency
AB Pripps Bryggerier Client
Stockholm. Sweden

107
Bruce Crocker Art Director
Patrick Blackwell Illustrator
Daniel Altman Copywriter
Altman + Manley Agency
Daniel Webster Medical Center Client
Cambridge MA

GISSA VILKET
STARKÖL SOM SKUMMADE
I SVENSKARNAS GLAS
REDAN NÄR INGO BLEV
VÄRLDSMÄSTARE.

Etiketten var blå då som nu. Smaken lika
frisk och balanserad. De mängder som
druckits av detta omtyckta starköl sedan
den minnesvärda natten 1959 då Radio
Luxemburg gav svenskarna glädjefnatt
skulle säkert räcka till att fylla en hel ocean.
Visst vet du vilket öl vi tänker på!

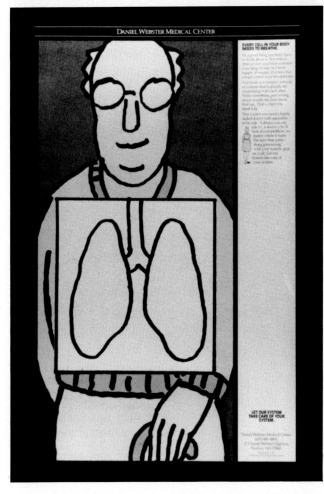

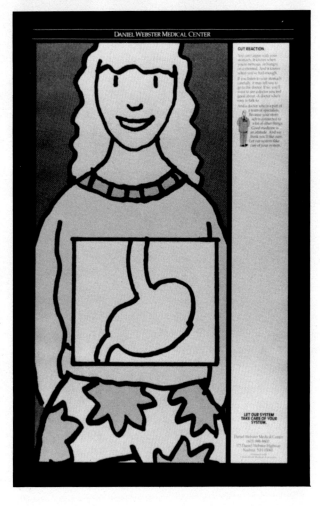

108
Rhonda Gainer Art Director
Daniel Hechter Designer
Dan Balioti Photographer
Billman & Associates Studio
Daniel Hechter Menswear Client
New York NY

109
Morten Saether, Tom Solbakken Art Directors
Tom Solbakken Copywriter
Einar Brathe Account
Benton & Bowles, Oslo Agency
Lee Norge A/S Client
Oslo. Norway

THE GREAT CHEESES OF EUROPE.
ONE TASTE IS WORTH A THOUSAND PICTURES.

Treat yourself to CHÈVRE & CHAMPAGNE.

THE GREAT CHEESES OF EUROPE.
ONE TASTE IS WORTH A THOUSAND PICTURES.™

Treat yourself to a SAINT PAULIN SANDWICH.

THE GREAT CHEESES OF EUROPE.
ONE TASTE IS WORTH A THOUSAND PICTURES.

Treat yourself to a ROQUEFORT RENDEZVOUS.

110
Gail Daniels Art Director/Designer
Michael Ives Photographer
Angus McQueen, Jeff Nauser Copywriter
Ackerman & McQueen Agency
Food & Wines From France Client
Oklahoma City OK

111
**Len Fink, Joe Cipolla, Alan Goodman
Dennis McClain** Art Directors
Jack Silverman Creative Director/Copywriter
Dennis McClain Designer
Anthony Edgeworth Photographer
Leber Katz Partners Agency
R.J. Reynolds Tobacco Company Client
New York NY

Could you seriously support a company
that insists there's a shortage of manpower
when the streets are full of potential employees?

Right now, in this country, improved employment
opportunities exist.
And yet, there are millions of would-be employees
who, because of the deficiencies
in the education system,
are unable to make use of them.
The attitude in some quarters seems to be,
it's too late to alter matters.
It is never too late.
And as an attitude, it is shortsighted
and not in the interests of the country.
At Shell, we are doing our best to help
change the situation.
We realise education is a long term project.
We know we won't change the status quo overnight.
But education and training continue to be
at the heart of our community
involvement programme.
It is an involvement that is not an exercise
in Black advancement for its own sake.
It merely reflects the cold reality
that the number of skilled people, of all races,
from current sources, will be inadequate
to meet the future demand of South Africa.
Our attitude is: If we don't help our country's
future manpower to achieve its full potential faster,
how can we expect others to do so?

A question of the right attitude.

What does the place you live in
have to do with a tankful of petrol?

It's one thing dreaming of owning your
own home some day.
It's another finding the money to get yourself
out of your present living conditions.
At Shell, we believe that one of the good things
about producing Supershell petrol
is that it gives us a chance to help
thousands improve their lives.
It means we can offer them jobs, education
and better housing.
Our attitude is: If by developing the best petrol
your money can buy, we also help the people
of this country, so much the better.
So the next time you fill up with Supershell,
think of what you're getting.
You're getting a petrol that meets
major motor manufacturers' requirements.
A petrol that works as well as you want it to,
and better.
So that when you put in Supershell,
you can be sure it will help keep your engine
clean and give you maximum kilometres
and power. You're also getting
the attitude of a company
whose aim it is to help
South Africans of all races
enjoy a higher standard
of living.

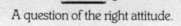

A question of the right attitude.

112
Jeff Vetter Art Director
Corson Hirschfeld Photographer
D'Arcy MacMAnus Masius, St. Louis Agency
Anheuser-Busch, Inc.-Budweiser Client
St. Louis MO

113
Hans Peter Weiss Art Director
Robert A. Parker Illustrator
Wolf D. Rogosky Copywriter
GGK New York Agency
Gunther Maier Studio
United Technologies Corporation Client
New York NY

114
Ian Blake Art Director/Designer
David Goldblatt, Georgina Karvellas, Iain Campbell,
 Harry De Zitter Photographers
Yvonne van Onselen Copywriter
Grey Phillips, Bunton, Mundel and Blake Agency
Shell S.A. Client
Johannesburg. RSA

Trade
SINGLE UNIT

Emerald Aisle.

A Tropitone original, our Irish River collection offers you a distinctively unique octagon design. Perfect in either commercial or residential installations.

Frames and virgin vinyl strap available in 20 designer colors. Use your imagination with chaises, dining tables, chairs, ottomans.

Write or call for our free 76 page 1984 catalog today. Your files may be obsolete without it.

Tropitone Furniture Company, P.O. Box 3197, Sarasota, FL 33578 (813) 355-2715;
5 Marconi, Irvine, CA 92714
(714) 951-2010

tropitone
Probably the finest

Straight Ahead. New directions in color reproduction.

The road to full color reproduction is very exacting and demands precise controls and skills. Our laser scan technology enables us to reproduce your color subjects with the highest degree of accuracy. In-line with our presses, Peake's scanner is part of a system that is our commitment to quality printing.

Peake, The last word in versatility.

Peake Printers, Inc.
2500 Schuster Drive
Cheverly, Maryland 20781
301/341-4600

Photography: David Sharpe
Design: Sparkman and Bartholomew Assoc.

115
Stephen S. Quine Art Director
Howard Smith Designer
Sparkman & Bartholomew Studio
Peake Printers Client
Washington DC

116
Mark Kent Art Director/Designer
Al Fisher Photographer
Brian Flood Copywriter
Cipriani Advertising Inc. Agency
Cole-Haan Client
Boston MA

117
John Waters Art Director
Linda Grimm Designer
Michael Meyers Photographer
Bob Bilek Illustrator
John Waters Associates, Inc. Agency
The Gunlocke Company Client
New York NY

118
Dan Scarlotto Art Director/Designer
Mik Granberry Photographer
Ed Korenstein Copywriter
Pringle Dixon Pringle Agency
Tropitone Furniture Client
Atlanta GA

HAVE YOUR CUSTOMERS BEEN INTRODUCED TO FLAVIA'S COTTAGE STREET MEMORIES?

The Balloon Lady was a street vendor who sold newspapers on a corner I passed daily on my way to school. She kept balloons tied to her newsstand and fresh flowers in a glass jar. She fascinated me because she was always so glad to be alive—and I thought of her as my secret friend although she never knew it.

The editorial for the card above reads: Thank you for everything
The editorial for the card below reads: The way we were/Remember?

"I used to wonder if anyone else on Cottage Street was aware that someone, sometime, loved this Balloon Lady very much and had given her this inner glow—this same love of life—that my uncle Jack had given to me.

"He was my Mama's kid brother, tall and good looking and only a few years older than I. During World War II, Jack joined the Air Force and became a B17 pilot. In 1944, at the age

of twenty-two, and while completing his last mission, he was killed as he was trying to help his crew to safety.

"At the moment his plane was shot down, a part of my world died with him—yet still to this day—he has a hold on my hopes and my dreams. Jack was a dream maker and he gave dreams away like a Pied Piper. He wore caps and funny old hats and suspenders and long scarves.

"He wrote poetry and songs, and used to direct Bill and me in plays he had written. I remember wondering if God had put Jack on Earth just so he could show others how wonderful life was. Being with him made me feel important.

"He had the unique capacity for seeing life as an adventure filled with wonder and new beginnings—and he cherished the right to live and to dream—for he knew how necessary dreams are to the heart." © Flavia Weedn

* * *

The stories of Flavia and the Balloon Lady and Jack are more parts of Cottage Street. Flavia's new card line explores all the moments lovingly remembered. The characters

The editorial for the card above reads: This is your magical day/May your wish come true.

rekindle those special feelings for friends and family. The editorials are familiar, hand-printed and direct. Printed on quality paper and featuring colored envelopes, each of the 48 designs serves more than one sending occasion. The entire selection is balanced to offer a variety of choices for any specific reason your customer may have in mind.

A fully illustrated catalogue is yours from a representative in your area. Call or write:
ROSERICH DESIGNS, LTD.
PO Box 1030 Carpinteria, California 93013-1030
Inside CA 805/684-6977 Outside CA 800/235-6931

Even the best skipper needs a good rudder.

FOR THE LAST 50 YEARS, The Associated Press has benefited from the advice of a unique organization in journalism—the Associated Press Managing Editors Association. Since 1933 members of APME have given freely of their time and talents, enabling the AP to produce the world's most respected news report. No other news service receives such scrutiny or support from the editors it serves. When they talk, we listen.

To everyone associated with APME over the years, we'd like to say thanks. Here's to the next 50 years.

AP Associated Press
ONE OF A KIND

119
Victor M. Bickmore Art Director/Designer
Kathleen C. Corby Designer
Flavia Weedn Illustrator
Design Management Agency
Roserich Designs, Ltd. Client
Carpinteria CA

120
Heidi Schmeck Art Director
Sheila Norman-Culp Copywriter
The Associated Press Client
New York NY

121
Robert C. Bogart Art Director/Designer
Willette Friday Creative Director
Michael Pateman Photographer
Pacificom Agency
Allergan Pharmaceuticals, Inc. Client
Irvine CA

It outsells Excedrin, Alka-Seltzer, Head & Shoulders...

"Retailing is one of the most competitive industry groups we follow. It is important that the retailer not only stock the products customers want but correctly anticipate future needs as well. To avoid tying up capital in expensive, unsold inventory, the most profitable companies emphasize products with a proven record of fast turnover and high profit margins."

—Edward Weller
Vice President, Equity Research
E.F. Hutton and Co.
New York, New York

Soflens Enzymatic
Contact Lens Cleaner
The profit-builder
New 36-tablet refill size now available

Allergan Pharmaceuticals, Inc.
Irvine CA 92713
© 1983 Allergan Pharmaceuticals, Inc.

122
Rune Ostberg Art Director
John Holmes Illustrator
Bjorn Borgstrom Copywriter
Anderson & Lembke Kungsgatan AB Agency
SKF Steel-Gustaf Holgersson Client
Stockholm. Sweden

123
Pamela Young Art Director
Marinella Bonini Illustrator
Stephen Dodds Copywriter
Sudler & Hennessey, Sydney Agency
Du Pont (Australia) Ltd. Client
North Sydney. Australia

124
Israel Fraiman Art Director/Designer
George Simhoni Photographer
Fraiman Design & Advertising Inc. Studio
Goodhost Foods Ltd. Client
Toronto. Canada

GREAT FOR GUNS

SKF Steel is great for guns and almost every other piece of equipment you use down the hole like subs, jars, packers, pup joints, couplings and casing connectors.

That's because SKF has developed a unique process, the SKF MR (melting and refining) method, that produces steel with a very low and controlled level of non-metallic inclusions.

The result is a steel that is extremely consistent from heat to heat. More consistent, and cleaner, than conventional steel.

And since it's cleaner, it's stronger, reducing the risk of fatigue failure and increasing the reliability of your tools even under the most demanding, and difficult operations.

And that's not all. The close chemical analysis of our steel and narrow tolerances of our products improve machining, which means

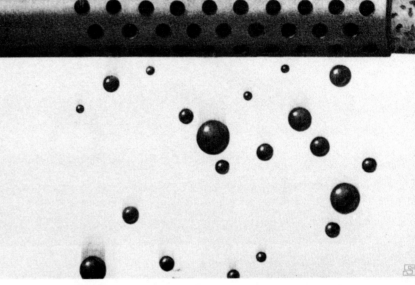

significantly lower production costs.

So, it's great for guns or any other oilfield equipment you manufacture.

For information about the possibilities of ordering from standard specifications adjusted to suit your particular production conditions, get in touch with SKF Steel, Box 133, S-182 12 Danderyd, Sweden, tel. (08)753 32 20.

We'll be happy to provide you with all the information you need.

SKF Steel
The Special Steel Specialist

SKF STEEL US, 963 NORTH BELT, SUITE 455, HOUSTON, TEXAS 77060, TEL. 713-847-2724
SKF STEEL US, P.O. BOX 745, AVON, CONNECTICUT 06001, TEL. 203-677-4423.

There are very few crops you cannot protect with Benlate.

Since its introduction over 10 years ago, Du Pont Benlate Fungicide has proved itself on more crops and more diseases than any other fungicide.

Today Benlate is still the most effective broad spectrum residual fungicide available. To give your crop the advantages of its proven systemic

action, alone or in combination with a contact fungicide, see your local Du Pont reseller.

Chances are, unless you grow Australia's most unusual crop, you can bank on Benlate.

Bank on Benlate, before it's too late.

DU PONT

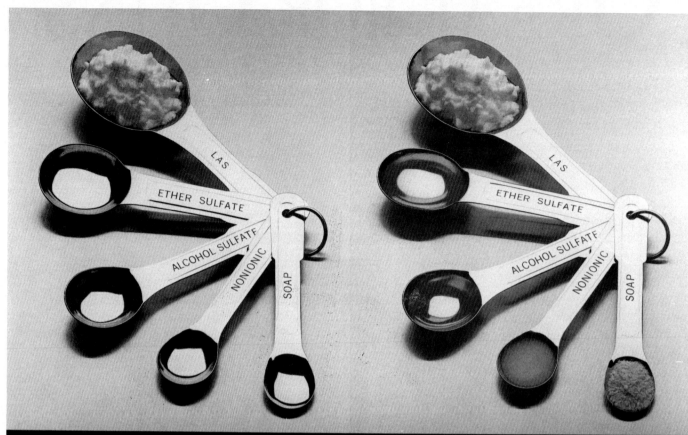

Single vs Mixed Actives. Does your detergent recipe call for linear alkylbenzene sulfonate alone? Or do you prefer to blend it with other active ingredients? No matter which choice you make, LAS measures up. For proof, write our Manager of Marketing, Surfactants, Post Office Box 19029, Houston, Texas 77224 or call (713) 531-3200.

(conoco)
Conoco Chemicals

125
Charles Hively Creative Director/Designer
Harvey Marks Copywriter
The Metzdorf-Marschalk Company Agency
Conoco Chemicals Client
Houston TX

126
Kerry Grady Art Director/Designer
Rhodes Patterson Copywriter
Container Corporation of America Agency/Client
Chicago IL

YOU ALWAYS GET A BIGGER CUT FROM ORE-IDA.

Ore-Ida

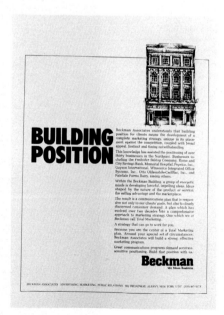

BUILDING POSITION

Beckman
We Mean Business

Dine on England's most beautiful border.

Wedgwood

127
Sharon L. Occhipinti Art Director/Designer
Stuart Heir Photographer
Pamel Sherman Copywriter
Doyle Dan Bernbach Agency
Ore-Ida Client
New York NY

128
Daniel Mark Fay Art Director/Designer
Betsy Comstock Creative Director
Jack Palancio Illustrator
Betsy Comstock, Caroline Meyers Copywriters
Beckman Assoc. Agency/Client
Albany NY

129
Debra Johnston Art Director
Connie Hansen Photographer
Candace Whitman Copywriter
J. Walter Thompson Agency
Wedgwood Client
New York NY

Timbers Tall
Start Small...

The whole marvelous process
begins with 12-inch seedlings.
Time and care take it from there. CCA
has been delivering expert care to
small timbers—and the resulting quality
products of tall timbers—for more than
half a century.
Helping America's forests stand
tall is our business—
and pleasure. **CCA**

Timber Division

Container Corporation of America
Fernandina Beach, Florida

WORKAHOLIC.

You know the type. Never leaves the office. Gives 100 percent day in and day out. Prefers a tough assignment over a good night's sleep. And wouldn't dream of taking a vacation.

Now you can get this kind of job dedication from, would you believe of all places, your telephone.

It's possible with an exciting business communication product called VMX®, the Voice Message Exchange™. A breakthrough in telephone technology that lets your phone work around the clock. To transfer and receive typical business information faster and more accurately than you ever thought possible.

With VMX® you can send or receive spoken messages at your convenience. You won't have to leave messages with a third party. So there's no room for misinterpretation.

And because VMX® has a user-friendly design that's years ahead of the competition, you get a system that's easier to operate at a lower cost per port.

In just minutes you'll learn how to reduce the number of memos you have to read and write. Shorten your response time to inquiries and requests. Reduce the number and length of everyday business calls. And minimize time zone problems.

Plus, with advance VMX® features such as personalized greetings, user to non-user messaging, and system to system networking you'll find even more ways to put us to work for your company.

The point is, by giving your phone new responsibilities, you can make better use of each precious moment in the day. So while VMX® does the necessary work like: storing, redirecting and broadcasting information, you can concentrate on the important decisions...such as, why do so many Fortune 500 companies have a VMX® system, and maybe your company doesn't?

Write or call today for more information on how VMX® can make your phone work harder for you.

Name _____ Title _____
Company _____
Address _____
City _____ State _____ Zip _____
Telephone _____

VMX VMX, Inc.
1241 Columbia Drive, Richardson,
Texas 75081 214/699-1461

©1983. VMX, Inc., VMX® and Voice Message Exchange™ are trademarks of VMX, Inc.

WHEN YOU PAY FOR WEED CONTROL IT SHOULDN'T HAVE TO COST YOU YIELD.

Lasso delivers full-season grass control with less herbicide stress.

Studies have shown that high performance herbicides can cause herbicide stress to corn and soybean plants.

But there is a full-season herbicide that puts less stress on your crops. Lasso® herbicide stresses young crops less than other grass herbicides.

And that fact can make a difference for you next harvest. Because the less stress on your crop, the better your yield will be.

Lasso provides full-season control of foxtails, fall panicum, crabgrass and other labeled weeds. It even controls tough weeds like pigweed and black nightshade. Yet it still gives you all the yield you're entitled to.

Don't miss out on a single bushel at harvest. Protect your yield with the high performance herbicide that stresses crops less. Protect your yield with Lasso. Monsanto

LASSO. THE YIELD PROTECTOR.

ALWAYS READ AND FOLLOW LABEL DIRECTIONS. Lasso® is a registered trademark of Monsanto Company © Monsanto Company 1984. LAS-4-149D

P E R R Y   E L L I S
P O R T F O L I O

OPENING MONDAY MARCH 12, 1984 575 SEVENTH AVENUE NEW YORK, NEW YORK 212·921·8500

135
Bryce Browning, Joan P. Browning,
  William Orr Designer/Writers
Peter Gerba Photographer
Browning 2 Studio
William Orr Client
San Francisco CA

136
Adrienne Y. Carlin Art Director
Andrew A. Oliver Copywriter
Carlin Advertising, Inc. Agency
Studio NoveNove Client
New York NY

134
Martha Voutas Art Director
Norico Kanai, Martha Voutas Designers
Lynn Kohlman Photographer
MVP et al, Martha Voutas Productions, Inc. Studio
Perry Ellis Portfolio Client
New York NY

137
Stavros Cosmopulos, Tom Demeter Art Directors/Designers
Ken Maryanski Illustrator
Sam Bregande Copywriter
Arrow Composition Tysetting
Cosmopulos Crowley & Daly, Inc. Boston Agency
Allendale Insurance Client
Boston MA

The J Factor.

It's an industry given: management of production systems; manufacturing processes; planning for business growth —whether strategic or tactical; monitoring worldwide market trends; directing research and development; the care for individual productivity and growth; all are the standard functions required of management.

However, we also know what makes the difference is what you can't define or plan for: Insight. Vision. Daring. And especially the ability to recognize the future. In short, the J Factor.

While it's awfully hard for me to say these things about myself, it is nevertheless true that I have been a moving force behind state of the art video editing systems; I was one of the first to understand the American and world potential for DBS.

Now I'm looking to be absorbed in a new endeavor: consumer and broadcast video products; home video programming; international and domestic marketing. It might be your idea. It might be mine.

Give me a call at 415/856-1341, or write me at 450 San Antonio Road, Suite 48, Palo Alto, California 94306.

"The man keeps his promises, that's important to me."
Julius Barnathan,
President,
Engineering,
American Broadcasting
Company, New York

"Smart, honorable, hard working."
Marty Irwin,
AF Associates, New Jersey

"Most knowledgeable and astute businessman I've had the pleasure of knowing."
Larry Finley,
LF Associates,
New York

"In a decade of close association, Bill has always impressed me with his vision of the future of television and with his grasp of video high technology."
Joe Royzen,
Telden, Palo Alto, Calif.

Allendale announces the only sprinkler in the world designed to prevent hell and high water.

It's called ESFR, Early Suppression Fast Response —a remarkable breakthrough in sprinkler technology, designed to respond to a fire faster and more effectively.

Under "high-challenge" fire conditions, flames must be knocked down quickly. If they aren't, everything goes to hell. And you get burned.

Or, present sprinklers can stop the flames but may operate in areas beyond the fire, flooding your inventory. Your company runs the risk of losing its share of the market. And you take a bath.

Either way, you can get hurt.

At Allendale, we've thought a lot about these problems. Enough to fund an extensive research program through the Factory Mutual System to develop ESFR sprinklers.

Entirely new testing methods were used in an effort to better understand the characteristics of high-challenge fires and how to suppress them. Years of research produced the ESFR program. These new sprinklers will be capable of meeting the task of a high-challenge fire, typical of highly combustible materials. And capable of greater cost-effectiveness.

ESFR's performance is designed to be twofold:

Early Suppression means this sprinkler will produce larger water drops resulting in better fire penetration. Fewer sprinkler heads should operate, so less water is needed overall.

Fast Response means the sprinklers have a greater thermal sensitivity and activate much earlier. So a fire is doused before it even has a chance to spread.

No hell or high water.

Prototype ESFRs are currently in development by several major sprinkler manufacturers and will soon be available for installation.

ESFR is just one way Allendale is showing you that we're more than an ordinary insurance company. Our concern for the companies we insure goes well beyond the property coverages we provide.

This is the Allendale approach. Working to take more of the risk out of risk management.

For an update on the ESFR program, write on your letterhead to Michael C. McIntyre, Sr. V. P. Marketing Staff, P.O. Box 7500, Johnston, Rhode Island 02919.

Allendale Insurance/Factory Mutual System

World leaders in risk management.

HEADLINE BROKERS IS GOING PUBLIC.

Headline Brokers, an acknowledged leader in private sales and syndications, is pleased to announce that it will now be available to represent sellers at public auction.

Headline Brokers is now accepting consignments under the management and supervision of John Bradley, formerly vice president/sales manager of Harness Breeders Sales Co., Inc.

Inquiries are welcome at (201) 866-2546.

138

Ted Burn Art Director
Clyde May Photographer
Alf Nucifora, Rich Maender Copywriters
Nucifora & Associates Agency
Headline Brokers, Inc. Client
Atlanta GA

Columbus Dental, Good As Gold.

You're a good businessman. You have your eye on the future. You're building your business, gaining the trust of your clientele, using only the very best products for your professional services. You're in it for the long run.

At Columbus Dental® we're right behind you. Providing you with the most dependable dental materials on the market – Dri-Clave® Ivory® Modern Materials® Steele's® and Surgident® Each the finest product of its kind.

We've been supplying the dental profession with quality products since 1887. You see, we're in it for the long run, too.

Columbus Dental
1000 Chouteau Ave.
P.O. Box 620
Saint Louis, MO 63188 USA
314-241-2988
800-525-7357
Telex 434090

139

David Bartels Art Director
Bill Kumke Designer
Michel Guirevaka Illustrator
Joe Hanrahan Copywriter
Bartels & Company, Inc. Agency
Columbus Dental Co. Client
St. Louis MO

AUGUST. FIRST.

First in quality shopping centers and industrial properties. First in caring for our tenants with attractive, high-traffic locations, competitive rents and the best in tenant services.

We are leasing space in more than a dozen quality centers in Northern and Southern California, in Washington, in New Mexico, and Illinois. Spaces range from 2,000 to 10,000 square feet, and occupancy in some locations can be immediate. Prime pad locations are available, also, for virtually every kind of commercial use.

Call or write us now. Tell us about your requirements and get our list of available locations. Call August. First.

August Management, Inc.
Post Office Box 22630
Long Beach, CA 90801 (213) 424-6131
(800) 352-3718 in California
(800) 821-3332 Continental U.S.

140

Dennis Tordini Art Director
R. Michael Ervin Designer
Tom O'Brien Photographer
Sterling Research Corporation Copywriter
Ervin Advertising and Design, Inc. Agency
August Management, Inc. Client
Seal Beach CA

Invest in a liquid growth fund.

There's never been a better time to make your move to Sugar Free Canada Dry® Ginger Ale. The sugar free category jumped 15% in 1983. And we more than tripled that rate, increasing our sales an incredible 46%!

Our sugar free ginger ale, which has never had caffeine, has always had a taste your customers love. And now we've added NutraSweet,™ so it tastes even better than before. Best of all, we'll be making our move to network TV starting in February. So invest in our liquid growth fund. And take advantage of a valuable asset.

MAKE YOUR MOVE TO CANADA DRY.

Someone was first to make a barn into a house.

When the first person dared to make a car barn a country house, little did they know they'd start a stampede. But what kind of person would ever think of it? Someone who's not part of the herd. A person who sees every part of life a little ahead of every one else. The one-in-a-million who's part of the 15 million "first people" of the Condé Nast Ltd. They don't follow trends. They start them. Where do they get started? The "first people" get page after page of stimulation and information ideas from Vogue, Vanity Fair, House & Garden and GQ.

THE CONDÉ NAST LTD.

THE FIRST PEOPLE. VOGUE VANITY FAIR HOUSE & GARDEN GQ

154
Virginia Halstead Art Director/Designer
Dennis Magdich Illustrator
Andrew Landorf Copywriter
Young and Rubicam, NY Agency
Canada Dry Client
New York NY

155
Herman Davis Art Director/Designer
Christoph Blumrich Illustrator
Frankie Cadwell Copywriter
Cadwell Davis Partners Agency
Conde Nast Publications Client
New York NY

156
Stephen Brothers Art Director
Julius Galian Illustrator
Robin Silverman Copywriter
Sudler & Hennessey, Inc. Agency
Craftsman Color Lithographers Production
Parke-Davis Client
New York NY

157
Bo Zaunders Art Director
Jim Johnston Designer/Copywriter
Jim Marchese Photographer
Jim Johnston Advertising Agency
The Wall Street Journal Client
New York NY

"Hemostasis is a major problem in excision..."

STERILE
THROMBOSTAT
THROMBIN, USP

A controlling factor in tangential excision

During tangential excision, when eschar is removed in sequential layers, capillary bleeding becomes profuse. Rapid-acting THROMBIN, USP (THROMBOSTAT®) controls capillary bleeding on the wound site—preventing excessive blood loss. It is a valuable hemostatic aid, especially where a tourniquet has been used. THROMBIN, USP (THROMBOSTAT) is equally effective in maintaining hemostasis at the donor site, where the removal of a layer of healthy skin prompts excessive capillary oozing.

PARKE-DAVIS

Bill of Particulars.

Bill Backer, Co-founder and president of Backer & Spielvogel. Beneath a soft accent and gentle Southern ways are sharp views about advertising and the agency business. Here, from a recent conversation, are the views of the man whose thoughts and actions have long filled the bill.

On leaving home:
I had an idyllic childhood in Charleston, South Carolina. Charleston specializes in looking backward, in venerating the past. I don't denigrate that, but when you're young and you want to do something creative, you need a different environment. I left to attend Episcopal High in Alexandria, Virginia; then after the Navy, went off to Yale. Finally to New York where I've been ever since. This is the place to be if you're creative; it's where it all happens.

On how it all happened:
My first agency job was at McCann-Erickson. After three years I went to Young & Rubicam. But McCann called back with an attractive offer. So I went back to stay, or so I thought. The last few years, though, I wasn't writing. I was meeting. I wanted to get back to what I'm good at doing. That's making advertising, not talking about it. So I left, planning to go into the music business. I bumped into Carl Spielvogel who'd left Interpublic and—as the trade press might say—the rest is advertising history.

On goals and ideals:
At the start, Carl and I had one goal: to return to a "classic agency" where top management works at a client's business, not their own. Our personal goals? To have some fun, and make some money. We don't intend to be the largest agency in the world. We want clients with good products. We want to keep working. We don't want to become "managers." We don't try to be all things to all people. We believe that what we do, we do better than anyone. We want to keep doing it—for clients who need and want it.

On thinking and the idea:
To work, advertising needs an idea. That requires sharp thinking, about the product and the problem. Television lends advertising people to substituting glitz for ideas. We won't let a tv commercial go to a client until we've done it as a print ad. Print strips away the show business. You find out if there's an idea. With music, we won't take a jingle to a client until we've played the tune with one finger. People don't hum chords and rhythm. There have to be melodic and lyric ideas. You need ideas, in music and all forms of advertising.

On advertising and sales:
Advertising is a substitute for a salesperson, so it should be likable. You wouldn't buy from a salesperson who's rude, arrogant, insulting, would you? Americans like to shop and they like to buy from people they like. That's why we want our advertising to be the best liked in its category. Over the long term, consumers like to do business with people they like, and they respond to advertising created by people who like people.

On dressing our advertising right:
We try to dress our advertising to fit the occasion. How you dress your sales force is very important. So is how you dress your advertising. We call that tone and mood. Some clients may think that sounds arty. But it's critically important to your sales message.

On hiring and firing:
Good people are hard to find—and hiring the wrong person is worse than having no person at all. We want decent people with talent who make life

exciting when they come in all revved up in the morning, self starters who don't need prodding. Some people need tension and crisis. They won't like it here. When they don't work out, we tell them they don't have as bright a future here as they might somewhere else. After all, it's not a matter of who's right or wrong. The environment has to fit the person—and vice versa.

On invisible advertising:
Much advertising seems based on the theory you can beat the clutter if you only yell loud enough. There's no idea, just more noise. The result is advertising that's invisible. To beat clutter, you need advertising that isn't part of the din, advertising that works harder on the third exposure than the first. You don't get it with the boring formulas on which so much advertising is based.

On advertising as an energy business:
Advertising is described as a people business, but I believe it's an energy business. Sure, we depend on people but the differences in talent count only if you can turn on the energy. If you can get eighty percent of anyone's red corpuscles working, you're going to have a big edge. I don't believe you can hope to get one hundred percent of anyone's energy—most agencies get ten percent, maybe twenty percent at the most. All of us get up in the morning with just so many ergs in us. If eighty percent of those ergs can be applied constructively and not destructively you're going to feel the difference.

On The Wall Street Journal:
I've been reading The Journal for years—oh, not every story on every page, but day-in and day-out for what I think is a good reason. The Journal gives me the most unbiased news in print. I'm anti-news media for the most part because too many let their biases show—and not on the editorial pages where bias belongs but in the news reporting. The Journal is remarkably free of bias; you get the facts, straight-on, with no slant. I can count on The Journal to give me the important news, the real news that matters. It's the one publication most apt to become the world's number one news source—not simply for business but for everyone who needs the news. There's no glitz to The Journal, so I wouldn't put a glitzy ad into The Journal. But if I have a good product that's made to appeal to thoughtful people, there couldn't be a better place to advertise it than The Journal. As I said, there's more than chords and rhythm to music, and to a medium. You need ideas. And nothing carries an idea like The Journal.

The Wall Street Journal.
It works.

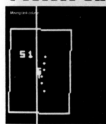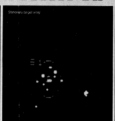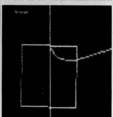

IF IT MOVES AT ALL, WE PICK IT UP. IF IT DOESN'T MOVE, WE STILL PICK IT UP. IF WE CAN'T PICK IT UP, IT'S NOT THERE.

Moving tank column · Stationary target array · No target

For Joint-STARS, nobody else delivers the kind of high-resolution, high-accuracy performance from stand-off distances that we do. Our radar system is the only one with a three-port antenna and CSI (Clutter Suppression Interferometry). It makes real-time, stand-off weapons delivery a sure thing.

Surveillance, target detection/tracking, information processing, and weapons control from the Grumman • Norden • TRW team. Proved in PAVEMOVER. Ready for Joint-STARS.

UNITED TECHNOLOGIES NORDEN SYSTEMS

Fluid bed combustion is the most environmentally acceptable way to get rid of municipal sludge. Nothing else comes close.

You can't bury it cleanly. You can't dump it in the ocean safely. You can't burn it in a multiple hearth incinerator economically.

In fact, the most environmentally acceptable way to get rid of sludge is through fluid bed combustion.

At Dorr-Oliver we've been designing and building fluid bed systems for more than 40 years. We've supplied over 100 communities that are successfully using fluid bed technology right now.

Of course, it's easy to understand why fluid bed systems are so popular. Their reactor design means a low capital investment. Autogenous burning means low fuel bills.

But fluid bed systems don't just save energy. They produce it. Just add on waste heat boilers or other heat recovery equipment, and you've got steam for use as energy.

And fluid bed combustion is clean. Perfectly clean. The stack emission is a colorless, odorless vapor (1500°F exit temperature from the reactor). And there is virtually no particulate matter. All that's left of sludge is inert ash that can easily be carted away for landfill.

For more information on the only way to go with municipal sludge, contact Dorr-Oliver, Stamford, CT 06904.

DORR-OLIVER
A step ahead in process equipment

"My daddy says this place is gonna be mine. I already got a baby calf — you oughta see him!"

Photo by William Albert Allard

BEEF
A Webb Publication

We reach cattlemen.
More important,
cattlemen reach for BEEF.

COSMOPULOS, CROWLEY & DALY, INC.
ADVERTISING/MARKETING
250 BOYLSTON ST., BOSTON, MASS. 02116
266-5500

164
Stavros Cosmopulos Art Director/Copywriter
Arrow Composition Tysetting
Cosmopulos, Crowley & Daly, Inc. Boston Agency/Clie
Boston MA

165
Valrie Lesley Art Director
Richard Haymes Designer/Illustrator
Les L. Lieberman Copywriter
Lesley-Hille, Inc. Agency
Hilson Management Corp. Client
New York NY

166
Karen Kerski Art Director
Michael Garlitz Designer
Michael Costello Copywriter
Thompson Recruitment Advertising, Inc. Agency
RCA Government Systems Division Client
Baltimore MD

Trade
CAMPAIGN

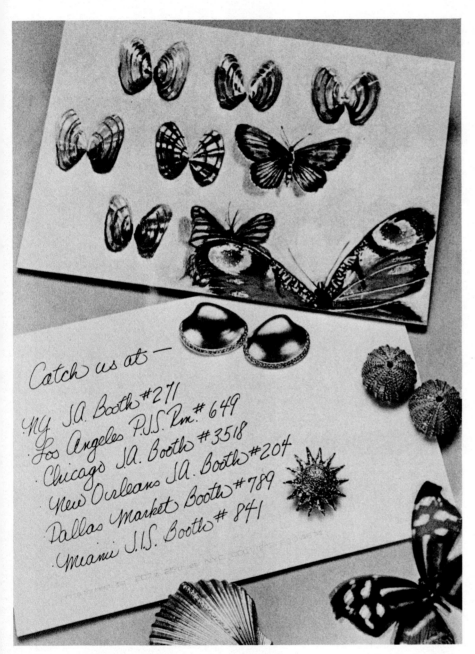

167
Jairo Botero Art Director/Illustrator
Michelle LeGrand Photographer
Mad Comp Design, Inc. Studio
John A. Forrest, Ltd. Client
New York NY

168
Gregory Cutshaw Art Director/Designer
Dawson Jones Photographer
Jon J. Hooper Copywriter
D.W.C. Enterprises Typesetter
The Icon Group Agency
Jim Nelson/Copeland Corporation Client
Dayton OH

SYSTEM SELECTIONS FROM SYVA

SELECT, DON'T SETTLE. **SYVA**

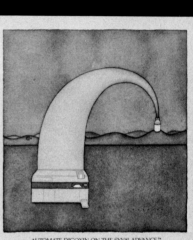

AUTOMATE DIGOXIN ON THE SYVA ADVANCE™

SELECT, DON'T SETTLE. **SYVA**

ROUTE STAT TRAFFIC TO THE SYVA QST SYSTEM

SELECT, DON'T SETTLE. **SYVA**

169
John Schwarz Art Director/Designer
Ariel Skelley Photographer
Kit McCracken Copywriter
Pluzynski & Associates Agency
Aspetuck Trading Co. Client
New York NY

170
Orin Kimball Art Director/Designer
Lonni Sue Johnson Illustrator
Marietta Abrams Copywriter
Gross Townsend Frank, Inc. Agency
Syva Company Client
New York NY

Galina Panova, balle-
rina on Broadway
in "On Your Toes,"
wears our Shape
Maker nylon/Lycra®
Camisole leotard with
criss-cross back, fish-
net tights and silver
ballroom shoes.
For a free copy of our
catalogue, write:
Ballet Makers, Inc.,
Dept. BN384, 1860
Broadway, New York,
New York 10023.

CAPEZIO'S
BEEN DANCING
SINCE 1887.®

The best bodies in the dance world wear Capezio.

171
Frank Young Art Director
Lois Greenfield Photographer
Regina Ovesey Copywriter
Ovesey & Co., Inc. Agency
Capezio by Ballet Makers, Inc. Client
New York NY

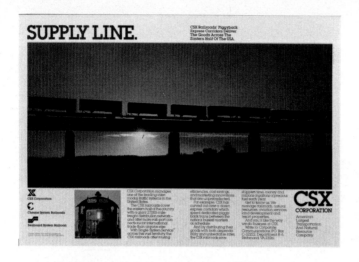

SUPPLY LINE.

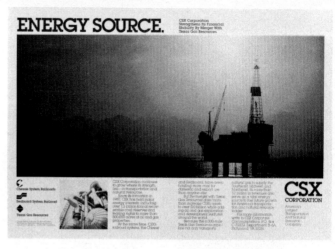

ENERGY SOURCE.

LAUNCHING PAD.

TIMBERLINE.

173

Tony Anthony, Johnny Clark Art Directors
Al Clayton, David Brill, L.D. Gordon-Image Bank Photographers
Mack Kirkpatrick Copywriter
Tucker Wayne & Company Agency
CSX Corporation Client
Atlanta GA

THE DETROIT PIGGY BANK.

SAVING THE NAVY WAY.

THE CINCINNATI PIGGY BANK.

174

Tom Roth Art Director
Gina Federico Designer
John Chang McCurdy Photographer
Erik Gronlund Illustrator
Anderson, Lembke, Welinder, Inc. Agency
Tour & Andersson, Inc. Client
Stamford CT

Now the original is guaranteed twice as long as the imitators.

175

Don Nagel Art Director/Designer
Anthony Arciero Photographer
Millie Alexander Copywriter
D'arcy MacManus Masius Agency
Boulevard Photographic Studio
The Budd Company Client
Bloomfield Hills MI

176

Elissa Querze Art Director
Irv Bahrt Photographer
Karen Irland Copywriter
Sudler & Hennessey, Inc. Agency
L.P. Thebault Production
Parke-Davis Client
New York NY

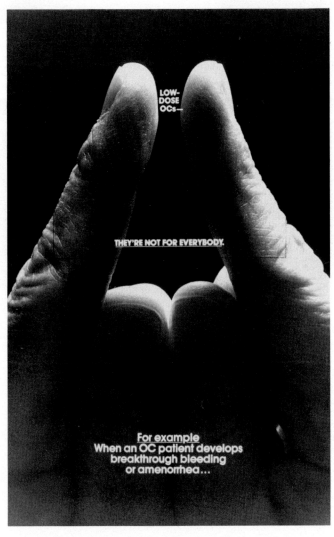

Troubled by fuel separation?

Here's the simple solution.

THE CUTTING TOOL DECISION: WHERE IS THE SENSE IN CARRYING MORE THAN YOU NEED?

Unsure about fuel density?

Here's the simple solution.

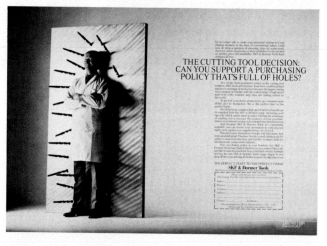

THE CUTTING TOOL DECISION: CAN YOU SUPPORT A PURCHASING POLICY THAT'S FULL OF HOLES?

Worried about fuel quality?

Here's the simple solution.

THE CUTTING TOOL DECISION: WHAT MUST YOU DO TO FIND THE PERFECT SOLUTION?

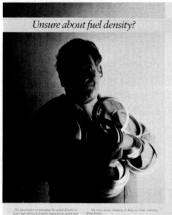

THE CUTTING TOOL DECISION: HOW LONG DOES IT TAKE TO SEE WHAT YOU COULD BE SAVING?

177
John Connolly Art Director/Designer
Graham Ford Photographer
Chris Howden Copywriter
Ronny Nicholas Accounts Director
Ehrenstrahle + Co. Agency
Alfa-Laval Client
London. England

178
John Connolly Art Director/Designer
Graham Ford Photographer
Per Ehrenstrahle Copywriter
Ronny Nicholas Accounts Director
Ehrenstrahle + Co. Agency
SKF + Dormer Tools Client
London. England

BLAIR HAS ONLY ONE RECORD TO BEAT.

OUR OWN.

Talking about winning doesn't make it happen. You've got to go for it. Blair people train to win. At Blair, we prove our record weekly with a computerized Sales Activity Report that tracks every piece of business until it is resolved. Only Blair is organized to sell with knowledge, consistency and believability. Separate network and independent teams sell in New York, Chicago and Los Angeles. Regional specialists are ready to close when money's on the line in their markets. Every Blair salesperson is backed up by a trained sales assistant. Each sales team is supported by its own research group. Experts in sales promotion, agri-marketing, sports, market development and programming to boost station sales. When it comes to competing for Spot TV dollars, there's only one winner. **BLAIR. ONLY BLAIR.** Television

BLAIR HAS ONLY ONE RECORD TO BEAT.

OUR OWN.

Talking about winning doesn't make it happen. You've got to go out and do it. At Blair, we have to run that extra mile just to maintain our pace. We were the first to set up a rep operation exclusively for TV. And we're the rep firm rated #1 among ad agencies. Only Blair talks to media buyers on their own terms. Because we have network, independent and regional experts where it counts. Our people know their stations and their markets. Blair-repped stations have been with us an average of 13 years! And 33 more stations chose Blair to sell for them in the last three years. Our record is their record. Together, we'll keep breaking it. **BLAIR. ONLY BLAIR.** Television

179

Dale Calvert Art Director/Designer
Flip Chalsant, The Image Bank,
Janeart Ltd. Photographers
Dale Calvert Chris Moseley Copywriters

George Gray Studio, Spano/Roccanova Retouching
Muller, Jordan, Weiss Agency
Blair Television Client
New York NY

In air travel, you look good when you stay in control.

The Air Travel Card lets you stay in control of your company's air travel expenses.

That's because it's exclusively for air travel and related expenses. Unlike conventional credit cards, it won't let business and pleasure mix. That gives you control.

For still more control, you get just one statement per billing period that may even be customized to your specific auditing

format. And in most cases, you pay just one refundable deposit with no annual fee or monthly charges, whether you issue 5 cards or 5000.

Join the over 100,000 businesses who fly under control on more than 200 airlines with the Air Travel Card. Return this coupon for complete details.

Get control with the Air Travel Card. You'll look good.

Please send me more information about the Air Travel Card.

Name/Title

Company

Business Address

City   State   Zip

Phone

Mail to: Air Travel Card
525 East Oliver Street
Baltimore, MD 21202

The Air Travel Card

In air travel, control means everything.

The Air Travel Card gives you everything you need to control your company's air travel expenses.

It gives you control because it's exclusively for air travel and related expenses. Unlike conventional credit cards, it won't let business and pleasure mix.

For still more control, you get just one statement per billing period that may even be customized to your specific auditing

format. And in most cases, you pay just one refundable deposit with no annual fee or monthly charges, whether you issue 5 cards or 5000.

Join the over 100,000 businesses who fly under control on more than 200 airlines with the Air Travel Card. Return this coupon for complete details.

The Air Travel Card. It means control. Which means everything.

Please send me more information about the Air Travel Card.

Name/Title

Company

Business Address

City   State   Zip

Phone

Mail to: Air Travel Card
525 East Oliver Street
Baltimore, MD 21202

The Air Travel Card

Only one frequent flyer dares take off without the Air Travel Card.

If you're a mere mortal, you need the Air Travel Card.

When you use it, your company is billed directly. So you can charge air travel expenses without tying up your personal line of credit. And without tying up your time with reimbursement hassles.

What's more, the Air Travel Card gives you a prestigious

piece of identification honored instantly by over 200 airlines worldwide.

Give this coupon to the people who run the numbers in your company. Tell them you want the card that sends you around the world without sending you the bill.

The Air Travel Card. It's superior.

Please send me more information.

Name/Title

Company

Business Address

City   State   Zip

Phone

Mail to: Air Travel Card
525 East Oliver Street
Baltimore, MD 21202

The Air Travel Card

Help your clients fly with the greatest of ease.

Recommend the Air Travel Card.

Every time it is used through your agency you get a full commission. And since the airlines bill your clients directly, you avoid the credit responsibility. What could be easier?

The Air Travel Card makes things easy for clients too. It

gives them precise control of air travel expenses. The simplicity of single-statement billing. And prestigious identification accepted instantly by over 200 airlines worldwide.

The Air Travel Card really works. For satisfying old clients. For getting new clients. And

for building a solid relationship between the airlines and travel agents.

Join the thousands of agents and airlines who market the Air Travel Card. It makes flying easy for us all.

The Air Travel Card

Ken Joy Art Director
Ken Joy, D.C. Comics (Superman) Illustrators
Scott Rasmussen Copywriter
VanSant Dugdale & Co. Agency
Universal Air Travel Plan Client
Baltimore MD

Glen James Art Director/Designer
Mark Simkins Creative Director
Sonya Geyer Illustrator/Copywriter
Geffen Simkins & Marrington Agency
Siemens S.A. Client
Johannesburg RSA

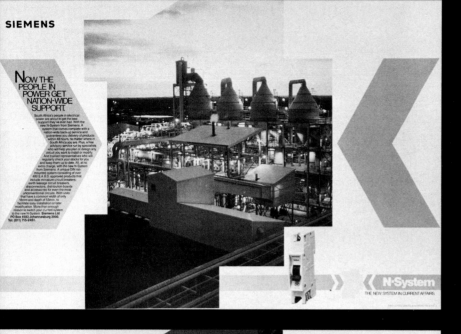

SIEMENS

NOW THE PEOPLE IN POWER GET NATION-WIDE SUPPORT

N·System
THE NEW SYSTEM IN CURRENT AFFAIRS

SIEMENS

PREPARE FOR NEW POWER CONTROL IN SOUTH AFRICA.

N·System
THE NEW SYSTEM IN CURRENT AFFAIRS

SIEMENS

THERE'S ABOUT TO BE A REVOLUTION IN SOUTH AFRICA'S CURRENT SYSTEM.

N·System
THE NEW SYSTEM IN CURRENT AFFAIRS

PROWL

PROWL HANDLES WILD PROSO MILLET AT THE LOWEST COST EVER.

PROWL. YOUR BEST HERBICIDE VALUE.

PROWL

PROWL GIVES GUARANTEED WEED CONTROL AT THE LOWEST COST PER ACRE.

NOW! $5 PER GALLON REBATE.

PROWL

PROWL. GUARANTEED WEED CONTROL. LOWER COST THAN TREFLAN.

PROWL. YOUR BEST HERBICIDE VALUE.

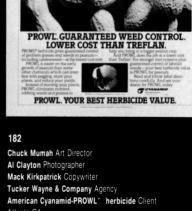

182

Chuck Mumah Art Director
Al Clayton Photographer
Mack Kirkpatrick Copywriter
Tucker Wayne & Company Agency
American Cyanamid-PROWL herbicide Client
Atlanta GA

SUNDSTRAND ACTUATION SYSTEMS. A SWEEPING ADVANCE FOR THE B-1.

184
Dan Scarlotto Art Director/Designer
Richard Hoflich Photographer
Daniel Russ Copywriter
Pringle Dixon Pringle Agency
B.P. Britches Client
Atlanta GA

185
Bob Tanaka Art Director
Buddy Endress, Jan Edmondson Copywriters
Cole & Weber, Inc. Agency
Sundstrand Client
Seattle WA

THE TIGERSHARK FLIES WITH SUNDSTRAND.

183
John Brunner Art Director
Bjorn Keller Photographer
Anders Joost Copywriter
Anderson & Lembke Kungsgatan AB Agency
The Swedish State Railways (SJ) Client
Stockholm, Sweden

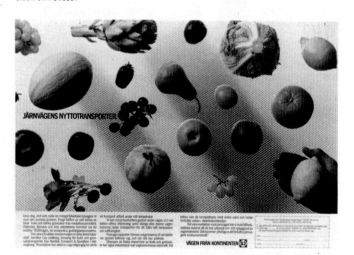

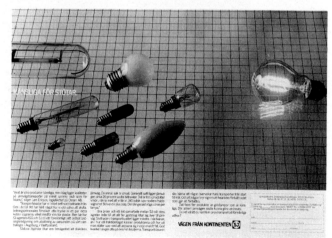

s. It goes without saying.

B.P. Britches. It goes without saying.

We
Made
It.

A new company
entered the
5¼" Winchester
market.

And closed
the door
behind them.

186

Dennis Gagarin, Ottip Ramos, Mike Shennon
  Art Directors/Designers
Del Tycer Creative Director
Rudi Legname, Dow, Clement & Simison Photographers
Tycer-Fultz-Bellack Agency
Maxtor Corporation Client
Palo Alto CA

We've taken
the 5¼" Winchester
from 140 to 380 MB
in six months flat.

And it's only
the beginning.

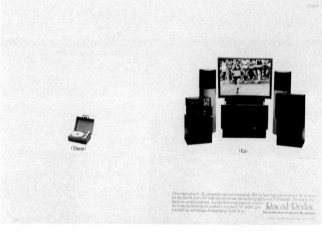

187

Bill Hoo, Jim Fitts Art Directors
Frank Foster Photographer
Carolyn Acterio Illustrator
Charles McAleer, Jon Goward Copywriter
ClarkeGowardFitts Agency
Racal-Redac Client
Boston MA

188
Cynthia Brower Walker Art Director/Designer
Walter Gray Photographer
Martha Kelly Copywriter
J. Walter Thompson Agency
Wilton/Copco Client
Chicago IL

189
Anne Prochazka Art Director
Image Bank, Woodfin Camp, Animals/Animals Photographers
Scott Rasmussen Copywriter
VanSant Dugdale & Co. Agency
Westinghouse Client
Baltimore MD

190
Mogens Sorensen Art Director/Designer
Finn Rosted Photographer
Fred Preston Illustrator
Bill Riley Copywriter
Bergsoe 3, Copenhagen Agency
ScanDutch I/S, Copenhagen Client
Klampenborg, Denmark

191
Michael Cheney Art Director/Designer
George Kase Copywriter
Lou Beres & Associates Agency
Rudy Munis Studio
Lake Shore Bank Client
Chicago IL

Magazine
Covers

Industrial
Launderer
April
1984

Glove
Renovation
In the
Personal
Protection
Market

Spring 1964
Vol. 6. No. 4
ISSN 0163-710X

Family Advocate
A Practical Journal by the ABA Family Law Section

Trial of a
Custody Case

The Child
as Witness

Spotting
the patients
most likely to sue

How
to drive a
car thief crazy

My cleaning
woman was
an extortionist

Don't get
sidetracked by
financial pipe dreams

DECEMBER 12, 1980

medical
economics

WHAT WE CAN
ALL LEARN FROM
MY DAUGHTER'S
BATTLE WITH
COCAINE

195

Karl W. Heuschel Art Director/Designer
Gerd W. Thiel Photographer
Studio Sign Studio
GWP Wirtschaftswoche Client
Frankfurt. Germany

196

Gary Gretter Art Director/Designer
Winslow Homer Artist
SPORTS AFIELD Magazine Client
New York NY

197

Paula Greif Art Director/Designer
Paul Lange Photographer
MADEMOISELLE Magazine-Conde Nast Client
New York NY

198

David Bartels Art Director
Bill Kumke Designer
Shannon Kriegshauser Illustrator
Bartels & Company, Inc. Agency
ART DIRECTION Magazine Client
Saint Louis MO

199

Richard Schemm Art Director
Harold Naideau Photographer
Harold Naideau Studio Studio
Service Publications Client
New York NY

200

Al Foti, Merrill Cason Art Directors
Al Foti Designer
Aleksandr Rodchenko Photographer
MD Publications Client
New York NY

201

Robert V. Engle, Ron Meyerson Art Directors
Melchior DiGiacomo Photographer
NEWSWEEK Magazine Client
New York NY

202

Tony Gregson, Derrick Clinton Carter Art Directors
Barbara Pulling Copywriter
**Association of Book Publishers of
  British Columbia** Client
Vancouver. Canada

The Hairstylist

NOVEMBER/DECEMBER 1983   FIVE DOLLARS

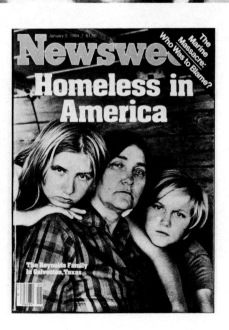

THE JEWISH WOMEN'S MAGAZINE

Issue #11 $3.00
Fall/Winter '83/5744

Lilith

Unmasking Pornography in Israel

Are Feminists Changing Judaism?

Children of Intermarriage: Raising Them as Jews

203
Barbara Taff Art Director/Designer
Jay Manis Photographer
Yona Levine Artist
Lilith Publications Client
New York NY

204
Edwin Torres Art Director/Designer
Linda Obvchoska Photographer
ISLAND Magazine Client
New York NY

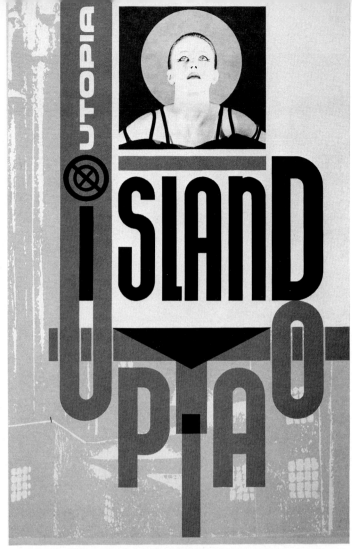

205
Stanley Braverman Art Director/Designer
David Doubilet Photographer
SIGNATURE Magazine Client
New York NY

206
M. Christian Guillon Art Director
Bruno J. Zehnder Photographer
ZOOM Magazine, Paris Client
New York NY

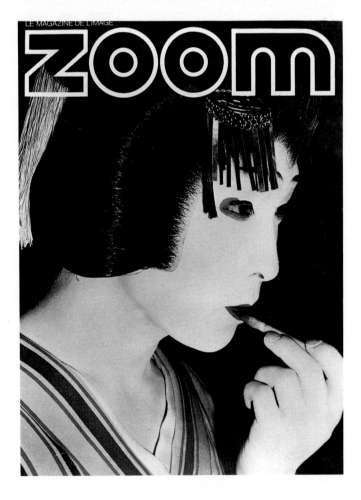

November 1983

MEETINGS & CONVENTIONS
INCLUDING INCENTIVE WORLD

SPECIAL SUPPLEMENT:
1983 Gold Key Hotels

UPBEAT IT&ME
Optimism Marks
Incentive Show

Traditional Hotels

Convention Centers

Anaheim
Atlanta
Orlando
Ohio
Oklahoma

WOMEN AT WORK
*Life on the Edge
of a Social Revolution*

Progressive Architecture

March 1983

THE **W** WORKBOOK

DIRECTORY

AMERICAN AGRICULTURIST

Founded 1842   The Magazine of Northeastern Agriculture   September 1983

207
Lee Ann Jaffee Art Director
Laura Smith Illustrator
MEETINGS & CONVENTIONS
  Magazine-Ziff-Davis
  Publishing Co. Client
New York NY

208
Ken Windsor Art Director/Designer
Eleonore Littasy Photographer
PROGRESSIVE ARCHITECTURE,
  Reinhold Publishing Co., Client
Stamford CT

209
Betsy Rodden Designer
Craig Butler Creative Director
Bob Seidemann Photographer
Lou Beach, Pearl Beach Illustrators
THE WORKBOOK/California Edition Client
Hollywood CA

210
Maureen Viele Art Director/Designer
Alan R. Knight Photographer
Alice Goldfarb Typographer
AMERICAN AGRICULTURIST Client
Ithaca NY

211
Eric Seidman Art Director/Designer
Henry Wolf Photographer
DISCOVER Magazine Client
New York NY

212

Michael Waitsman & Liane Sebastian Art Directors
W.B Parker Illustrator
Synthesis Concepts Studio
A.B.A. Section of Litigation Client
Chicago IL

213

Crit Warren Art Director/Designer
Jay Paris, Lois Abel Harlamert Photographers
OHIO Magazine Client
Columbus OH

214

Karl W. Henschel Art Director/Designer
Gerd W. Thiel Photographer
Studio Sign Studio
HORIZOUT ADVERTISING AGE, Deutschland Client
Frankfurt. Germany

215

Michael Grossman Art Director/Designer
James Wojcik, AP/Wide World Photographer
NATIONAL LAMPOON Magazine Client
New York NY

216

Barbara Solowan Art Director
Walter Chin Photographer
Yanis Ertmanis Chair and Concept
Karen Hanley Editor
CITY WOMAN Magazines—Comac Communications Client
Toronto. Canada

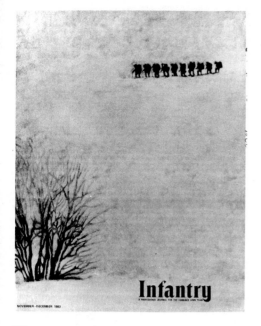

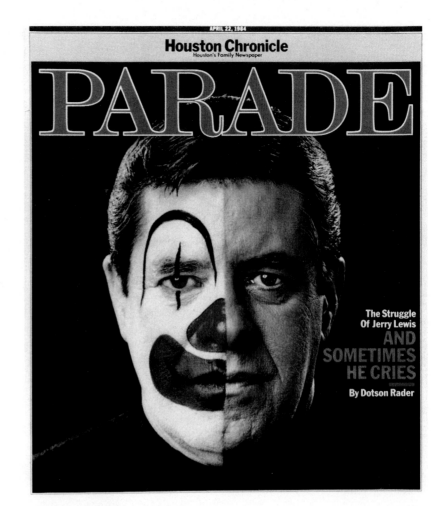

217

Charles Willis Art Director
Mary Ann Norton Designer/Illustrator
INFANTRY Magazine Agency
U.S. Army Client
Fort Benning GA

218

Ira Yoffe, Christopher Austopchuck Art Directors/Designers
Eddie Adams Photographer
Brent Petersen Photo editor
PARADE Magazine Client
New York NY

219

Hall Kelley Art Director/Designer
R.J. Muna Photographer
Nancy Pfund, Jon Rant Copywriter
Repro-Media Inc. Color Seps
Jaciow/Kelley Organization Agency
Intel Corporation Client
Menlo Park CA

220

Gerry Rosentswieg Art Director/Illustrator
The Graphics Studio Studio
Santa Monica Place Client
Los Angeles CA

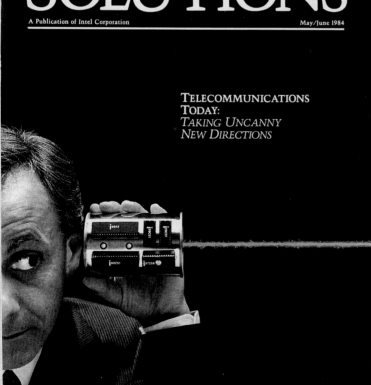

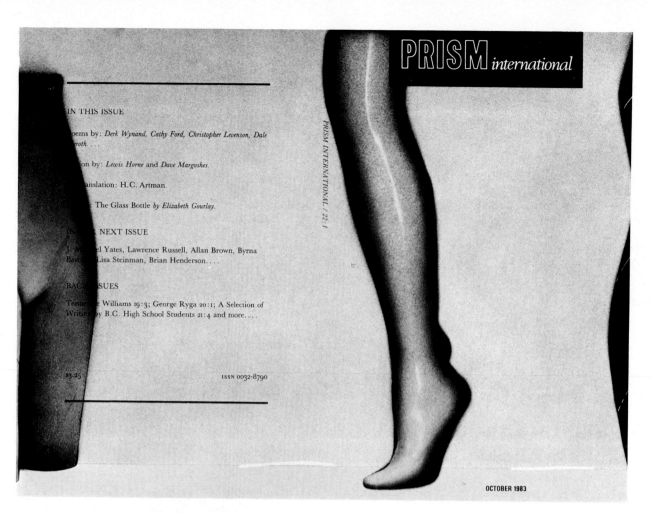

PRISM international

IN THIS ISSUE

Poems by: *Derk Wynand, Cathy Ford, Christopher Levenson, Dale ...roth....*

...on by: *Lewis Horne* and *Dave Margoshes.*

...anslation: H.C. Artman.

... The Glass Bottle *by Elizabeth Gourlay.*

IN ... NEXT ISSUE

J. ... el Yates, Lawrence Russell, Allan Brown, Byrna Bar... Lisa Steinman, Brian Henderson....

BACK ... SUES

Ten... e Williams 19:3; George Ryga 20:1; A Selection of Writing by B.C. High School Students 21:4 and more....

$3.25   ISSN 0032-8790

PRISM INTERNATIONAL / 22:1

OCTOBER 1983

Monthly update on the diagnosis and treatment of cardiovascular disease—Volume 2, Issue 3

CV REVIEW

Special Feature:

Preventing recurrence of cardiac arrest in young patients—Page 2

Continuous GIK infusion in suspected MI—Page 4

MI mortality higher in women—Page 5

Sodium in drinking water—important or not?—Page 9

2-D echo replaces catheterization in children—Page 10

"Smasher" stops heart for study—Page 11

Digital radiography pinpoints arterial structures—Page 12

221
Derrick Clinton Carter, Rick Stevenson Art Directors
Bill Hurst Designer
Jon Baturin Photographer
PRISM INTERNATIONAL Magazine Client
Vancouver. Canada

222
Alan Bottger Art Director/Designer
Ed Acuna Illustrator
Cee Jee Publishing, Inc. Agency
CV REVIEW Magazine Client
New York NY

Book Jackets

223
Ruth Kobert Art Director
Wendell Minor Designer/Photographer
Freundlich Books Client
New York NY

224
Jackie Merri Meyer Art Director/Designer
Alan Kaplan Photographer
MacMillan Publishing Company Client
New York NY

225
Sylvia Frezzolini Art Director
Diane de Groat Illustrator
Wm. Morrow & Co. Client
Yonkers NY

CALIFORNIA
MART

DIRECTORY AND
YELLOW PAGES
JANUARY 1984

THE SEASON OF THE
1984 SUMMER GAMES

110 E. 9TH STREET
LOS ANGELES, CA 90079
(213) 620-0260

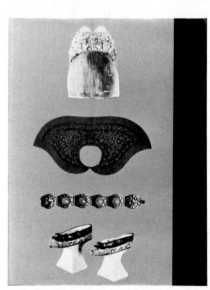

226
Eugene Cheltenham Art Director
Ben Kitay, Eugene Cheltenham Photographers
Eugene Cheltenham Design Agency
California Mart/Directory Office,
  California Mart/Public Relations Client
Los Angeles CA

227
Kan Tai-keung, May Lam Mei-yuen Designers
Zhou Xun, Gao Chunming, Zou Zhenya, Liu Yuemei Illustrators
SS Design & Production Studio
The Commercial Press Ltd. Client
Hong Kong

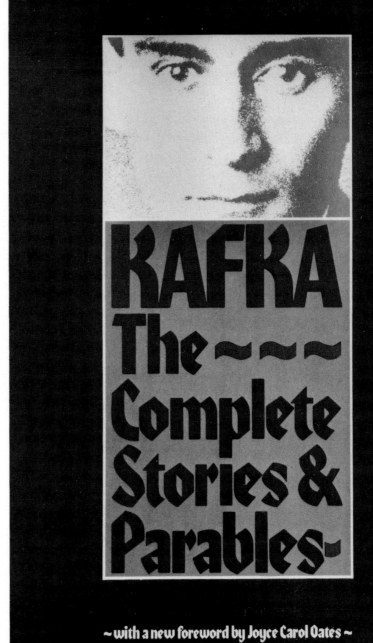

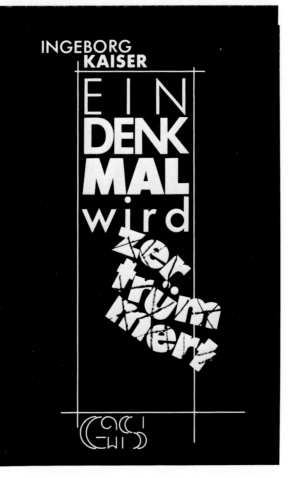

228
Don Munson Art Director
Ruth Ross Designer
George Davidson Production
Ballantine Books Client
New York NY

229
Jessica Weiber Art Director/Designer
Quality Paperback Book Club, A Division of
Book-of-the-Month-Club, Inc. Client
New York NY

230
Albert Gomm Art Director/Designer
GS Yerlag Basel Client
Basel. Switzerland

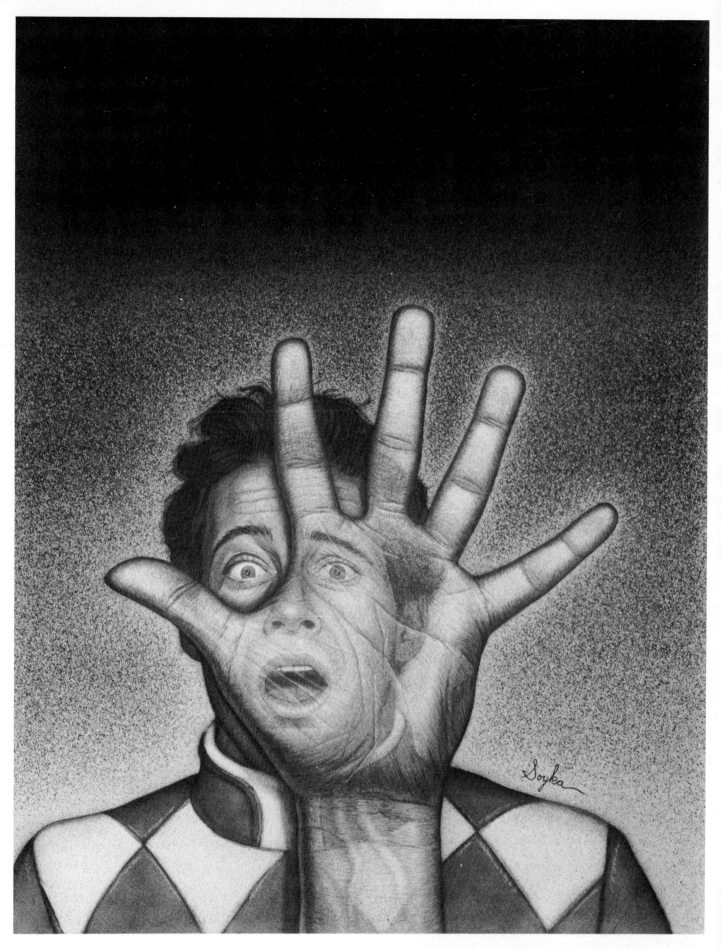

231
Milton Charles Art Director/Designer
Ed Soyka Illustrator
Pocket Books Client
Peekskill NY

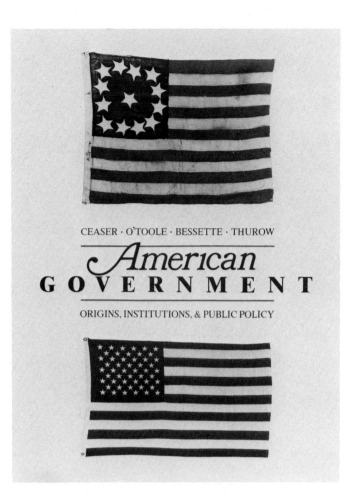

232
Robin Hessel, Nicholas Krenitsky Art Directors
Randy Matusow Photographer
McGraw-Hill Book Company Client
New York NY

233
Nicholas Krenitsky Art Director/Designer
McGraw-Hill Book Company Client
New York NY

234
Doug Bergstrasser Art Director
Nava Atlas Designer/Illustrator
Doubleday & Co., Inc. Client
New York NY

235
Nicholas Krenitsky Art Director/Designer
Annette Shaw Photographer
McGraw-Hill Book Company Client
New York NY

236
Jim Plumeri Art Director
Scott H. Osborne Designer/Illustrator
New American Library Client
New York NY

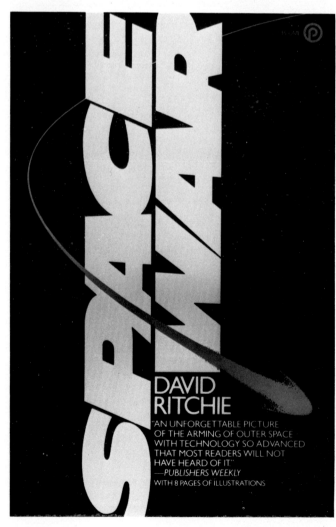

237
Marty Neumeier, Sandra Higashi Designers
Newmeier Design Team Studio
Creative Education, Inc. Client
Santa Barbara CA

238
Lidia Ferrara Art Director
Gun Larson Designer
Michael George Photographer
Alfred A. Knopf Client
New York NY

239
John Sposato Art Director/Designer
Rick Davis Photographer
Villard Books/Random House Client
New York NY

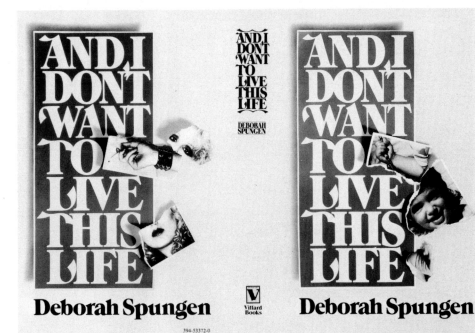

240
Milton Charles Art Director/Designer
Bruno Luchesi Illustrator
Pocket Books Client
New York NY

241
Milton Charles Art Director/Designer
Alan Magee Illustrator
Pocket Books Client
New York NY

242
Lisa Delgado Art Director
Megan Higgins Designer
Ken Karp Photographer
Delgado Design, Inc. Studio
Hayden Book Company Client
New York NY

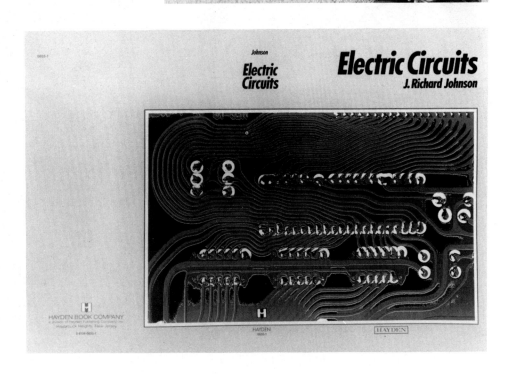

WATERLAND

Graham Swift

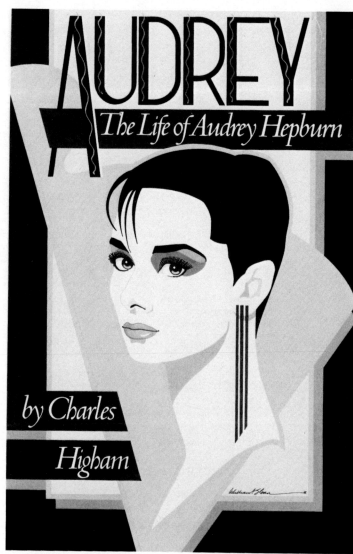

AUDREY

The Life of Audrey Hepburn

by Charles

Higham

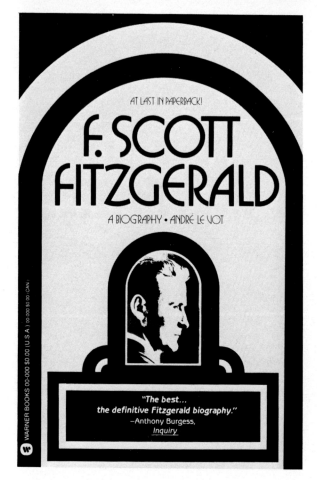

AT LAST IN PAPERBACK!

F. SCOTT FITZGERALD

A BIOGRAPHY • ANDRÉ LE VOT

*"The best...
the definitive Fitzgerald biography."*
—Anthony Burgess,
Inquiry

WARNER BOOKS 00-000 $0.00 (U.S.A.) 00-000 $0.00 (CAN.)

Magruder's

AMERICAN GOVERNMENT

McClenaghan

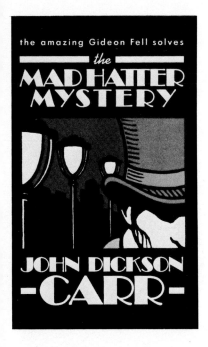

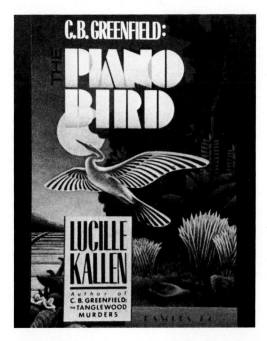

243

Milton Charles Art Director
Fred Marcellino Designer/Photographer
Pocket Books Client
New York NY

244

Jackie Merri Meyer Art Director
William Sloan/Three Designer/Illustrator
MacMillan Publishing Company Client
New York NY

245

Gene Light Art Director
James Laird Designer
Bettman Archive Photographer
James Laird Design Studio
Warner Books Client
N. Tarrytown NY

246

L. Christopher Valente Art Director
John Martucci Designer/Photographer
Allyn & Bacon, Inc. Client
Newton MA

247

Jacki Merri Meyer Art Director
Bascove Designer/Illustrator
MacMillan Publishing Company Client
New York NY

248

Bob Aulicino Art Director
David Tamura Designer/Illustrator
Random House, Inc. Client
New York NY

249

Jackie Merri Meyer Art Director
Mary Mietzelfeld Designer/Illustrator
MacMillan & Co. Client
New York NY

250

Sara Eisenman Art Director
David Tamura Designer/Illustrator
Alfred Knopf, Inc. Client
New York NY

University of Utah Press Poetry Series

Maura Stanton

Cries of Swimmers

DR. AARON HASS

LOVE, SEX, & THE SINGLE MAN

addresses

251
Scott Engen Art Director/Designer
Lewis Dreyer, Jack Churchill Photographers
University of Utah Press Client
Salt Lake City UT

252
Judie Mills Art Director
Nicholas Krenitsky Designer
Franklin Watts, Inc. Client
New York NY

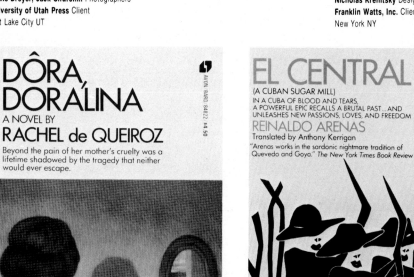

DÔRA, DORALINA
A NOVEL BY
RACHEL de QUEIROZ
Beyond the pain of her mother's cruelty was a
lifetime shadowed by the tragedy that neither
would ever escape.

EL CENTRAL
(A CUBAN SUGAR MILL)
IN A CUBA OF BLOOD AND TEARS,
A POWERFUL EPIC RECALLS A BRUTAL PAST...AND
UNLEASHES NEW PASSIONS, LOVES, AND FREEDOM
REINALDO ARENAS
Translated by Anthony Kerrigan
"Arenas works in the sardonic nightmare tradition of
Quevedo and Goya." The New York Times Book Review

AVON BARD 84822 $4.50

AVON BARD 86934 $3.50

253
Matt Tepper Art Director
Donna Pacinelli Illustrator
Avon Books Client
New York NY

254
Matt Tepper Art Director
Martha Sedgwick Designer
Avon Books Client
New York NY

Record Jackets

255

Jeff Ayeroff Art Director
Lynn Robb Designer
Lou Beach Illustrator
A + M Records Client
Los Angeles CA

256
Javier Romero/Rafael Rovira
 Art Directors
Javier Romero Illustrator
Periscope Studio, Inc. Studio
Memo Records Client
New York NY

257
Douglas Joseph, Clif Boule
 Art Director
Cliff Boule Illustrator
Montage Records Client
Los Angeles CA

259
David Byrne Designer/Photographer
Francie McBride Production
Warner Bros. Records Client
Burbank CA

258
Dawn Cooper, Glynn Bell Designers
Dawn Cooper Illustrator
Cooper Bell Limited Studio
William Tenn Management Client
Toronto. Canada

260
Javier Romero Art Director/Designer
Periscope Studio, Inc. Studio
Memo Records Client
New York NY

261
Gerd F. Setke Art Director/Designer
Atelier Setzke Studio
Albert Bauer KG Client
Hamburg. West Germany

262
John Berg Art Director/Designer
Marcus DeVoe Photographer
CBS Records Client
New York NY

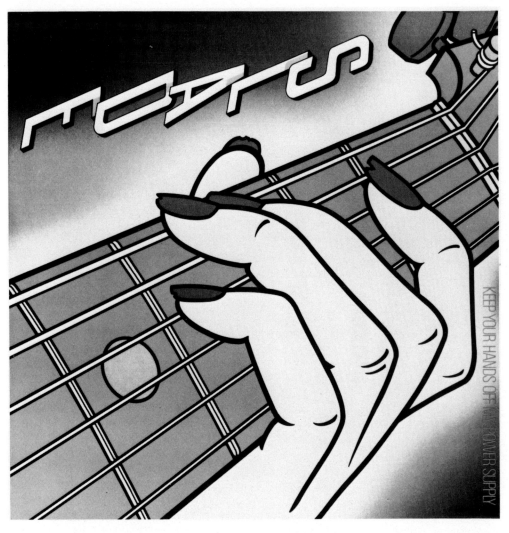

263
Josephine DiDonato Art Director/Designer
Lou Brooks Illustrator
CBS Records Client
New York NY

264
Rod Dyer Art Director
Clive Piercy Designer
Dyer/Kahn, Inc. Agency
Geffen Records Client
Los Angeles CA

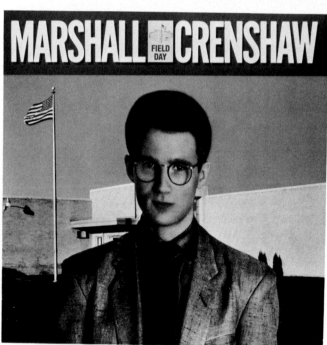

265
Michael Dexter Art Director/Designer
Dave Calver Illustrator
Salvato & Coe Studio
Earthtone Recording Company Client
Columbus OH

266
Tibor Kalman, Carol Bokuniewicz Art Directors
Larry Williams Photographer
M&Co. Agency
Warner Bros. Records Client
New York NY

267
Jeffrey Kent Ayeroff, Paula Greif Art Directors
Jeri McManus Designer
E.K.T.V. Photographer
Hugh Brown Special Thanks
Warner Bros. Records Client

268
Henrietta Condak Art Director/Designer
Mel Odom Illustrator
CBS Masterworks Client
New York NY

269
Patrick Florville Art Director/Designer
John Firman Photographer
Florville Design & Analysis Studio
Zekle Music Productions Client
New York NY

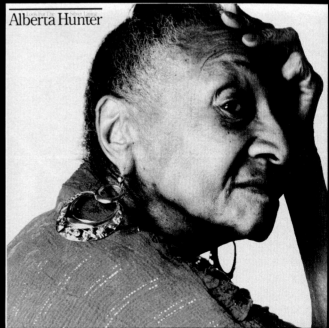

270
Cyd Kilbey Gorman Art Director
Sam Irvin Designer
Alain Venisse (Blk. & Wht.) Photographer
Mary Anne Shea (Hand Tinting) Illustrator
Graphix Studio
DRG Records Client
New York NY

271
Allen Weinberg Art Director/Designer
Bill King Photographer
CBS Records Client
New York NY

272
Christopher Lione Art Director/Designer
CBS Masterworks Client
New York NY

273
Spencer Drate, Judith Salavetz, Meryl Laguna, Joan Jett Art Directors
Dieter Zill Photographer
Dratedesign Inc. Agency
Blackheart Records/Jett Lag Inc. Client
New York NY

274
Spencer Drate, Judith Salavetz Designers
Stephen Durke Illustrator
DrateDesign Inc. Agency
Rocker Fella Productions, Inc. Client
New York NY

275
Michael Dexter Art Director/Designer
Roman Sapecki Photographer
Salvato & Coe Studio
Earthtone Recording Company Client
Columbus OH

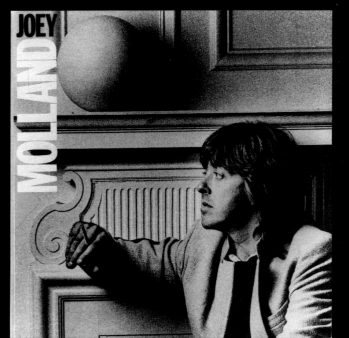

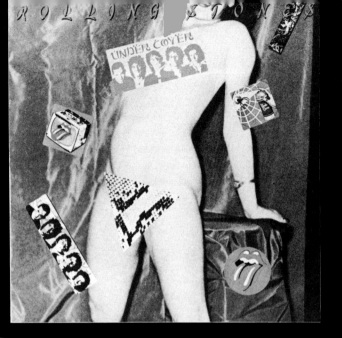

276
Hubert Kretzschmar Designer/Illustrator
Rolling Stones Records Client
New York NY

277
John Coy Art Director
John Coy, Kevin Consales Designers
Grant Mudford Photographer
David Levy Lithography Printer
COY, Los Angeles Studio
Museum of Contemporary Art, Los Angeles Client
Culver City CA

278
Janet Perr Art Director/Designer
Annie Leibovitz Photographer
CBS Records Client
New York NY

House Organs

279
Dean Morris Art Director/Designer
Judith Garten Editor
Kim Lyons Editorial Assistant
The Adams Group Production
Cooper Union Alumni Association Client
New York NY

At Art Center

280
Don Kubly Art Director
John Hoernle Designer
John Vince Photographer
Maxine Gaiber Copywriter
Art Center College of Design Client
Pasadena CA

281
Robert Cooney Art Director/Designer
R.A. Cooney, Inc. Agency
Continental Insurance/Marine Office of America Corp. Client
New York NY

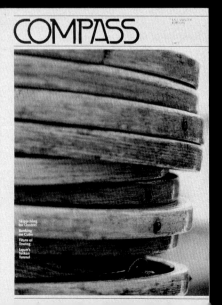

COMPASS

THE MORANS AND THE McCALLISTERS
TITANS OF TOWING

282
Gina Stone, Philip Gips Art Directors/Designers
Jean Marie Guyaux Photographer
Seymour Chwast Illustrator
Michael Mudd Copywriter

Gips + Balkind + Associates Agency
BBDO Client
New York NY

COMMUNIQUÉ

A NEWSLETTER OF THE COLLEGE OF FINE ARTS AND COMMUNICATION / TOWSON STATE UNIVERSITY / TOWSON, MARYLAND 21204 / VOLUME 2 NUMBER 1/NOVEMBER 1983

"THE GANG'S ALL HERE" . . .
Shown are the nearly 50 young-sters, ages 8-18, who participated in TSU's first Summer Dance Camp in August. Pictured with the group are members of the dance camp faculty. Work has already been started in planning next year's summer dance camp. For information, contact the dance office at (301) 321-2760. ■

PROFILE
CAMILLE IZARD
by Katie Ryan

It's really not surprising to her that she's in a university setting teaching, even though she has a fairly new college degree herself. Camille Izard, a new part-time faculty member in the dance department, has strong college/university ties. You might say they're hereditary! Her parents teach at the University of Delaware—her mother in the theater department and her father in psychology.

Education has been a part of her life since she can remember, but: "Ballet was, and is, my true love."

Dancing since she was a small child, Ms. Izard felt that ballet would be her life beginning when she was age 9. "I saw the movie 'The Red Shoes' when I was 9 and I knew that I wanted to be a dancer. I was always a well-motivated person, even as a child. And I still am," she says matter-of-factly.

Studying dance and performing became serious business for the young woman, so much so that she finished high school by correspondence. "It involved a lot of discipline—to dance all day and to do my high school work at night. It also took a lot of trust from my parents."

She has danced with several companies, but is probably best remembered locally for dancing with the Maryland Ballet Company from 1975-78. A graceful classic dancer, she often stole the show when performing "The Nutcracker," "Sleeping Beauty," "Don Quixote," and "LeCorsaire" at the Lyric Theater or at Kraushauer Auditorium at Goucher College.

It was during her time at the Maryland Ballet that she competed in the Third International Ballet Competition in Moscow and captured the award for artistic excellence. *Tass*, the official Soviet News Agency, reported that

"Camille Izard won over the Moscow public by her musicality, plasticity and purity of form." The chauvinistic Moscow audiences repeatedly gave her sustained applause and the Moscow critics loved her.

After leaving Baltimore, Ms. Izard joined the prestigious American Ballet Theater in New York. For two years, she performed with the company in New York as well as on national tours. She left the company primarily to resume her education.

"I have a pattern of doing one thing very intensely. There have been about three periods in my life that I have concentrated on one thing almost to the exclusion of others."

Resuming and completing her education became an area of concentration for about two years. She had started her degree program in psychology at the University of Maryland College Park while dancing with the Maryland Company. She resumed her studies at Hunter College and graduated summa cum laude in June of 1982 with her degree in psychology. While at Hunter, she was teaching and coaching dance on a free-lance basis and took a pedagogical course as well.

1983 — Why back in Baltimore and why TSU?

Her ties began to gravitate from New York to Baltimore. She was teaching free-lance in both Delaware and Pennsylvania and became the artistic advisor with the Delaware Dance Company in Newark, Delaware; and she also began teaching for a friend of hers—Caryl Maxwell who has studios in Ellicott City.

"My ties to this area have never been severed. When I began teaching for Caryl Maxwell, I began to look around for something else." Having heard of TSU's reputation for its dance program, she contacted Helene Breazeale, the director, and has now

had her first taste of teaching at TSU. She taught Beginning Ballet this summer. "In a nutshell, I loved it." She's looking forward to teaching another Beginning Ballet class as well as Intermediate Ballet in the fall.

And the future?

She recently choreographed a ballet "Zephras" which will be performed by the Ellicott City Ballet Company. "Ultimately, my goal is to stay balanced with dancing as the rubric. I would like to pursue an advanced degree in psychology here at Towson and keep a balanced social life. Dancing will always be a part of my life. I'm psychologically motivated to dance."

Ms. Izard will be performing here at Towson on November 5 when the Faculty Dance Show is presented. ■

TAKING A TURN AT THE BARRE *are students in the fall Saturday Children's Dance Program, sponsored by the dance department. The program, which continues through December 17, is designed for children, ages 4-17. It consists of courses in creative movement, introduction to dance and the different styles of dancing, including tap, jazz, modern dance and ballet. The spring 1984 Saturday children's dance program begins February 11. For information, call the TSU dance office at (301) 321-2760.*

283
W. Michael Dunne Jr. Art Director
Lois A. Toulette, Bertin Toulette Designers
J. Michael O'Neill Photographer
Daniel Walsch, Katie Ryan Copywriters
Towson State University College of Fine Arts & Communication Client
Towson MD

284

Albert Cullere Art Director/Designer
ADG-FAD Client
Barcelona, Spain

285

Susan Borgen Art Director/Designer
Jennifer Jecklin Photographer
Susan Gilbert Executive Editor
Timothy Connor Managing Editor
Metro-North Commuter Railroad Agency/Client
New York NY

Para el estudio y la modernización racional de la tipografía.

El Supertipo Veloz

ADGFAD BUTLLETÍ

9
Febrer 1984

On Track

The Monthly News Publication for Metro-North Employees   December 1983

Metro Roadrunners Run Away with Top Honors in Challenge

On Track

The Monthly News Publication for Metro-North Employees   January 1984

Rail Tours Give Employees First-Hand Look at Operations

On Track

The Monthly News Publication for Metro-North Employees   February 1984

Repairs on the Run

BEST·TIMES

Volume VIII
Number 9

October
1983

For employees of
Best Products Co., Inc.

Customer service is our No. 1 priority, J. Lee Hawks, senior vice president—operations, says emphatically. And to help Best Products employees give customers the very best service during the nine-week holiday selling season that runs from Oct. 30 to Dec. 31, a comprehensive program called "Best Spirit"

(please turn to page 3)

inside: Lotsa on page 3, Rogers' 30th anniversary on page 4 . . .

286
Rob Carter Art Director/Designer
Mallory Callan Illustrator
Laura Cameron Copywriter
Rob Carter Design Studio
Best Products Co., Inc. Client
Richmond VA

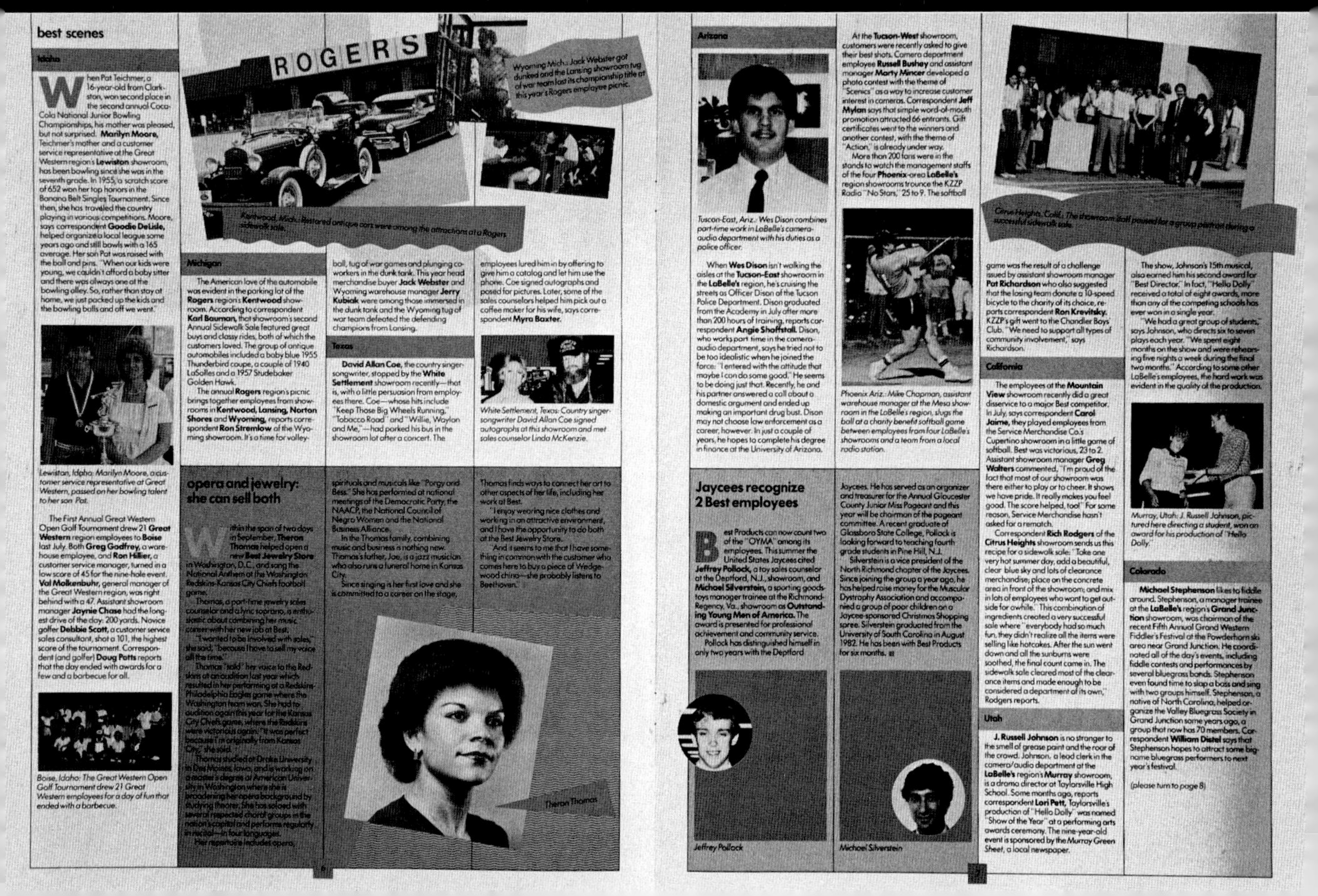

best scenes

Idaho

When Pat Teichmer, a 16-year-old from Clarkston, won second place in the second annual Coca-Cola National Junior Bowling Championships, his mother was pleased, but not surprised. **Marilyn Moore,** Teichmer's mother and a customer service representative at the Great Western region's **Lewiston** showroom, has been bowling since she was in the seventh grade. In 1955, a scratch score of 652 won her top honors in the Banana Belt Singles Tournament. Since then, she has traveled the country playing in various competitions. Moore, says correspondent **Goodie DeLisle,** helped organize a local league some years ago and still bowls with a 165 average. Her son Pat was raised with the ball and pins. "When our kids were young, we couldn't afford a baby sitter and there was always one at the bowling alley. So, rather than stay at home, we just packed up the kids and the bowling balls and off we went."

Lewiston, Idaho: Marilyn Moore, a customer service representative at Great Western, passed on her bowling talent to her son Pat.

The First Annual Great Western Open Golf Tournament drew 21 **Great Western** region employees to **Boise** last July. Both **Greg Godfrey,** a warehouse employee, and **Ron Hillier,** a customer service manager, turned in a low score of 45 for the nine-hole event. **Val Molkenbuhr,** general manager of the Great Western region, was right behind with a 47. Assistant showroom manager **Jaynie Chase** had the longest drive of the day: 200 yards. Novice golfer **Debbie Scott,** a customer service sales consultant, shot a 101, the highest score of the tournament. Correspondent (and golfer) **Doug Potts** reports that the day ended with awards for a few and a barbecue for all.

Boise, Idaho: The Great Western Open Golf Tournament drew 21 Great Western employees for a day of fun that ended with a barbecue.

Kentwood, Mich.: Restored antique cars were among the attractions at a Rogers sidewalk sale.

Wyoming Mich.: Jack Webster got dunked and the Lansing showroom tug of war team lost its championship title at this year's Rogers employee picnic.

Michigan

The American love of the automobile was evident in the parking lot of the **Rogers** region's **Kentwood** showroom. According to correspondent **Karl Bauman,** that showroom's second Annual Sidewalk Sale featured great buys and classy rides, both of which the customers loved. The group of antique automobiles included a baby blue 1955 Thunderbird coupe, a couple of 1940 LaSalles and a 1957 Studebaker Golden Hawk.

The annual **Rogers** region's picnic brings together employees from showrooms in **Kentwood, Lansing, Norton Shores** and **Wyoming,** reports correspondent **Ron Stremlow** of the Wyoming showroom. It's a time for volleyball, tug of war games and plunging co-workers in the dunk tank. This year head merchandise buyer **Jack Webster** and Wyoming warehouse manager **Jerry Kubiak** were among those immersed in the dunk tank and the Wyoming tug of war team defeated the defending champions from Lansing.

Texas

David Allan Coe, the country singer-songwriter, stopped by the **White Settlement** showroom recently—that is, with a little persuasion from employees there. Coe—whose hits include "Keep Those Big Wheels Running," "Tobacco Road" and "Willie, Waylon and Me,"—had parked his bus in the showroom lot after a concert. The employees lured him in by offering to give him a catalog and let him use the phone. Coe signed autographs and posed for pictures. Later, some of the sales counselors helped him pick out a coffee maker for his wife, says correspondent **Myra Baxter.**

White Settlement, Texas: Country singer-songwriter David Allan Coe signed autographs at this showroom and met sales counselor Linda McKenzie.

opera and jewelry: she can sell both

Within the span of two days in September, **Theron Thomas** helped open a new **Best Jewelry Store** in Washington, D.C., and sang the National Anthem at the Washington Redskins-Kansas City Chiefs football game.

Thomas, a part-time jewelry sales counselor and a lyric soprano, is enthusiastic about combining her music career with her new job at Best.

"I wanted to be involved with sales," she said, "because I have to sell my voice all the time."

Thomas "sold" her voice to the Redskins at an audition last year which resulted in her performing at a Redskins-Philadelphia Eagles game where the Washington team won. She had to audition again this year for the Kansas City Chiefs game, where the Redskins were victorious again. "It was perfect because I'm originally from Kansas City," she said.

Thomas studied at Drake University in Des Moines, Iowa, and is working on a master's degree at American University in Washington where she is broadening her opera background by studying theater. She has soloed with several respected choral groups in the nation's capital and performs regularly in recital—in four languages.

Her repertoire includes opera, spirituals and musicals like "Porgy and Bess." She has performed at national meetings of the Democratic Party, the NAACP, the National Council of Negro Women and the National Business Alliance.

In the Thomas family, combining music and business is nothing new. Thomas's father, Joe, is a jazz musician who also runs a funeral home in Kansas City.

Since singing is her first love and she is committed to a career on the stage, Thomas finds ways to connect her art to other aspects of her life, including her work at Best.

"I enjoy wearing nice clothes and working in an attractive environment, and I have the opportunity to do both at the Best Jewelry Store.

"And it seems to me that I have something in common with the customer who comes here to buy a piece of Wedgewood china—she probably listens to Beethoven."

Theron Thomas

Arizona

Tuscon-East, Ariz.: Wes Dison combines part-time work in LaBelle's camera-audio department with his duties as a police officer.

When **Wes Dison** isn't walking the aisles at the **Tucson-East** showroom in the **LaBelle's** region, he's cruising the streets as Officer Dison of the Tucson Police Department. Dison graduated from the Academy in July after more than 200 hours of training, reports correspondent **Angie Shaffstall.** Dison, who works part time in the camera-audio department, says he tried not to be too idealistic when he joined the force: "I entered with the attitude that maybe I can do some good." He seems to be doing just that. Recently, he and his partner answered a call about a domestic argument and ended up making an important drug bust. Dison may not choose law enforcement as a career, however. In just a couple of years, he hopes to complete his degree in finance at the University of Arizona.

At the **Tucson-West** showroom, customers were recently asked to give their best shots. Camera department employee **Russell Bushey** and assistant manager **Marty Mincer** developed a photo contest with the theme of "Scenics" as a way to increase customer interest in cameras. Correspondent **Jeff Mylan** says that simple word-of-mouth promotion attracted 66 entrants. Gift certificates went to the winners and another contest, with the theme of "Action," is already under way.

More than 200 fans were in the stands to watch the management staffs of the four **Phoenix**-area **LaBelle's** region showrooms trounce the KZZP Radio "No Stars," 25 to 9. The softball game was the result of a challenge issued by assistant showroom manager **Pat Richardson** who also suggested that the losing team donate a 10-speed bicycle to the charity of its choice, reports correspondent **Ron Krevitsky.** KZZP's gift went to the Chandler Boys' Club. "We need to support all types of community involvement," says Richardson.

Phoenix Ariz.: Mike Chapman, assistant warehouse manager at the Mesa showroom in the LaBelle's region, slugs the ball at a charity benefit softball game between employees from four LaBelle's showrooms and a team from a local radio station.

Citrus Heights, Calif.: The showroom staff posed for a group portrait during a successful sidewalk sale.

California

The employees at the **Mountain View** showroom recently did a great disservice to a major Best competitor. In July, says correspondent **Carol Jaime,** they played employees from the Service Merchandise Co.'s Cupertino showroom in a little game of softball. Best was victorious, 23 to 2. Assistant showroom manager **Greg Walters** commented, "I'm proud of the fact that most of our showroom was there either to play or to cheer. It shows we have pride. It really makes you feel good. The score helped, too!" For some reason, Service Merchandise hasn't asked for a rematch.

Correspondent **Rich Rodgers** of the **Citrus Heights** showroom sends us this recipe for a sidewalk sale: "Take one very hot summer day, add a beautiful, clear blue sky and lots of clearance merchandise; place on the concrete area in front of the showroom; and mix in lots of employees who want to get outside for awhile." This combination of ingredients created a very successful sale where "everybody had so much fun, they didn't realize all the items were selling like hotcakes. After the sun went down and all the sunburns were soothed, the final count came in. The sidewalk sale cleared most of the clearance items and made enough to be considered a department of its own," Rodgers reports.

Utah

J. Russell Johnson is no stranger to the smell of grease paint and the roar of the crowd. Johnson, a lead clerk in the camera/audio department at the **LaBelle's** region's **Murray** showroom, is a drama director at Taylorsville High School. Some months ago, reports correspondent **Lori Pett,** Taylorsville's production of "Hello Dolly" was named "Show of the Year" at a performing arts awards ceremony. The nine-year-old event is sponsored by the *Murray Green Sheet,* a local newspaper.

The show, Johnson's 15th musical, also earned him his second award for "Best Director." In fact, "Hello Dolly" received a total of eight awards, more than any of the competing schools has ever won in a single year.

"We had a great group of students," says Johnson, who directs six to seven plays each year. "We spent eight months on the show and were rehearsing five nights a week during the final two months." According to some other LaBelle's employees, the hard work was evident in the quality of the production.

Murray, Utah: J. Russell Johnson, pictured here directing a student, won an award for his production of "Hello Dolly."

Colorado

Michael Stephenson likes to fiddle around. Stephenson, a manager trainee at the **LaBelle's** region's **Grand Junction** showroom, was chairman of the recent Fifth Annual Grand Western Fiddler's Festival at the Powderhorn ski area near Grand Junction. He coordinated all of the day's events, including fiddle contests and performances by several bluegrass bands. Stephenson even found time to slap a bass and sing with two groups himself. Stephenson, a native of North Carolina, helped organize the Valley Bluegrass Society in Grand Junction some years ago, a group that now has 70 members. Correspondent **William Distel** says that Stephenson hopes to attract some big-name bluegrass performers to next year's festival.

(please turn to page 8)

Jaycees recognize 2 Best employees

Best Products can now count two of the "OYMA" among its employees. This summer the United States Jaycees cited **Jeffrey Pollock,** a toy sales counselor at the Deptford, N.J., showroom, and **Michael Silverstein,** a sporting goods-toys manager trainee at the Richmond-Regency, Va., showroom as **Outstanding Young Men of America.** The award is presented for professional achievement and community service.

Pollock has distinguished himself in only two years with the Deptford Jaycees. He has served as an organizer and treasurer for the Annual Gloucester County Junior Miss Pageant and this year will be chairman of the pageant committee. A recent graduate of Glassboro State College, Pollock is looking forward to teaching fourth grade students in Pine Hill, N.J.

Silverstein is a vice president of the North Richmond chapter of the Jaycees. Since joining the group a year ago, he has helped raise money for the Muscular Dystrophy Association and accompanied a group of poor children on a Jaycee-sponsored Christmas Shopping spree. Silverstein graduated from the University of South Carolina in August 1982. He has been with Best Products for six months.

Jeffrey Pollock

Michael Silverstein

287

Larry Lamm, Don Denny, Mike Huntley Designers
Bill Thomson Editor
Philip Morris Design Group Studio
Philip Morris USA, Richmond, VA Client
Richmond VA

288

Jim Sanders, Lee Heidel Art Directors
Bruce Bollinger Photographer
Bud Huntoon Illustrator
Jennie Storey Editor
Provident Client
Chattanooga TN

289

Denise Halpin, Robert Webster Art Directors/Designers
Darryl Zudeck, Robert Webster Illustrators
Robert I. Greene Editor
Catherine Gonick Managing Editor
Rick Young, Enid Goldberg, Marc Frankel,
  Jim Carey Copywriters
Robert Webster, Inc. Studio
Chase Manhattan Bank N.A. Client
New York NY

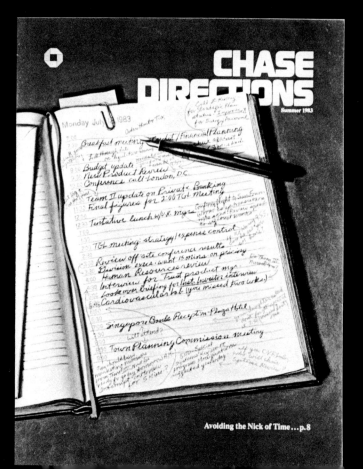

PM thrives under "adverse, highly competitive conditions"

Employees continue efforts to reduce accidents

record sales

290
Anthony Russell Art Director
Kevin McPhee Designer
Eric Sauter Editor
Squibb Corporation Client
New York NY

291
Gordon Mortensen Art Director/Designer
Gary Pierazzi Illustrator
Terri Hodges Copywriter
Mortensen Design Agency
Austin Assoc./Triad Systems Client
Palo Alto CA

292
Zane Carter, Ken Cosgrove Art Directors/Designers
Cameron Davidson Photographer
Carter/Cosgrove Agency
Bell Atlantic Client
Washington DC

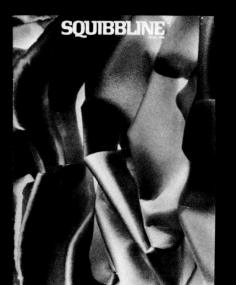

Triad Expands Customer Education Program

Ligature

THE TYPOGRAPHIC COMMUNICATION JOURNAL. PUBLISHED BY WORLD TYPEFACE CENTER INC., VOLUME TWO, NUMBER TWO, SEPTEMBER 1983

293
Jason Calfo, Doug May Designers
Tom Carnase Editor
Carnase, Inc. Design Firm
World Typeface Center, Inc. Client

Volume 26 No. 4

294

Bruce Withers, Laure Torrisi Designers
Jeff Aranita, et al Photographers
David Koningsberg Copywriter
Bruce Withers, Inc. Agency
Fischbach Corporation Client
New York NY

295

Robert Meyer, Julia Wyant Art Directors/Designers
Nicolas Muray Photographer
Michael Hager, John Kuiper Copywriters
Robert Meyer Design, Inc. Studio
**International Museum of Photography at George
  Eastman House** Client
Rochester NY

296

Keith Blissett Art Director
Ross Gervais Designer/Illustrator
Acart Graphic Services Inc. Studio
Solicitor General of Canada Client
Ottawa, Canada

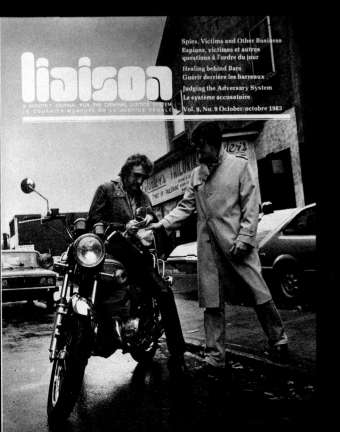

Contents

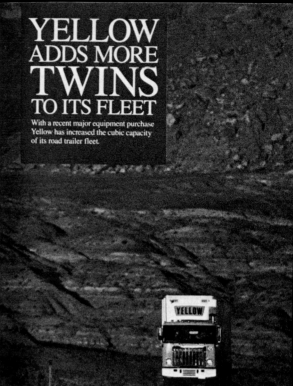

YELLOW ADDS MORE TWINS TO ITS FLEET

With a recent major equipment purchase Yellow has increased the cubic capacity of its road trailer fleet.

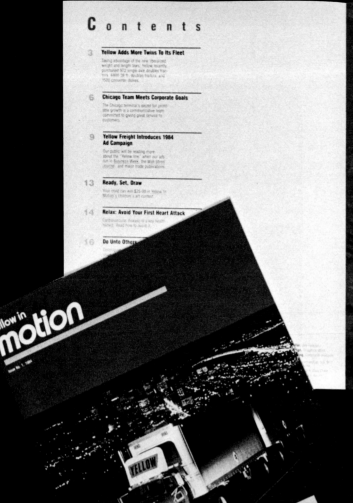

yellow in motion

Yellow Adds More Twins
P. 3

297

Stan Chrzanowski Art Director
Frank Addington Designer
Jim Felkner Copywriter
West & Associates Agency
Yellow Freight Client
Mission KS

298

Berdie Stein, Jitsuo Hoashi Designers
Ron Tweel Photographer
Mario Stasolla, Norm Bendel Illustrator
Judi Adolino Editor
Burson-Marsteller Agency/Client
New York NY

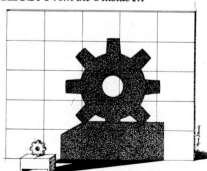

Burson·Marsteller

Published quarterly for employees of Burson-Marsteller worldwide

ideas

Spring 1984
Volume 1

Synergenics: *From the Outside In*

It's not easy being a corporate giant these days. With worldwide economic pressures, increasing technological advances, and competitors that run harder and smarter—well, it's enough to give any self-respecting CEO an ache from his head to his bottom line.

While the business environment has changed, demands on corporate management have not, says Geoff Nightingale, creative director/Americas and head of our new internal involvement program capability.

"Companies still have to get their balance sheets in order—just do it faster than ever before," he says. "There's a tremendous sense of urgency."

Developing the business

Management really has two options to strengthen the company's position, Geoff explains.

"They can make an impact in the marketplace by pushing sales, developing new or better products and services.

"Or, they can make improvements where the bottom-line impact is almost immediate: with employees. The smart companies are doing both."

For years, Burson-Marsteller has been involved in internal communications programs for our clients. But, last year, we decided to develop that service as a true line of business.

We retained a well-known behaviorist (a specialist in organizational dynamics) and began exploring traditional behavior-modification systems, often used by the consulting firms who'd be our new "competitors." At the same time, we reviewed our own programs to learn what has worked in the past, and why.

A program called "Synergenics" grew out of this six-month search. The term, Geoff says, refers to the core concept of the program: market affiliation, or the sense of kinship between employees at all levels and the marketplace.

As Geoff explains, our research revealed that traditional employee relations approaches rarely answer the needs of management.

"CEOs today are asking for programs that encourage entrepreneurial behavior by employees. They want their people to act and feel as if they own the company," he says.

"Most traditional programs that focus on organization, structure, or incentives tend to have the opposite effect. They build bureaucracy, not creativity; and inflexible behavior, not a sense of ownership, in employees."

The outside-in view

What's the right approach, then? The research showed success comes from first creating an environment that allows people to get close to customers. Then, companies must build in opportunities for people to grow in their efforts to meet those customers' needs.

That's the essence of a Synergenics program, and it differs from traditional employee programs in its view of the company's situation.

Traditional programs tend to look at the company almost exclusively from the inside—its structure, organization chart, benefits package. But Synergenics looks at it from the *outside in*, from the marketplace in which the company exists.

"It's the only way to develop a realistic picture and gain perspective on the company's internal problems and opportunities," Geoff says.

Burson-Marsteller views the selling process that way automatically, from a marketing communications perspective. "That's why this approach has been so successful," he adds.

Once the premise was clear—that the greater employees' market affiliation, the greater the chance for success—Geoff says they turned to B-M's research department and asked Dr. Lloyd Kirban to develop a specialized measurement tool.

The result was called MACS (Market Affiliation Climate Study), a four- to six-week process that reaches employees at all levels of the client company with interviews and questionnaires. MACS can be offered as a separate study, or part of an overall employee program. Either way, the client receives an in-depth report with specific recommendations at the conclusion of a MACS review.

Who has benefited from our unique outside-in approach? Geoff can cite companies from a wide range of industries: Sikorsky Aircraft, Ingersoll-Rand, Armco, Piper Aircraft and St. Regis Paper.

During the past few months, Geoff has been out on the road, meeting with a number of new and existing B-M clients about Synergenics. At present, he reports, we're working with Eastern Airlines, Flying Tigers, National Distribution and Digital Equipment in this critical area.

A core of specialists

Geoff says the plan is to develop a core unit of specialists in employee involvement programs, trained to sell and service such programs in key offices around the world. For the moment, Geoff and Barbara Smith, creative director/Eastern region, will continue to handle Synergenics, with the addition of a third team member this quarter.

A formal slide presentation has been developed to explain Synergenics and market affiliation to clients and other prospects. Geoff says we've never failed to win a positive response whenever the presentation has been shown.

If you have a client who's looking for help in communicating with or motivating employees, give Geoff or Barbara a call in the New York office.

Braggin' Rights

The test to come

Hobcaw Barony:

Baruchs' rich legacy to Georgetown

'I don't believe there is any place else like this in the United States...and it is going to stay untouched forever.'

Current research

Best regards,

H. Ann Silvernail

299

Marshall Harmon Art Director
Lucille Tenazas Designer
Eric Poggenpohl Photographer
H. Ann Silvernail Editor
Harmon Kemp Inc. Agency
Internation Paper Company Client
New York NY

The Multinational Account

Taking Searle's NutraSweet across the Atlantic was a lesson in global public relations

The challenge: create one cohesive program for six European countries.

Beyond the language barrier

Putting it all together

Knowledge helps build a level of confidence, for the client and yourself.

No substitute for face-to-face

A strong example

Research assistance by John Duggleby, B-M/Cgo.

MEDIA CLIMATES

	UK	W. GERMANY	SWEDEN	DENMARK	NORWAY	SWITZ.
TV	4 national 22 regional	2 national 6 regional	2 national	1 national	1 National	3 national (German, French & Italian)
RADIO	4 national 80 independent	1 national 7 regional	3 national	1 national	2 national Several regional	2 national Trial with 30 regionals
NEWSPAPER	130 daily-Sun. 1,500 weeklies	4 national 120 local	10 national 100 regional	A few nat'l Lots of small locals	4 national 230 region.	No national 10 dailies
CONSUMER/ TRADE	6,000 publications	Variety & growing	About 20	Variety	Lots of consumer; one trade or prof.ess.	Variety & growing
COMMENTS	Most like U.S. Tough editorial policies	Best opportunities in print, but none get into from TV	Potential in print. Central news agency	Love negative news & controversy	Rules for advertising/ sponsorship and marketing strict. Press independence fiercely defended.	Radio is reaching out with trial; may have potential

A Guide To Burson Buzzwords

There it was. Right between *buzz saw* and *B.V.D.* underwear. "Buzzword, *n.* (1967): an important-sounding usually technical word or phrase, often of little meaning, used chiefly to impress laymen." Even Webster's *Ninth New Collegiate Dictionary* couldn't ignore the impact buzzwords have had on our language.

The dictionary's editors may have been a bit harsh, though. Every business has its own jargon, lingo, shoptalk, patois. It's a form of verbal shorthand, and a colorful one, at that. And while every language has its own peculiar set of buzzwords, Americans may produce the most amusing—at least, in the ears of the rest of the world.

We thought we'd poke a little fun at ourselves, so we crept about the hallways, flipped through memos and gathered some of our favorite Burson Buzzwords.

Eventually, we'd like to start a column called "Esperanto," for the international language, to take a look at the way words work around the globe. It's one way we can be a bit more sensitive to our international neighbors and, perhaps, broaden our personal horizons.

Research assistance by Eliot Sloane, B-M/NY.

300
Holland Macdonald Art Director/Designer
CBS Records Client
New York NY

Posters

301
Allen Weinberg Art Director/Designer
CBS Records Client
New York NY

302
Heather Cooper Designer/Illustrator
Burns, Cooper, Hynes Ltd. Studio
Herzig-Sommerville Ltd. Printer
Toronto International Festival Client
Toronto. Canada

303
Albert Gomm Designer/Photographer
Gerwerbemuseum Client
Basel Switzerland

To borrow the United Way slogan, thanks to you it's working.

We as the Business Communications Systems division of Ontario Region Marketing Services, count on you to help us provide maintenance activities on behalf of customers with data, dedicated voice, video and radio services.

Because of your help we are better able to meet customer needs for integrated telecommunications services and compete more effectively in the marketplace.

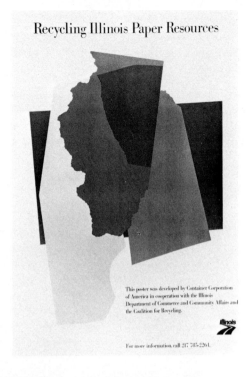

Recycling Illinois Paper Resources

This poster was developed by Container Corporation of America in cooperation with the Illinois Department of Commerce and Community Affairs and the Coalition for Recycling.

Illinois

For more information, call 217 785-2264.

308
Michael Hodgson Art Director/Designer
Adelle Lutz Photographer
Warner Bros. Records Client
Burbank CA

309
Kerry Grady Art Director
Container Corp. of America Agency
Illinois Dept. of Commerce Client
Chicago IL

310
Marco DePlano Designer/Illustrator
Marco Deplano & Associates Agency
Hoashi Studio
IVECO Client
New York NY

311
David Bartels Art Director/Designer
Gary Overacre Illustrator
Bartels & Company Inc. Agency
Leonard J. Waydeck Client
St. Louis MO

REVLON
UNTAMED EYES

Revlon's newest
Super Shadow
fashions and
color tipped lashes

Model is wearing colors from the S...
Unequaled Eyes Kit and Red Royal...
Super Lustrous Smudgeproof Masc...

Dress by Junko Koshino, Hat by Pat...
Jewelry by M. J. Savitt

312
Fred J. DeVito Art Director
Larry Damato Designer
Steven Meisel Photographer
Revlon Creative Marketing Dept Agency
Revlon Inc. Client
New York NY

TREK.
FURTHER
THAN YOU'VE
EVER GONE.

313
Jon Rost, Frank Melf Designers
Image Studios Photographer
Marc Braunstein Copywriter
Sports Marketing Group at Jacobson
   Advertising Agency
Trek Bicycle Corporation Client
Sheboygan WI

THE
PRETENDERS

LEARNING
TO
CRAWL

314
Simon Levy Art Director/Designer
Paul Cox Photographer
Warner Bros. Records Client
Burbank CA

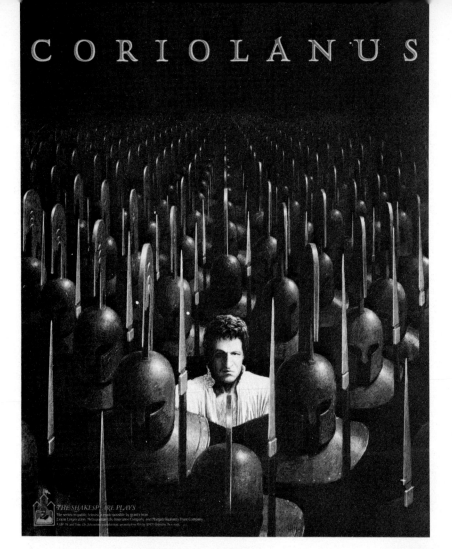

CORIOLANUS

THE SHAKESPEARE PLAYS

MY DAD IS THE BEE'S KNEES

FATHER'S DAY JUNE 19TH

SOMETIMES THE ONLY THING TO DO IS THE IMPOSSIBLE. THE TERRY FOX STORY

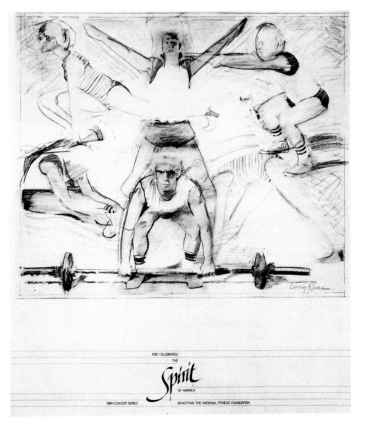

OIE BAY

Prince Edward Island Tourism, P.O. Box 940, Charlottetown, Prince Edward Island, Canada, C1A 7M5. Te—

Discover an Island **PRINCE EDWARD ISLAND**

321
Mary Ada Upstone Art Director/Designer
Lionel Stevenson Photographer
Prince Edward Island Dept. of Finance & Tourism Client
Charlottetown, Canada

322
Marty Neumeier Art Director/Designer
Sandra Higashi Illustrator
Neumeier Design Team Studio
Zipatone, Inc. Client
Santa Barbara CA

323
Bob Conge Art Director/Designer
Conge Design Studio
Corn Hill Arts Festival Client
Rochester NY

324
McRay Bagleby Art Director/Illustrator
Graphic Communications Studio
Brigham Young University Client
Provo UT

When you risk becoming an artist,
you risk taking your talent seriously.

School of Visual Arts

325

Silas Rhodes Art Director
Bill Kobasz Designer
Robert Weaver Illustrator

Dee Ito Copywriter
School of Visual Arts Agency/Client
New York NY

326
Gene Bramson, Harold Burch Art Directors
Harold Burch, Doug Brotherton Designers
Charles Pigg Illustrator
Gene Bramson Copywriter
Bramson + Associates Agency
M. David Paul + Associates Client
Fullerton CA

327
Jill Hawkins, Kent Kirkley Art Directors
Kent Kirkley Photographer
Jill Hawkins Design Studio
USA Film Festival Client
Dallas TX

328
Paul Gauthier Art Director/Designer
Cossette Communication-Marketing Agency
Grapheme Communication-Design Studio
Place Laurier Client
Quebec. Canada

329
Douglas Boyd, Paul Pruneau Art Directors
Paul Pruneau Designer
Michael Ruppert Photographer
Douglas Boyd Design & Marketing Agency
Condat Paper Company Client
Los Angeles CA

330
Primo Angeli Art Director/Designer
Primo Angeli Graphics Studio
San Francisco Arts Commission Client
San Francisco CA

331
Lauren Smith Art Director/Designer
Cliff Rusch, Lauren Smith Illustrators
Lauren Smith Design Studio
Dudley, Anderson, Yutzy Client/Copywriter
Mountain View CA

332

Tim Girvin Art Director/Designer
Tim Girvin Design Inc. Studio/Client
Seattle WA

333

Guy Salvato Art Director/Designer
Mike Dexter, Guy Salvato Illustrators
Salvato & Coe Assoc. Inc. Studio
Lazarus Dept. Stores Client
Columbus OH

334

Zand Gee Art Director/Designer
Calvin Roberts, Crystal Huie Photographers
Znd Gee Studio
Chonkmoonhunter Productions Client
San Francisco CA

335

Mark Anderson, Denys Gustafson Art Directors
Tom Suitor Creative Director
Henrik Kam, Steve Unze, Phillip Dixon Photographers
Tony Dirksen Copywriter
Kendra Brotherton Production Manager
Apple Computer Inc. Client
Cupertino CA

Booklets/Brochures

The Apple IIc

336
Cheryl Watson Art Director/Designer
Tom Clayton Photographer
Ann Olson Copywriter
Dayton's In-House Studio
Dayton's Client
Minneapolis MN

337
Bob Tanaka Art Director
Aaron Jones, Lis DeMarco Photographers
Hal Newsom Copywriter
Cole & Weber, Inc. Agency
Weyerhauser Wood Company Client
Seattle WA

338
Hinsche + Associates Art Direction
Steve Hulen Photographer
Clarion Corporation Client
Santa Monica CA

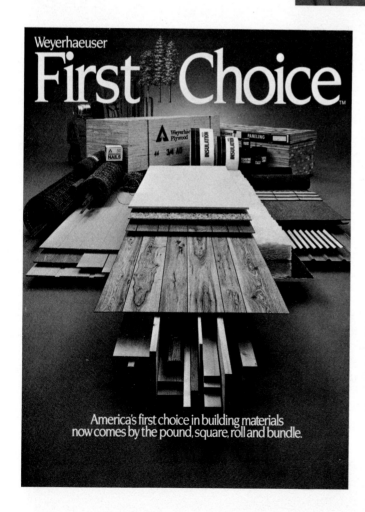

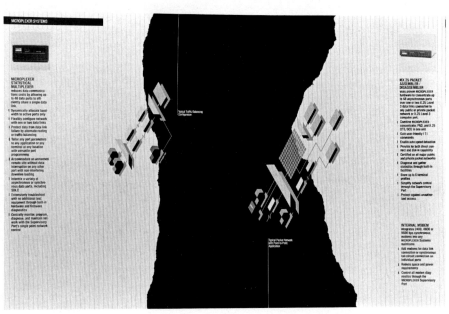

339
Russell Tatro Art Director/Designer
John Camden Copywriter
Russell Tatro Design Agency
Timeplex, Inc. Client
Danbury CT

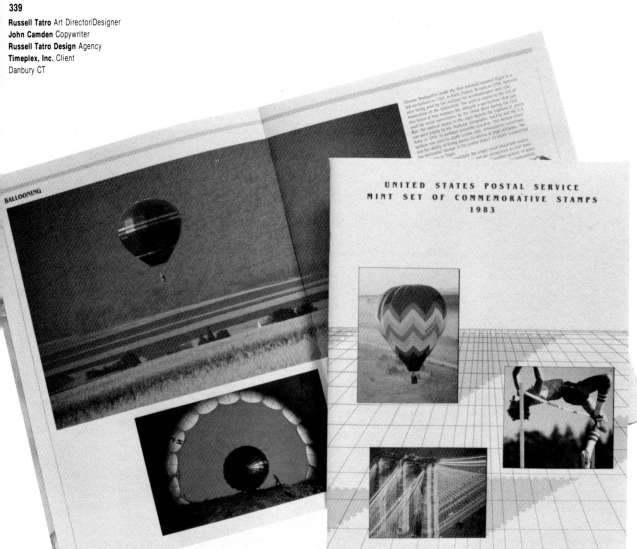

340
Terrence W. McCaffrey Art Director/Designer
U.S. Postal Service Client
Washington DC

S.S.Universe
*Adventurous lecture cruises to Alaska
and the grand South Pacific*

From quaint
fishing
villages to
bustling cities,
the past and
present are
yours to
explore.

Alaska.
The new frontier.

Cruise the S.S. Universe to Prince Rupert, British Columbia's busiest port, and to Juneau. Accessible only by ship or airplane, Juneau is perhaps the most unusual capital city in the U.S. and the site of one of the largest lodes of gold ever mined. After disembarking at Whittier, you'll ride a private railway to Anchorage through some of the loveliest scenery in the state — an "extra" part of your tour included at no extra charge. Once you're there, the sophistication of Alaska's largest city is a delightful contrast to its pioneer charm. Baskets and beadwork, scrimshaw and soapstone carvings, often of museum quality, are available in shops and galleries. Yet the beauty of the Alaskan wilderness lies just beyond the city limits. Valdez, called the "Switzerland of Alaska" because of its ring of snowcapped mountains, was discovered in 1790 by a Spanish explorer.

341

Steve Ditko, Barry Shepard Art Director
Rick Rusing, Rick Gayle Photographer
Barry Shepard Illustrator
Karen Swearingen Calligraphy
SHR Communications Studio
World Explorer Cruises Client
Phoenix AZ

342

Primo Angeli, Michael LaBash Designers
Charles Callister, Jr. Photographer
Claire Harrison Associates Agency
Primo Angeli Graphics Studio
Claire Harrison Assoc., Vintage Club Properties Client
San Francisco CA

343
Ellen Snyder Art Director/Designer
Thomas L. Fenton Photographer
James Hood Marketing Director
Lehman Brothers Graphics Client
New York NY

345
Tim Hartung Art Director/Designer
Marion Thatch Illustrator
David Palmer Copywriter
Hartung & Associates Ltd. Agency
Interwest Properties Client
San Ramon CA

344
John Markey Art Director
Ted Beck Photographer
McCathern McKinnly Studio
Brooklyn Union Gas Co. Client
Brooklyn NY

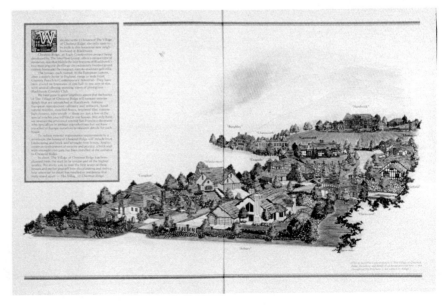

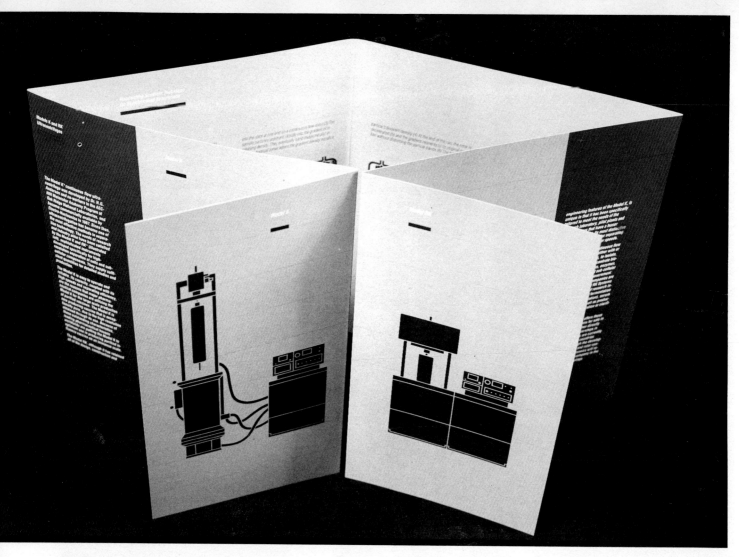

346
Jerold E. Fox Jr. Art Director/Designer
Dorothea Trecroce-Fox, Jerold E. Fox Jr. Illustrators
Judee Roth Copywriter
Roth + Associates Agency
Electro-Nucleonics, Inc. Client
Bloomfield NJ

347
John Coy, Tracey Shiffman Designers
Sidney B. Felsen, Douglas Parker Photographers
Henry Geldzahler Copywriter
Aldus Type Studio, Ltd. Typographer
COY, Los Angeles Studio
Gemini G.E.L. Client
Culver City CA

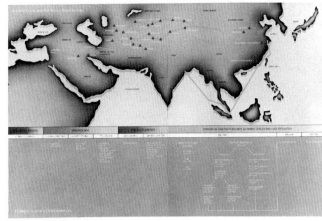

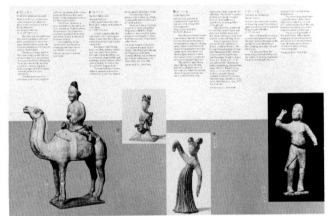

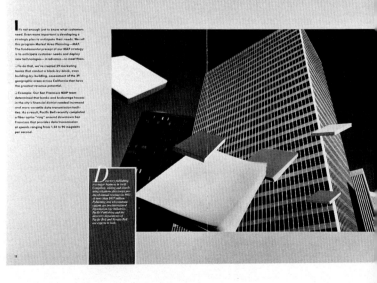

348

Patric SooHoo, Ken Kerr Art Directors
Paul Ison Designer
Marilyn Shimokochi Illustrator
Marc Nowadnick Copywriter
Patrick SooHoo, Inc. Agency
WED Enterprises, Inc. Client
Los Angeles CA

349

Neil Shakery, Sandra McHenry Designers
Charly Franklin Photographer
Margaret Bradford Copywriter
Jonson Pederson Hinrichs & Shakery Studio
Pacific Telesis Group Client
San Francisco CA

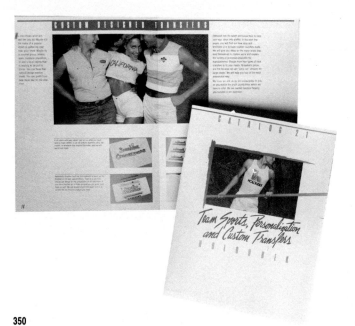

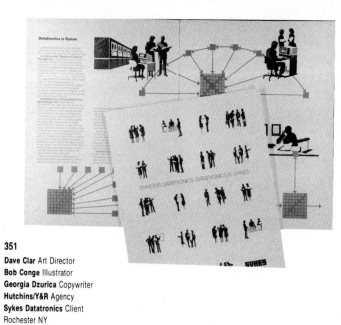

351

Dave Clar Art Director
Bob Conge Illustrator
Georgia Dzurica Copywriter
Hutchins/Y&R Agency
Sykes Datatronics Client
Rochester NY

350

Joe Hausch, Thomas Noll, Gary Haas Designers
Beckett Photography Photographer
Holoubek Inc. Studio/Client
Waukesha WI

352

John Brunner Art Director
Warren Madill Illustrator
Anders Joost Copywriter
Anderson & Lembke Kungsgatan AB Agency
Ingela Radstrom Production
Swedish State Railways Client
Stockholm, Sweden

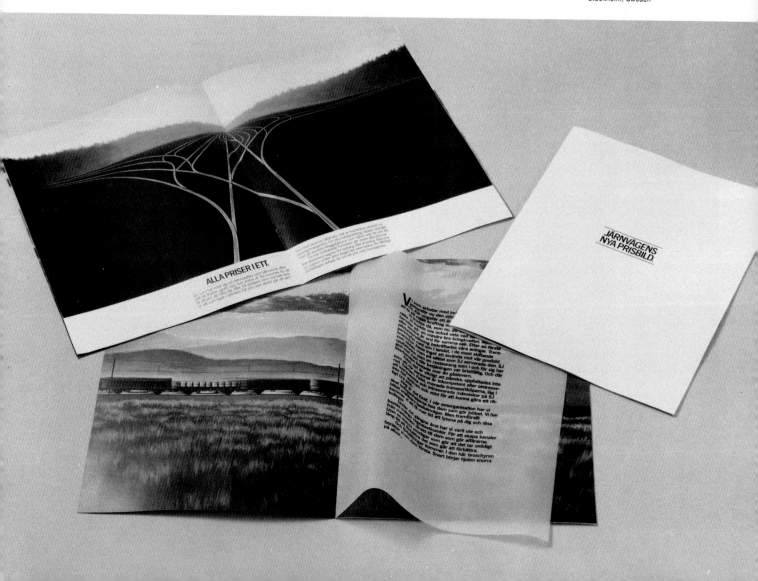

PORTS OF THE WORLD
A GUIDE TO CARGO LOSS CONTROL

Thirteenth Edition

353
Michael Rogalski, Bob Warkulwiz Designers
Michael Rogalski Illustrator
Bill Shirley, Barry Tarneff Copywriters
Warkulwiz Design Studio
CIGNA Client
Philadelphia PA

357
Martha Voutas, Norico Kanai Designers
Lynn Kohlman Photographer
MVP et al, Martha Voutas Productions Inc. Studio
Perry Ellis Portfolio Client
New York NY

354
Bridget De Socio Art Director/Designer
Henry Wolf Photographer
Claudia Hart Copywriter
Henry Wolf Productions Photo Studio
Stendig Client
New York NY

355
Hans Green Art Director
AI Studios Illustrator
Per-Erik Ohlsson Copywriter
Wendelbo & Green AB Agency
ALFA-LAVAL AB Client
Helsingborg Sweden

356
James Sebastian, Michael McGinn, Jim Hinchee Designers
Bruce Wolf Photographer
Designframe Inc. Studio
Martex/West Point Pepperell Client
New York NY

The elephant
and the blind men
are no different
than you and I.

358
Stavros Cosmopulos Art Director/Designer
Robert Crowley Copywriter
Arrow Composition Typesetting
Cosmopulos Crowley & Daly Agency
The Cambridge Group Client
Boston MA

359
John Connolly Art Director/Designer
Graham Ford Photographer
Chris Howden Copywriter
Ronny Nicholas Account Director
Ehrenstrahle & Company Agency
Alfa-Laval Client
London England

Worried about fuel density?

Parents' Survival Kit

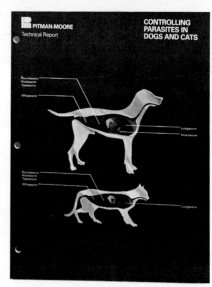

361
Hans Boye Boyesen Art Director/Designer
Howard Owen Photographer
Boye Communications, Inc. Agency
Pitman Moore Client
Rutherford NJ

360
Penelope Murphy Art Director
Seymour Chwast Illustrator
Eileen Simas Copywriter
N.Y.S. Health Promotion Group Agency
Push Pin Studios Studio
New York State Social Services Department Client
Albany NY

362
Meg Levine Art Director/Designer
Joel Spector Illustrator
Frank Hughes Copywriter
Wm. Joseph Bologna, International Agency
Key Pharmaceuticals, Inc. Client
New York NY

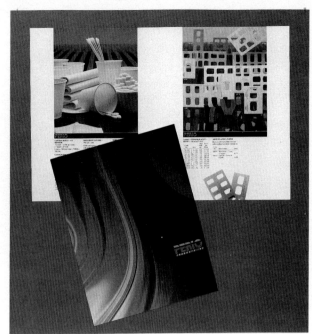

363
John Luckett Art Director/Designer
Naomi Kaltman Photographer
Rod Jones Illustrator
Tim Hawkins Copywriter
Luckett & Associates Inc. Agency
Members Only Client
New York NY

364
Bill Kumke Art Director/Designer
David Bartels Creative Director
Larry Willett Photographer
Joe Hanrahan Copywriter
Bartels & Company Inc. Agency
Perio Products Inc. Client
St. Louis MO

365
Gerald Olson, Julian Naranjo Designers
David Krammer Photographer
Julian Naranjo Illustrator
Mike Shirk Copywriter
Olson Design Inc. Studio
The Naiman Company Client
Del Mar CA

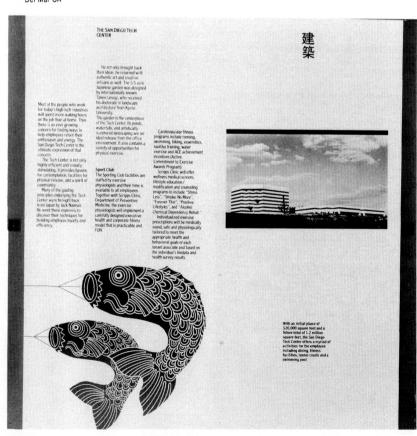

366

Jack Anderson, Terri Small Art Directors
Cliff Chung Designer
Susan Ryan Illustrator
Jon Bell Copywriter
Hornall-Anderson Design Works, Elgin Syferd Agency
HealthPlus Client
Seattle WA

367

Margie Mayer Art Director/Designer
Ian Birnie, Barbara Bejna Creative Directors
**Peter Cowie, Andrew Sarris, Jane Hennessey,
  Samantha Davis** Copywriters
Webcrafters Inc. Production
Films Incorporated Client
Wilmette IL

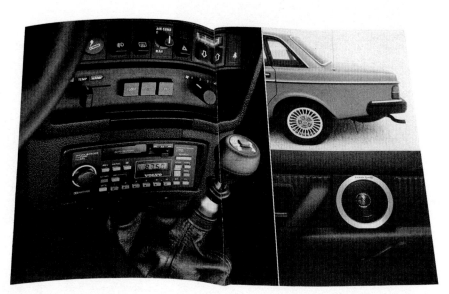

368
Torbjorn Winckler Art Director
Johnny Johansson Photographer
Goran Gardfeldt Copywriter
Stendahls Agency
Volvo RS Client
Gothenburg, Sweden

369
Lennart Soderqvist Art Director/Designer
Bengt Hoglund, Peter Ahlen Photographers
Gyula Buvary Illustrator
Urban Falkmarken Acc. Supervisor
Welinder Information AB Agency
HIAB-FOCO AB Client
Stockholm. Sweden

370
Michael Dexter, Guy Salvato Art Directors
Dan Miller Photographer
Salvato & Coe Studio
St. Joseph Medical Center Client
Columbus OH

372
Neil Probala Art Director/Designer
Greg Sereta Photographer
Chris Lee Copywriter
Carr Liggett, Inc. Agency
Falcon Art Studio
Society National Bank Client
Cleveland OH

373
Jeffrey C. Marienthal Art Director
Mark Shawver Designer
Norm Fisher, Jeffrey C. Marienthal Photographers

Leslie Hoppe-Glosser Copywriter
A.S.K. Design Agency
Encinal Terminals Inc. Client
Alameda CA

374
Joan F. Klimo Art Director
Claudia Julian Designer
Rik Van Glintenkamp Photographer

Terrie Cacciapoli Copywriter
Lord & Taylor Direct Mail/Catalogue Department Studio
Lord & Taylor Client
New York NY

375
Milton Glaser Art Director/Designer
Matthew Klein Photographer
Myrna Davis Copywriter
Milton Glaser Inc. Studio
Solow Development Corporation Client
New York NY

376
Mary Beth Cybul, Jacqueline Kohn Art Directors
Mark McMahon Illustrator
Lynne Strode Print Coordination
Hill and Knowlton, Inc. Agency
Rubloff, Inc. Client
Chicago IL

377
Kai Andersson Art Director
Marten Gullstrand Photographer
C-A Enefalt Copywriter
Ogilvy & Mather, Malmo Agency
Perstorp AB Client
Malmo, Sweden

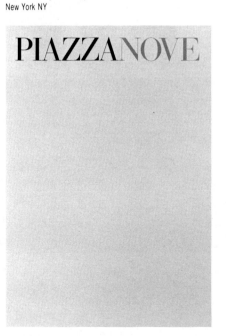

THE TRANSPORT FACTOR

Quality

Price

Assortment

Sales

Communications

LOOK AT YOUR SHIPPING LINE
AS PART OF YOUR STRATEGY

ScanDutch

378
Mogens Sorensen Art Director/Designer
Finn Rosted Photographer
Pino Migliazzo Illustrator
Bill Riley Copywriter
Bergsoe 3 Agency
ScanDutch I/S Client
Klampenborg Denmark

379
Cheryl Lewin Art Director/Designer
Ben Rosenthal Photographer
Cheryl Lewin Design Studio
Heller Client
New York NY

380
Bruce Wolfe Art Director/Designer
Terry Heffernan Photographer
Sandra Matsukawa Hu Editor
Ketchem Food Center Agency
Terry Heffernan Inc. Studio
Beef Industry Council Client
San Francisco CA

381
Jon Rost, Frank Melf Designers
Image Studios Photographer
Nachriener-Boie Art Factory Illustrator
Marc Braunstein Copywriter
Sports Marketing Group at Jacobson Advertising Agency
Trek Bicycle Corporation Client
Sheboygan WI

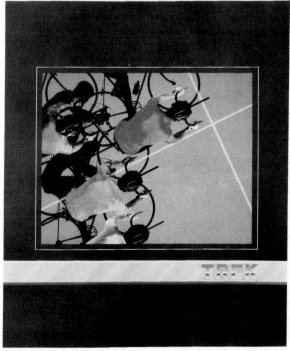

382
Jim Bertz, Laura Chisari Designers
Rick Becker Photographer
Susan Loren Copywriter
Pluzynski & Associates Agency
Community Coffee Company Client
New York NY

383
Larry Jennings Art Director/Designer
Charles Collum, Albert Watson Photographers
Vivien Flesher Illustrator
Macy's New York Client
New York NY

384
Robert Manley Art Director/Designer
Mark Fisher Illustrator
Daniel Altman Copywriter
Altman + Manley Agency
Quadex Corporation Client
Cambridge MA

385
Elizabeth Marks Art Director
Carl Turner Designer/Illustrator
Elizabeth Marks & Assoc. Inc. Agency
Olde English Tourism Commission Client
Columbia SC

386

Fritz Haase, Harald Schweers Designers
Dieter Kahl, Fritz Haase, Herr Sommerfeld,
 Nicolay Zurek Photographers
Atelier Haase & Knels Agency
Druckerei Holterdorf Production
Brillantleuchten AG Client
Bremen. West Germany

387

Tom Roth Art Director
Erik Gronlund Designer/Photographer
Temple Williams Copywriter
Anderson, Lembke, Welinder Agency
Talco Metals Inc. Client
Stamford CT

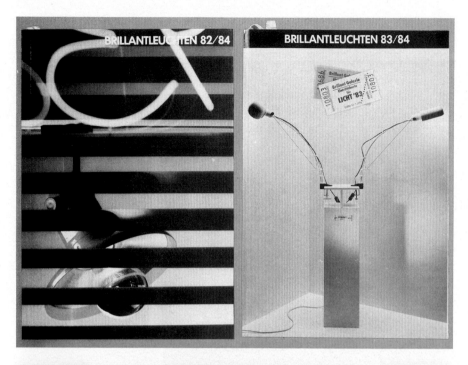

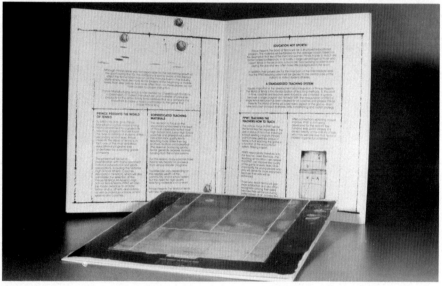

388

Ellen Woliner Art Director
Martine Harmouch Designer
Fred Mullane Photographer
Alan Cober Illustrator
Corchia Woliner Associates Agency
Prince Manufacturing Inc. Client
New York NY

389

Joseph Martino Art Director
Don Hummerston Designer/Illustrator
Neil Hickey Copywriter
TV GUIDE Magazine Client
Radnor PA

JAZ
PARIS

The watch that turned quartz into fashion.

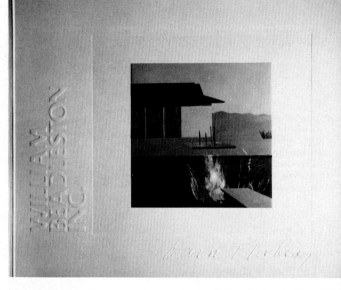

392
Bruce Bloch Art Director/Designer
Chris Callis, Doug Fraser Photographers
Carol Tudor Copywriter
A C & R Advertising Agency
JAZ Paris Client
New York NY

393
Edward Lamport Designer
David Hockney Illustrator
Communication Design Co. Studio
Wiliam Beadleston Gallery Client
New York NY

391
Schaeffer Boehm Ltd. Art Director
**Richie Williamson, Phillipe Houze, James Cohen,
   Robert Grant** Photographers
Jim Fulmer Illustrator
Schaeffer Boehm Ltd. Agency
Bloomingdale's Client
New York NY

390
Jeremy Sampson Art Director
Karen Hofmeyr Designer
Berna Jersich Photographer
Natalie Knight, Suzanne Priebatsch Copywriters
Jeremy Sampson Associates Studio
The South African Breweries Limited Client
Johannesburg, RSA

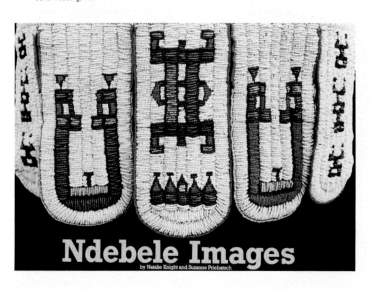

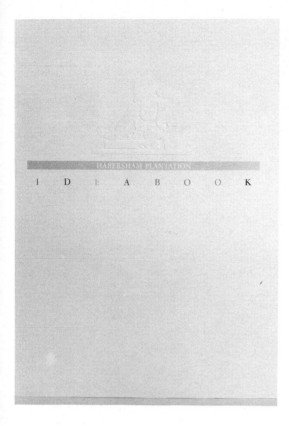

394
Brad Copeland Art Director/Designer
Mike Granberry Photographer
George Hirthler Copywriter
Cooper-Copeland Inc. Studio
Habersham Plantation Inc. Client
Atlanta GA

395
Jim Prokell Art Director/Designer
Chuck Fuhrer, Jack Wolf, Marc Romanelli Photographers
Jim Prokell Studio Studio
Broudy Printing, Inc. Production
Thorp, Reed & Armstrong Client
Pittsburgh PA

LOOKING TOWARD OUR SECOND CENTURY

Thorp, Reed & Armstrong traces its origins to 1895 when Ferdinand Weil and Charles M. Thorp established the partnership of Weil & Thorp with the opening of their offices in Pittsburgh's Union Trust Building. In 1929 the firm, then known as Thorp, Bostwick & Stewart, was retained to incorporate National Steel Corporation and become its general counsel

The firm became known as Thorp, Reed & Armstrong in 1947, with a staff of 16 lawyers providing a wide range of corporate legal services that emphasized labor relations, litigation, taxation and finance. In 1970 the firm marked its three-quarter century milestone, with a staff of 35 lawyers expanding into new areas of law including environmental regulation, international commerce, pension reform and employment discrimination.

To provide clients with legal services in the areas of international trade, international taxation and federal administrative proceedings, the firm opened a Washington, DC Office in 1976. To service the increasing business and personal needs of clients on Florida's Gulf Coast, offices in Sarasota and Bradenton were opened in 1982 and in Tampa in 1983.

Today, Thorp, Reed & Armstrong consists of more than 80 lawyers supported by a staff of paralegals, a 100,000 volume law library, computerized legal research, and modern word processing and tele-communications equipment.

THE LAW FIRM

Thorp, Reed & Armstrong is a partnership engaged in the general practice of law. The firm is made up of 40 partners and about an equal number of associates.

Of Counsel relationships are maintained with eight additional attorneys, and the firm has a staff of highly skilled paralegals. Approximately 60% of the firm's practice emanates from the Pittsburgh Office.

The more than 3,700 clients served by Thorp, Reed & Armstrong range from individuals and small businesses to multi-national Fortune 100 corporations, and the diversity of their business is illustrated below:

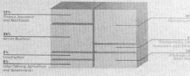

Thorp, Reed & Armstrong's areas of practice are as broad as the interests of its clients. Attorneys have experience in virtually every facet of law, including the specialized areas of patent and admiralty law. To manage this diversity of practice, the firm is organized into four departments: Business, Tax and Estate, Labor and Litigation.

A partner heads each department and, with the coordination of a Practice Management Committee, assures that an appropriate number of attorneys and paralegals are trained, experienced and available to meet client needs.

The following pages briefly describe these basic areas of practice and, more specifically, detail the firm's experience and capabilities in the fields of law falling into each of these areas. To best meet the needs of clients, the firm avoids the rigid departmentalization of its attorneys. While attorneys are assigned to a department for organization purposes, many Thorp, Reed & Armstrong lawyers have a practice which bridges two or more departments.

396
Tim Girvin, Rikki Conrad, Chris Spivey Designers
Victor Gardava Photographer
Jim Olson Copywriter
Tim Girvin Design, Inc. Studio
Olson/Walker Architects Client
Seattle WA

397
Urs Schwerzmann Art Director
Dietmar Henneka, Burkhard Leitner Designers
Buro Schwerzmann Agency
Leitner GmbH, Dr. Cantz sche Druckerei Production
Freelance Stuttgart Client
Stuttgart. West Germany

Annual Reports

398
Morava & Oliver Design Office Art Direction
Emmett Morava Designer
Tom Blay, Scott Fujikawa, Joan Gaynor Photographers
Spencer C. Boise, Deanna Xavier Copywriters
Mattel Inc. Client
Santa Monica CA

Overview
Worldwide
Leadership

Mattel Toys International Sales Growth

While the percent of sales increase for Mattel Toys International was substantial in 1983 in terms of U.S. dollars, the growth rate is much higher when expressed in terms of local currencies.

Worldwide Manufacturing and Distribution Capabilities

Countering Seasonality

Effective management of Company facilities to assure product quality, ready availability and higher gross margins.

Recognition of the importance of managing seasonality in the toy business by shifting a larger percentage of sales into the first half of the year, thereby improving profits.

In the domestic market, Mattel has extended its leadership position significantly by increasing its market share and growing at a faster rate than the rest of the toy industry over the past three years.

As Mattel's organization capabilities have been developed and refined overseas, the Company has aggressively sought special opportunities and has applied its resources to the expansion of international markets. Net sales for Mattel Toys International last year rose 28% in U.S. dollars (39% in local currencies). Profits more than doubled during the same period.

Shares of market have increased substantially to 16% in Australia, 12% in Canada and 11% in Italy. The Company gained market leadership positions in Mexico, the Philippines, Taiwan and Hong Kong and is expanding its base in other foreign markets.

Mattel's leadership in the toy industry is dramatically illustrated by the worldwide popularity of the Barbie doll, 25 years after introduction still the world's best-selling toy.

Brooklyn Union Gas   Annual Report 1983

Our Customers

Metal Box   Annual Report/Jaarverslag 1983

399
John Markey Art Director/Designer
Ted Beck Photographer
Brooklyn Union Gas Company Client
Brooklyn NY

400
Jeremy Sampson Art Director/Designer
Karen Hofmeyr Designer
Edward Russell-Walling Copywriter
Jeremy Sampson Associates Studio
Metal Box South Africa Ltd. Client
Johannesburg, RSA

401
Kay Woon Designer
Larry Keenan Photographer
George E. Browne & Assoc. Agency
Genentech Client
San Francisco CA

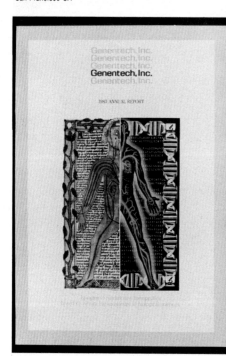
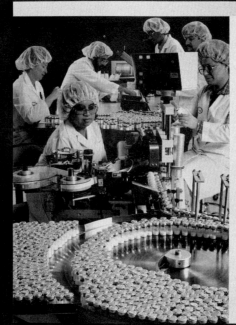

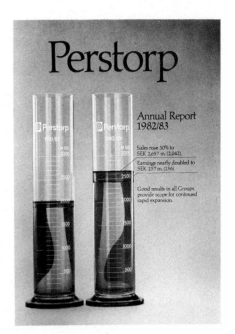

402
Wayne C. Roth Art Director/Designer
Jeff Smith, Lonny Kalfus Photographers
Roth + Associates Agency
Baker Industries Inc. Client
Bloomfield NJ

403
Kai Andersson Art Director
Lars Davidsson, Martin Gullstrand Photographers
C-A Enefalt Copywriter
Ogilvy & Mather, Malmo Agency
Perstorp AB Client
Malmo. Sweden

404
Milton Glaser Art Director
Karen Skelton Designer
Jim McMullan Illustrator
Seth McCormack, Jean Claude Comert Copywriters
Milton Glaser, Inc. Studio
Schlumberger Limited Client
New York NY

405
Gosta Enhammar Art Director
Martin Gullstrand Photographer
C-A Enefalt Copywriter
Ogilvy & Mather, Malmo Agency
PLM AB Client
Malmo. Sweden

During 1983, U.S. Bakery Products capitalized on its well-known brands to register a record year in sales and earnings.

406

Roslyn Eskind Art Director
Peter Scott Designer
Daniel Wiener Photographer
Maggie Dale Editor
Eskind Waddell Studio
Norcen Energy Resources Ltd. Client
Toronto, Canada

407

Len Fury Art Director
Barbara Cooper Designer
Andy Spreitzer, Gary Gladsone, David Vine Photographers
Corporate Annual Reports Inc. Agency
Nabisco Brands Inc. Client
New York NY

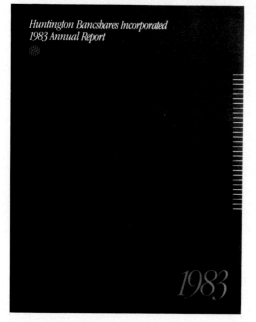

408

Eric Rickabaugh Art Director/Designer
Larry Sullivan Creative Direction
James Westwater, Roman Sapecki Photographers
Salvato & Co Associates Inc. Studio
Huntington Bancshares Inc. Client
Columbus OH

409

Mario G. Messina Art Director/Designer
David S. Jobrack Creative Director
Mikhail Ivenitsky Illustrator
D.T.C. Graphics Agency
Depository Trust Company Client
New York NY

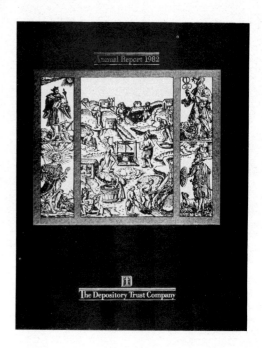

Heinz
THE H.J. HEINZ
COMPANY
1983
ANNUAL REPORT
BOOK OF COOKS

At-Home Conversations
With Ten
of the World's
Outstanding Cooks—
Wherein We Explore
Their Secrets
and Present
Some of Their Favorite
Family Recipes

410
Bennett Robinson Art Director
Naomi Burstein Designer
Bob Day Photographer
Daniel Schwartz Illustrator
Corporate Graphics, Inc. Agency
The J.J. Heinz Company Client
New York NY

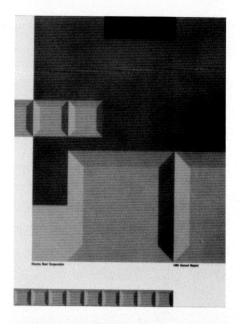

MegaOne
VLSI TEST SYSTEM

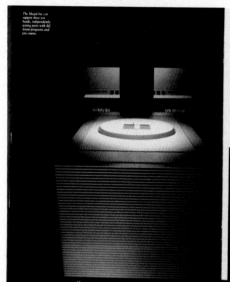

BENEFICIAL STANDARD CORPORATION

1983 ANNUAL REPORT

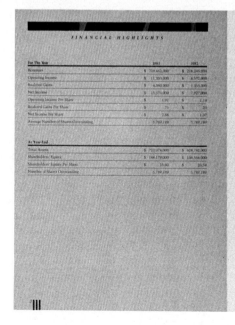

FINANCIAL HIGHLIGHTS

TO OUR SHAREHOLDERS

411

Rick Besser Designer
Besser, Bice Jr. Illustrators
Robert Miles Runyan & Associates Agency
Electro Rent Corporation Client
Playa del Rey CA

412

Craig Frazier, Jeff Hurn Art Directors
Rudi Legname Photographer
Megatest Corporation Client
San Francisco CA

413

Michael Kaiser Art Director
Susan Karasic Designer
James Hurley, Rhanda Kahawaii Copywriters
Kaiser McEuen Inc. Agency
Beneficial Standard Corporation Client
Los Angeles CA

414

Ernie Perich Art Director/Designer
Ann DeLaVergne Photographer
Matthew Thornton Copywriter
Group 243 Design Studio
Domino's Pizza, Inc. Client
Ann Arbor MI

415

Bryan Lahr Art Director/Designer
Pat Edwards Photographer
Lee Garth & Client Copywriters
Groseclose & Poindexter Adv. Agency
Dominion Bankshares Corp. Client
Roanoke VA

Products Research & Chemical Corporation

1983 Annual Report

417

Danielle Roy Art Director
Alain Senecal Designer
Patrice Puiberneau Photographer
Innovation Typography
Legault Nolin Larosée et associés inc Agency
The Prudential Assurance Co. Ltd. Client
Montreal. Canada

418

John Waters Art Director
Ed Walter Designer/Illustrator
Ron Blank Copywriter
John Waters Associates Inc. Agency
Curtiss-Wright Corporation Client
New York NY

419

Pierre Leonard Art Director/Designer
Alain Cornu Photographer
Grapheme Communication Design Agency
**Fédération des caisses populaires Desjardins
  de Montréal et de L'Ouest-du-Quebec** Client
Montreal, Canada

416

Jorge Alonso Art Director/Designer
Roger Marshutz Photographer
Farida Fotouhi Copywriter
Fotouhi Alonso Agency
Products Research & Chemical Corp. Client
Los Angeles CA

Major strides in proprietary polymers

PRC has over thirty-five years of experience in compounding sealants, adhesives and coatings based upon elastomeric polymers.

During the company's early years, it became apparent that the specific performance properties we were trying to achieve could not be totally met with conventional polymers. Therefore, about twenty-five years ago we started an in-house program to develop and manufacture our own proprietary polymer systems. Many of the major marketing breakthroughs which we have achieved are the direct result of our ability to custom design our own polymeric raw materials. Today, a major portion of our marine, industrial and construction urethane and polysulfide adhesives, sealants and coatings are based on our PRC Permapol® polymers.

The most notable product line to result from this effort in recent years is a new generation of high-performance insulating glass sealants based on PRC's Permapol P-2 polymers.

These innovative sealants have propelled PRC into the position of being the leading worldwide supplier of insulating glass sealants with our domestic market share in excess of 50%. PRC's P-2 based insulating glass sealants exhibit excellent adhesion, long-term elasticity and the ability to recover after compression. They have set new standards in long-term laboratory and field testing, and our insulating glass customers are achieving excellent performance results with them.

In 1983 PRC made further progress in P-3 polymer development and introduced a number of Permapol P-3 based products to the coatings and sealants markets.

Having patented these P-3 systems, the company has affiliated itself through licensing agreements with two major international companies, Société Nationale Elf Aquitaine (SNEA) and Nippon Shokubai Kagaku Kogyo Co., Ltd. (NSKK), to make available on a worldwide basis the complete line of Permapol polysulfide polymers.

Concurrently, PRC has begun an active effort to introduce our Permapol products to other specialty chemical manufacturers. P-2 polymers are now available to the adhesives industry for use in manufacturing advanced flexibilized epoxy adhesives. P-3 polyols were recently introduced to the coatings industry as a raw material to increase chemical, heat, fuel and corrosion resistance without forgoing flexibility, adhesion and impact resistance.

While still very much in the development stages, this ongoing program to broaden the use of our Permapol products has created many interesting and important applications. P-3 plasticizers are now recommended for use in the compounding of certain specialty synthetic rubbers to improve processability and physical properties. They are also used in the manufacture of certain dental impression materials. And a P-3 urethane coating is being tested as a possible replacement for fuel cell bladders in jet fighter aircraft.

These PRC products represent major technological improvements over other available systems and have already generated a high level of interest from the industry.

In order to meet the anticipated demand for PRC Permapol polymers, construction of a new manufacturing and development facility in Southern California has been started. This facility will be operating in early fiscal 1985, significantly adding to our existing manufacturing capacity for this growing family of products.

PRC has expanded its capacity to develop and manufacture polymeric raw materials, both for in-house use and for marketing to other specialty chemical manufacturers. PRC polymer reactors are shown in large photo. Proprietary polymers give PRC products major performance advantages.

CURTISS-WRIGHT CORPORATION ANNUAL REPORT 1983

MARKET PERSPECTIVES

Fédération des caisses populaires Desjardins de Montréal et de l'Ouest-du-Québec

Rapport annuel 1983

Prévoir les opportunités nouvelles

Les opérations internationales de la Fédération ont pris un essor significatif. Parmi les quelque deux millions de membres de nos caisses affiliées, de plus en plus d'entre eux voyagent à l'étranger; un nombre toujours croissant d'entreprises qui font affaire avec les caisses populaires ou de financement transigent sur les marchés extérieurs.

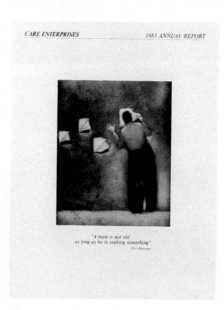

420

Arthur Zelvin Art Director/Designer
Kaimen Norman Ng, Donald R. Spiro, Matthew Klein,
 Don Hammerman, Steve Dunwell Photographers
Shareholder Reports Inc. Agency
Lithocraft Production
Beneficial Corporation Client
New York NY

421

Scott Griffiths, Jeff Burne Designers
Ken Whitmore Photographer
George Abe, Mark Penberthy, Matt Mahurin,
 Jacques Devaud Illustrators
Neii Frank Dale Stamos Griffiths Copywriters
Scott Griffiths Design Associates Inc. Agency
Care Enterprises Client
Studio City CA

422

Nelu Wolfensohn Art Director
Francine Gravel Designer
Peter Baumgartner, David Travers Photographers
Graphisme Lavalin Studio
Provigo Inc. Client
Montreal Canada

423

Bob Warkulwiz Art Director/Designer
Eugene Mopsik et al Photographers
Gerald Reimel Copywriter
Warkulwiz Design Studio
Citicorp Capital Markets Group Client
Philadelphia PA

424

Janet Nebel, Peggy Pugh Designers
Neal Slavin Photographer
Louise Hayman Copywriter
The Woods Group, Inc. Agency
Garamond Pridemark Production
Union Trust Bancorp Client
Baltimore MD

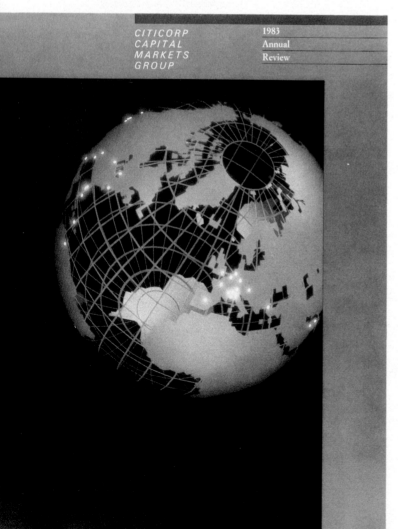

425
David A. Lozotte Art Director/Designer
John Carrier Photographer
Dan Page Copywriter
Gunn Associates Studio
Dunkin' Donuts, Inc. Client
Boston MA

426
Douglas Joseph Art Director/Designer
David Kimble Illustrator
John Halff, Craig Parsons Copywriters
Douglas Joseph Studio
Tylan Corporation Client
Los Angeles CA

427
Richard Foy Art Director
Julie Gerblick Designer
Communication Arts Incorporated Studio
Affiliated Bankshares of Colorado, Inc. Client
Boulder CO

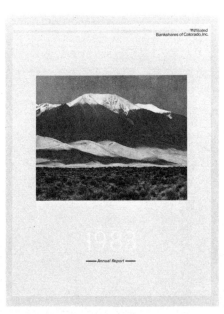

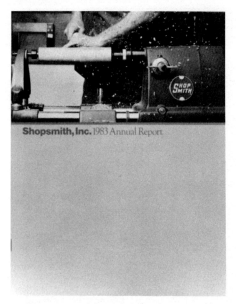

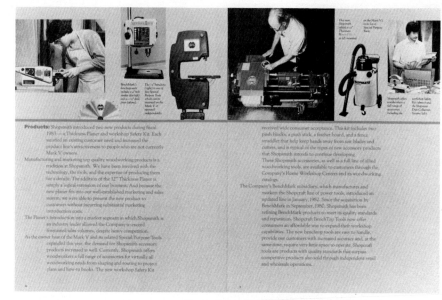

428
Robert A. Colaizzi, Jr., Mark P. Freytag Art Directors
Dirk Donson Photographer
Jeffrey C. Connor Copywriter
The Icon Group Agency
Shopsmith Inc. Client
Dayton OH

429
Marco DePlano Art Director/Designer
John Marmaras Photographer
Bob McDermott Copywriter
Groman, Glassberg, Inc. Agency
Citicorp Investment Management Client
New York NY

430
Jeff Moriber Art Director
Victoria McNamee, Diane Wasserman Designers
Jeff Holtzman Major Photographer
Lou Bori Illustrator
Hill and Knowlton, Inc. Agency
C.R. Bard, Inc. Client
New York NY

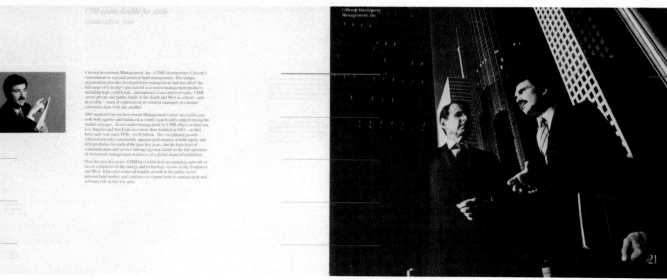

431

Henry Epstein Art Director
Susan Schatz Designer
ABC Visual Communication Photographer
James T. MacGregor, Huntington Williams, Betsy Freeman
  Copywriters
ABC, Inc. Client
New York NY

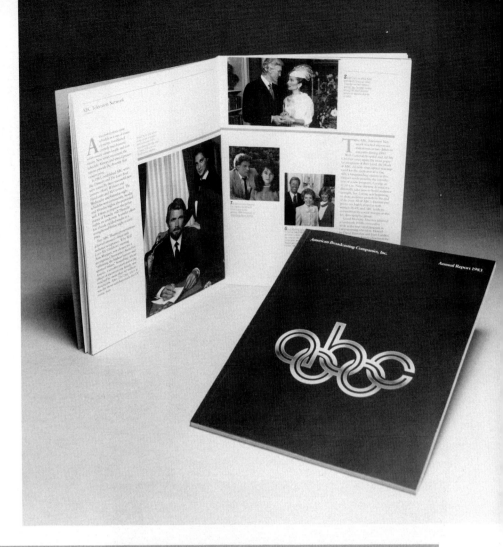

432

Richard M. Kontir Art Director/Designer
Camille Vickers Photography Photographer
Lee Stearns Copywriter
Lee & Young Communications Agency
Heritage Federal Savings & Loan Client
New York NY

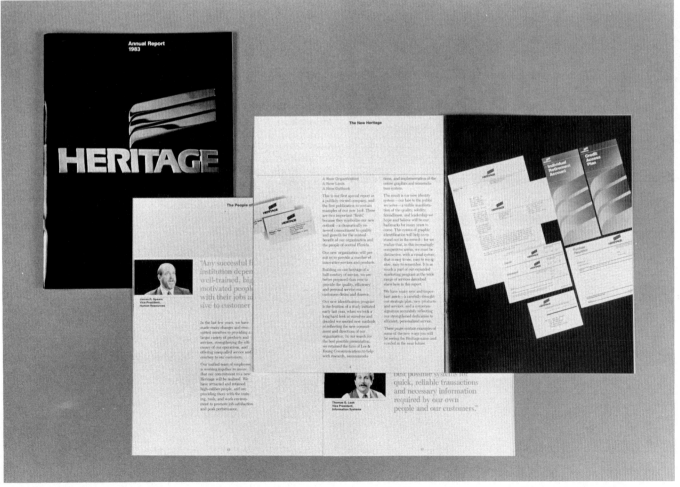

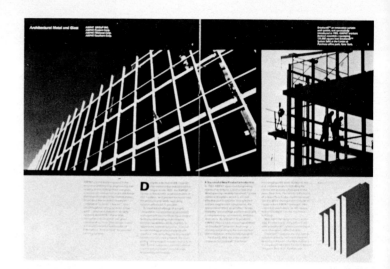

433
Duane Anders Art Director
Ted Young Creative Director
Bob Frink Designer
Peter James Samerjan Photographer
Red Barron, Inc. Agency
MEI Corporation Client
Minnetonka MN

434
Martin Miller Art Director/Designer
Chuck Slade Principal Photographer
Frank Pagani Copywriter
Michele Miller Editor
Miller + Pagani, Inc. Agency
Gemco National, Inc. Client
New York NY

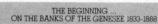
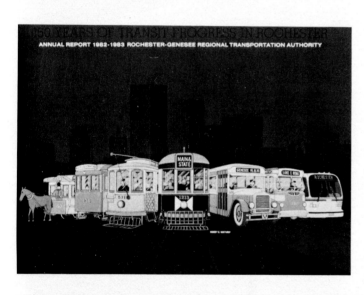

435
Shirley D. Zimmer Art Director/Designer
Robert G. Northrup Illustrator
Howard Gates Copywriter
Hart/Conway Co., Inc. Agency
Rochester-Genesee Regional Transportation Authority Client
Rochester NY

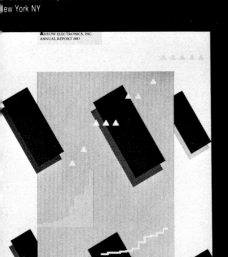

Caring for people.

436
Jim Berte Art Director/Designer
Deborah Meyer Photographer
Dave Johnson Copywriter
Robert Miles Runyan & Associates Agency
Home Health Care of America Inc. Client
Playa del Rey CA

437
Stephen Farrari, Jill Melchione Designers
Peggy & Ron Barnett Photographers
Bill Polito Illustrator
Mark Strage Copywriter
The Graphic Expressions, Inc. Agency
Liz Claiborne, Inc. Client
New York NY

1983

ANNUAL REPORT

LIZ CLAIBORNE

438
John Waters Art Director/Designer
John Waddell Copywriter
John Waters Associates, Inc. Agency
Arrow Electronics, Inc. Client
New York NY

ARROW ELECTRONICS, INC.
ANNUAL REPORT 1983

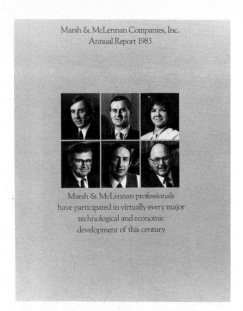

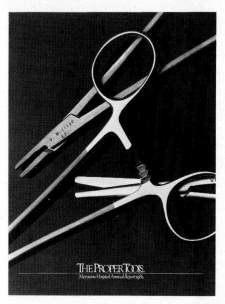

439

Beverly F. Schrager Art Director/Designer
Jeff Smith Photographer
Dong Kingman, Jr. Copywriter
Corporate Annual Reports Inc. Agency
Marsh & McLennan Companies Inc. Client
New York NY

440

Mike McMahon Art Director/Designer
John Whitehead Photographer
Bill Campbell, Mark McKenna Copywriters
Barker Campbell + Farley Agency
Maryview Hospital Client
Virginia Beach VA

441

Bennett Robinson Art Director
Peter Deutsch Designer
Bob Day Photographer
Barbara Banthien Illustrator
Corporate Graphics, Inc. Agency
Consolidated Foods Corporation Client
New York NY

442

Diana Graham, Michelle Aranda Designers
John Hill Photographer
Francis X. Piderit Copywriter
Gips + Balkind + Associates Agency
Crafton Graphics, Inc. Production
Macmillan, Inc. Client
New York NY

443

Beverly F. Schrager Art Director/Designer
Jeff Smith Photographer
Norma B. Walter Copywriter
Corporate Annual Reports, Inc. Agency
Lebanon Valley Offset Production
Sterling Drug, Inc. Client
New York NY

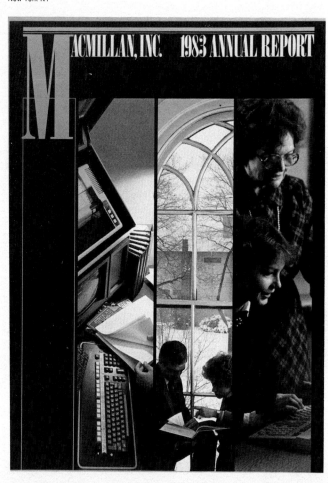

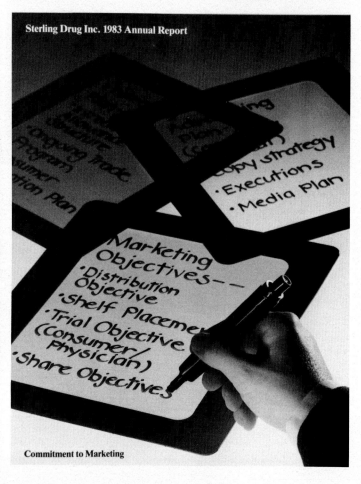

444
Jonathan Frewin Art Director/Designer
Bruno Hubschmid Photographer
Performance Communications, Inc. Agency
L. Givaudan & Cie S.A. Client
New York NY

445
Terry Lesniewicz, Al Navarre Art Directors/Designers
Carole Birndorf Copywriter
Lesniewicz/Navarre Agency
Elizabeth A. Zepf Community Health Center Client
Toledo OH

Imperial Industries, Inc. 1983 Annual Report

446

Susan Spivack Art Director/Designer
James Broderick Photographer
Bobie Goldwire Copywriter
Michael Goldwire Associates Agency
Newman Design Associates Studio
Imperial Industries Client
New York NY

447

Robert Manley Art Director
Steven Guarnaccia Illustrator
Daniel Altman Copywriter
Altman + Manley Agency
MultiGroup Health Plan Client
Cambridge MA

Premix-Marbletite is Florida's largest manufacturer of stucco products.

Premix-Marbletite Manufacturing Co.

Allied Electric Supply, Inc. provides a comprehensive array of electrical supplies and devices for residential, commercial, and industrial electrical contractors.

Allied's 21,000 line items include wire and conduit, lighting fixtures, safety switches, panel boards and motor controls. Responding to the age of technology, Allied is adding electronic and telecommunications items to its product line, building on its reputation as a full-line supplier. Both contractors and public utilities project engineers benefit from Allied's expertise and products.

For more than a quarter of a century, Allied has provided electrical supplies to builders and contractors from Key West up the Gold Coast to Jupiter. Today, Allied has extended operations well into Florida's West Coast to take advantage of dramatic population growth. Central and North Florida's electrical supply markets have been tapped by Allied in several locations including Cocoa, Orlando, Daytona Beach, and Jacksonville.

Premix-Marbletite Manufacturing Co. is the oldest and largest manufacturer of stucco products in the southeastern United States. Providing stucco for many exterior finishes in all types of buildings and swimming pools, Premix also provides plaster and drywall products for interior walls and surfaces.

Products provided by Premix for building and pool surfaces include those in The New Fontainebleau Hilton Resort pool and the Grand Bay Hotel building in Coconut Grove.

Current technology allows Premix to maintain the highest standards of uniformity and quality in color blends. Builders know the quality of Premix products and services and depend on the knowledge and experience of the Company.

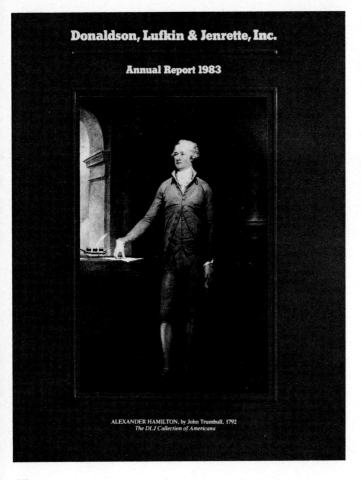

448

Paul Waner Art Director/Designer
Stuart Smith, Grant Peterson, Steven Wilkes Photographers
Richard H. Jenrette Copywriter
Case-Hoyt/Rochester Printer
Donaldson, Lufkin & Jenrette, Inc. Client
New York NY

449

Jay Tribich Art Director
Jerry Laufman Designer
Gary Perweiler Photographer
Tribich Design Associates, Inc. Agency
Athlone Industries, Inc. Client
New York NY

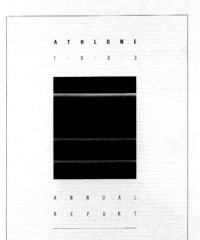

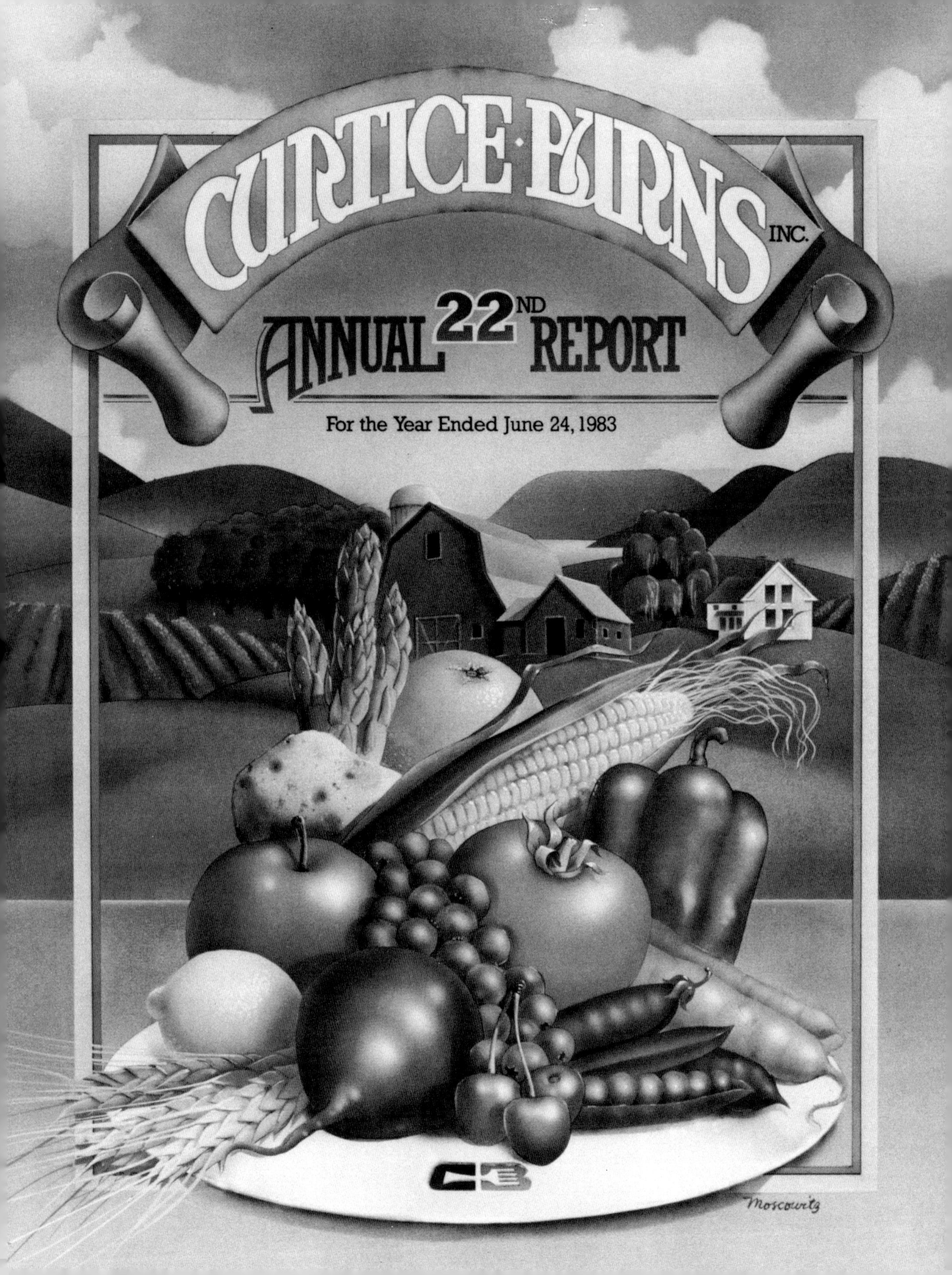

CURTICE·BURNS INC.

ANNUAL 22ND REPORT

For the Year Ended June 24, 1983

Moscowitz

450

Robert Meyer, Julia Wyant Designers
Ron Wu Photographer
Steve Moscowitz Illustrator
Ted Holmgren Copywriter
Robert Meyer Design, Inc. Studio
Curtice-Burns, Inc. Client
Rochester NY

451

Carl Seltzer Art Director
Cross Associates Designers
Dick Luria Photographer
Judith P. Wheeler Copywriter
Lockheed Corporation Client
New York NY

452

Nicholas Zarkades, Susan Cummings Art Directors
Louis Bencze Photographer
Zarkades Cummings Chasen Agency
Genetic Systems, Inc. Client
Seattle WA

453

Martin Miller Art Director
Laura Stoll Designer
Andrew Popper Photographer
Lawrence R. Tavcar, Carl Byoir & Assoc. Copywriters
Miller + Pagani Inc. Agency
Ampad Corporation Client
New York NY

454

David Bloch, Irwin Graulich Art Directors/Designers
Harry Benson Photographer
Bloch Graulich Whelan, Inc. Studio
Republic New York Corporation Client
New York NY

Lockheed
Corporation
1983
Annual Report

In high technology
we value people above all,
for our primary resource
is the human mind.

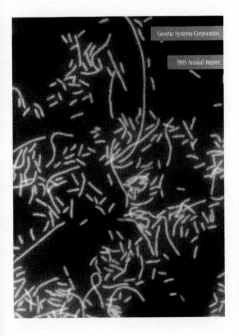

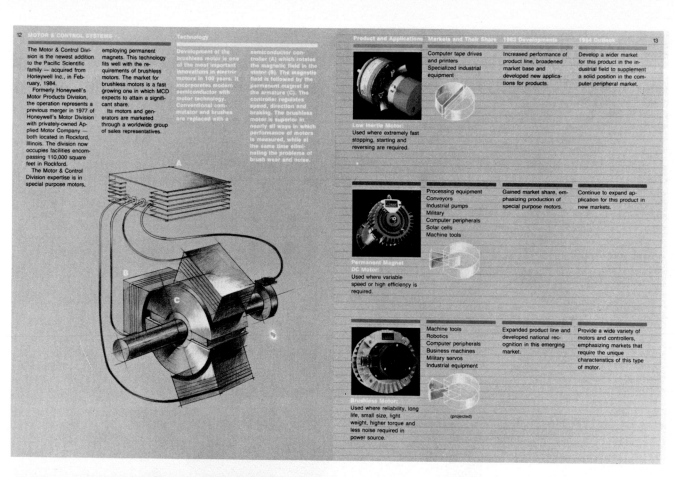

The Motor & Control Division is the newest addition to the Pacific Scientific family — acquired from Honeywell Inc., in February, 1984.

Formerly Honeywell's Motor Products Division, the operation represents a previous merger in 1977 of Honeywell's Motor Division with privately-owned Applied Motor Company — both located in Rockford, Illinois. The division now occupies facilities encompassing 110,000 square feet in Rockford.

The Motor & Control Division expertise is in special purpose motors,

employing permanent magnets. This technology fits well with the requirements of brushless motors. The market for brushless motors is a fast growing one in which MCD expects to attain a significant share.

Its motors and generators are marketed through a worldwide group of sales representatives.

Technology

Developments of the brushless motor is one of the most important innovations in electric motors in 100 years. It interpretes modern semiconductor with motor technology. Conventional commutator and brushes are replaced with a

semiconductor controller (A) which rotates the magnetic field in the stator (B). The magnetic field is followed by the permanent magnet in the armature (C). The controller regulates speed, direction and braking. The brushless motor is superior in nearly all ways in which performance of motors is measured, while at the same time eliminating the problems of brush wear and noise.

Product and Applications	Markets and Their Share	1983 Developments	1984 Outlook
Low Inertia Motor: Used where extremely fast stopping, starting and reversing are required.	Computer tape drives and printers / Specialized industrial equipment	Increased performance of product line, broadened market base and developed new applications for products.	Develop a wider market for this product in the industrial field to supplement a solid position in the computer peripheral market.
Permanent Magnet DC Motor: Used where variable speed or high efficiency is required.	Processing equipment / Conveyors / Industrial pumps / Military / Computer peripherals / Solar cells / Machine tools	Gained market share, emphasizing production of special purpose motors.	Continue to expand application for this product in new markets.
Brushless Motor: Used where reliability, long life, small size, light weight, higher torque and less noise required in power source.	Machine tools / Robotics / Computer peripherals / Business machines / Military servos / Industrial equipment	Expanded product line and developed national recognition in this emerging market.	Provide a wide variety of motors and controllers, emphasizing markets that require the unique characteristics of this type of motor.

(projected)

PACIFIC SCIENTIFIC
1983 ANNUAL REPORT

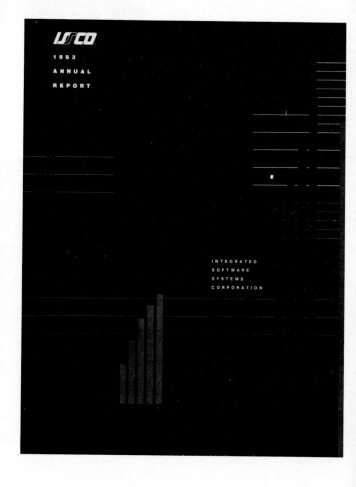

ISSCO
1983
ANNUAL
REPORT

INTEGRATED
SOFTWARE
SYSTEMS
CORPORATION

455

Ron Jeffries Art Director
David Sapp, Kenton Lotz Designers
William Warren Photographer
Steve Sherer, David Sapp Illustrators
The Jeffries Association Studio
Pacific Scientific Corporation Client
Los Angeles CA

456

John Benelli, Jim Crouch Art Directors
David Kramer Photographer
Joe Bowen, Joe Rauh Illustrator
Design Group West Agency
Crouch + Fuller, Inc. Studio
Integrated Software Systems Corporation Client
Del Mar CA

457
Craig Sheumaker Art Director/Designer
Jay Freis Photographer
Peter Braddock Copywriter
Unigraphics Agency
Crown Zellerbach Client
Sausalito CA

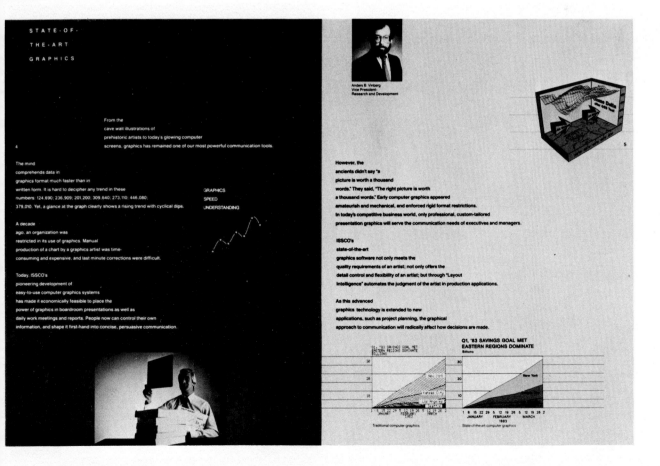

Packaging

458
A. Schechter, R. Wong Art Directors
R. Cruanas Designer
Schechter Group Inc. Agency
R.J. Reynolds Tobacco Co. Client
New York NY

459
Peter Schmidt Art Director
Peter Schmidt Studios Studio
Jil Sander Cosmetics Client
Hamburg, West Germany

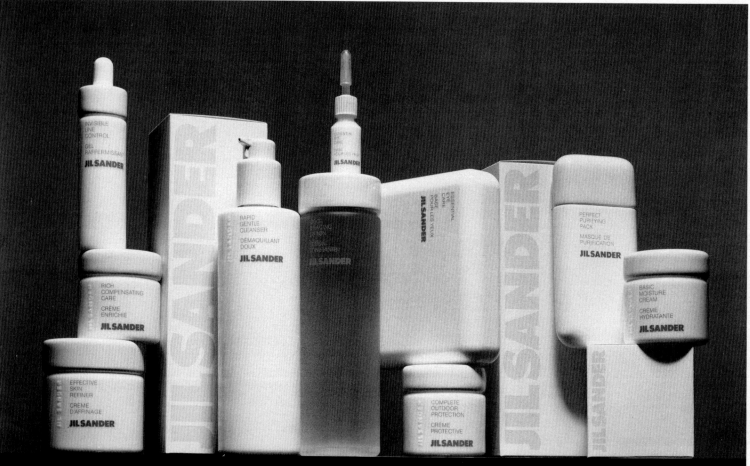

460
Janice Breisacher Art Director
Rich Strand Designer
Georgia Deaver Calligrapher
Wilton Coombs & Colnett Agency
Embarcadero Center Client
San Francisco CA

461
Louisa Sugar Art Director/Designer
Dover Archives Illustrator
Carme, Inc. Agency/Client
Novato CA

462
Heather Cooper Designer/Illustrator
Burns, Cooper, Hynes Ltd. Studio
Kimberly-Clark of Canada Ltd. Client
Toronto. Canada

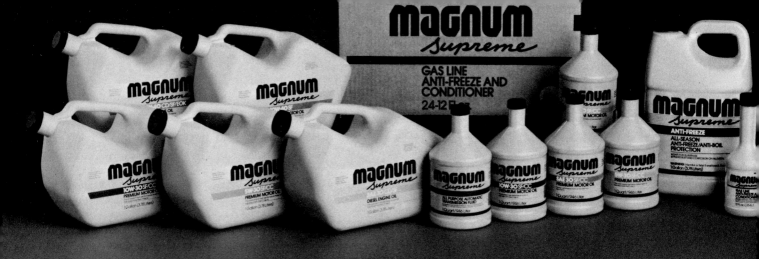

463
Robert Wages Designer
Bard Wrisley Photographer
Nucifora & Associates Agency
CW Petroleum & Chemical, Inc. Client
Atlanta GA

464
John Erickson Art Director/Designer
Jan Franks Copywriter
Young & Rubicam NY Agency
United States Postal Service Client
New York NY

465
Millie Falcaro, Mary Tiegreen Designers
Falcaro & Tiegreen Ltd. Studio/Client
New York NY

466
Laura Otani Art Director/Designer
Yasumara & Associates/CYB Agency
General Foods Le Cafe Client
New York NY

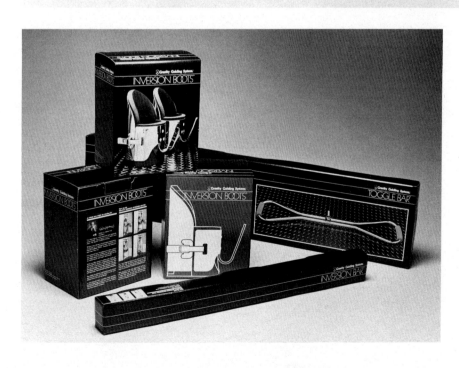

467

John Benson, John LeDuc Designers
Stephen Graham Photographer
Benson-LeDuc Agency
Clancy's Fancy Hot Sauce Client
Ann Arbor MI

468

Joy Greene, Ellen Spivak Designers
Kei Ogata Photographer
Yasumura & Associates/CYB Agency
Sunstar, Inc. Japan Client
New York NY

469

Greg Resler Art Director/Designer
Neal Higgins Photographer
John H. Harland Co. Agency/Client
Decatur GA

470

Ken Meek Art Director/Designer
Ken Biggs Photographer
Paula Johnson Copywriter
Gravity Guidance, Inc. Client
Pasadena CA

471
Jack Anderson, Reynaldo Sabado Designers
Hornall-Anderson Design Works Agency
Jay Jacobs Client
Seattle WA

472
Yves Simard Art Director
Pierre Leonard Designer
Cossette Communication-Marketing Agency
Grapheme Communication-Design Studio
Cooperative Federee Client
Montreal, Canada

473
Peter Schmidt Art Director
Peter Schmidt Studios Studio
Cerruti Client
Hamburg, West Germany

474
Donn Munson Art Director
Sylvain Michaelis Designer
Michaelis/Carpelis Design Assoc. Studio
Ballantine Books Client
New York NY

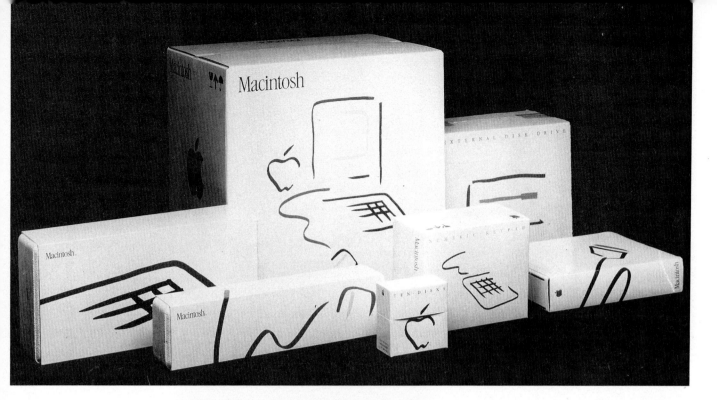

475

Dominick Sarica Art Director/Designer
One & One Design Consultants, Inc. Agency
Coty International Div. Pfizer Client
New York NY

476

Tom Hughes Art Director
Clement Mok, E. Romano Designers
John Casado Illustrator
Apple Creative Services Agency
Apple Computers Studio/Client
Cupertino CA

477

Tim Girvin Art Director/Designer
Anton Kimball Illustrator
Elizabeth Purser Copywriter
Tim Girvin Design Inc. Studio
The Hogue Cellars Client
Seattle WA

478

Tim Girvin Art Director
Mary Jean Radosevich Designer
Anton Kimball Illustrator
Beth Brosseau Copywriter
Tim Girvin Design, Inc. Studio
P & G Plant Company Client
Seattle WA

479

Patrick Florville Art Director/Designer
Florville Design & Analysis Studio
Fuego Cosmetics Inc. Client
New York NY

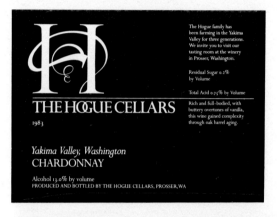

The Hogue family has been farming in the Yakima Valley for three generations. We invite you to visit our tasting room at the winery in Prosser, Washington.

Residual Sugar 0.2% by Volume

Total Acid 0.75% by Volume

Rich and full-bodied, with buttery overtones of vanilla, this wine gained complexity through oak barrel aging.

THE HOGUE CELLARS
1983

Yakima Valley, Washington
CHARDONNAY

Alcohol 13.0% by volume
PRODUCED AND BOTTLED BY THE HOGUE CELLARS, PROSSER, WA

PLEXI TRIVET

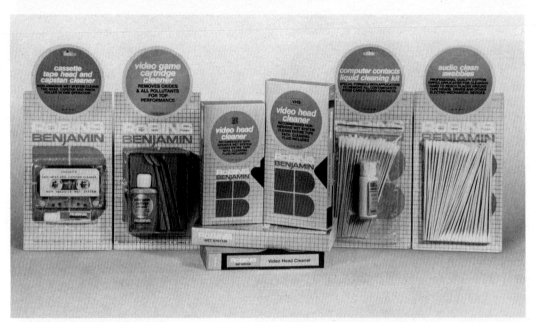

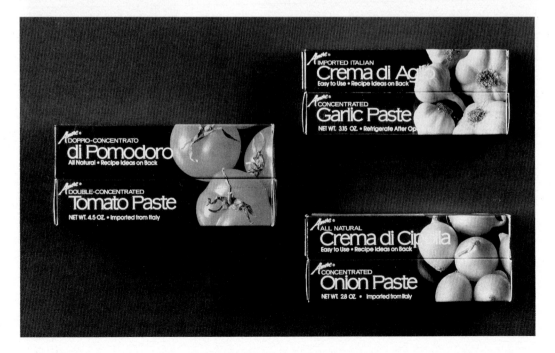

480

Marjorie Green Art Director/Illustrator
Gunn Associates Studio
Wang Client
Boston MA

481

Jack Schecterson Art Director/Designer
Jack Schecterson Associates, Inc. Agency
Benjamin Electroproducts, Inc. Client
New York NY

482

Millie Falcaro, Mary Tiegreen Designers
Falcaro & Tiegreen Ltd. Studio
Universal Foods Client
New York NY

483

Bruce Crocker, Robert Manley Art Directors
Matthew Imperiale Illustrator
Altman + Manley Agency
Sweet Micro Systems Client
Cambridge MA

484

Pat Garling Art Director/Designer
Diane Von Furstenberg Studio Studio/Client
New York NY

485

Rick Weiler Art Director
Skip Hartzell Creative Director
Paul Schnabel Photographer
The Linden Agency Agency
Stoney Point, Inc. Client
Virginia Beach VA

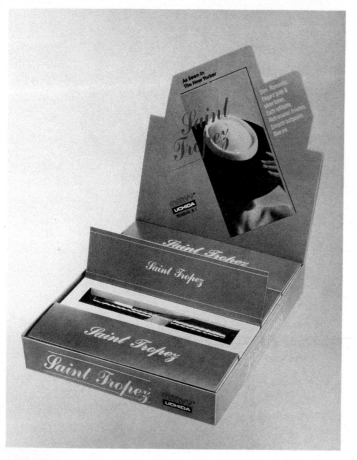

486
Liz Fischl-Nasta Art Director/Designer
Pete Glasheen Photographer
Glasheen Advertising Agency
Uchida of America Client
New York NY

487
Lee Lefever Art Director
Scott W. Hershey Creative Director
Brian Tolbert Photographer
Hershey, Philbin Assoc., Inc. Agency
Casa Di Bertacchi Corporation Client
Harrisburg PA

488
Judy Tipton Art Director/Copywriter
Barbary Shelley Designer
Norman Greene Illustrator
Tipton & Maglione Agency
Salt Free Gourmet Co. Client

489
Tina Fritche Art Director
James Gabel Designer
Libby, Perszyk, Kathman Studio
Totes, Inc. Client
Cincinnati, OH

490
Barbara Martocci Art Director/Designer
Davis A. Gaffga Photographer
Costich & McConnell Inc. Agency
Garfield Williamson—Wonderlawn Client
Hauppauge NY

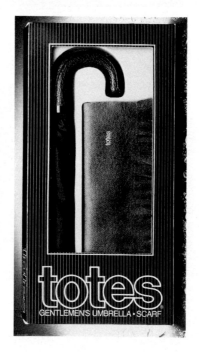

491
Lito Art Director
Paulo Rocha Photographer
Mario Nascimento Copywriter
Alcantara Machado, Periscinoto Com. Ltda. Agency
Alcantara Machado Nordeste Ltda. Client
Sao Paulo, Brazil

492
Cal Anderson Art Director/Designer
Georgia Deaver Calligrapher
Georgia Deaver Studio Studio
LeChamp Cellars Client
San Francisco CA

493
Juan Concepcion Art Director
Bob Tabor Designer
Gerstman + Meyers, Inc. Agency
E.R. Squibb & Sons, Inc. Client
New York NY

494
Amy Leppert Designer/Illustrator
Sheldon Rysner Account Supervisor
Murrie, White, Drummond, Lienhart Studio
McDonald's Corporation Client
Chicago IL

496
John Coy Art Director/Artist
COY, Los Angeles Studio
David Levy Lithography Printer
Quady Winery Client
Culver City CA

495
Judi F. Niemann Art Director
Sheri L. Bireley Designer
T Square Studios Studio
M. Gross & Co., Outfitters Client
Pennington NJ

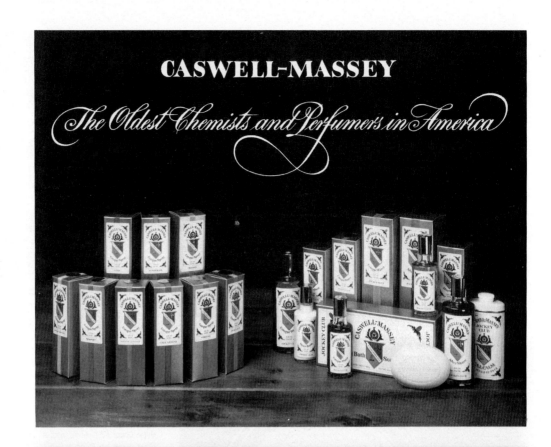

497
Victor Liebert Art Director/Designer
Joshua Taylor Production
Caswell-Massey Co., Ltd. Client
New York NY

498
John Digianni Art Director
Art Accardi Designer
Gianninoto Associates, Inc. Studio
H.P. Hood, Inc. Client
New York NY

499
Milton Glaser Art Director/Designer
Milton Glaser, Inc. Studio
The Grand Union Co. Client
New York NY

500
David Coven Art Director/Illustrator
Don Snyder Photographer
Leadworks, In-House Studio
Leadworks, Inc. Client
Beachwood OH

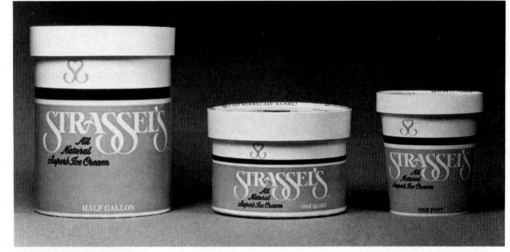

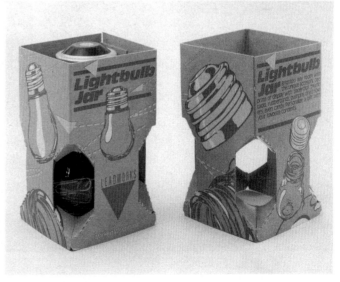

501
Marty Neumeier, Sandra Higashi Designers
Neumeier Design Team Studio
Knapp Communications Client
Santa Barbara CA

502
Cheryl Lewin Art Director/Designer
Cheryl Lewin Design Agency
Pintchik Paints Client
New York NY

503
Milton Glaser Art Director/Designer
Milton Glaser Inc. Studio
Caspian Caviar Client
New York NY

504
**Primo Angeli, Mark Jones, Jamie Davidosn,
  Eric Read** Designers
Primo Angeli Graphics Studio
Dreyer's Ice Cream Client
San Francisco CA

505
Alston Anderson Art Director/Designer
Mike Bull Illustrator
Anderson Miller & Hubbard Consumer Services Agency
Almond Board of California Client
San Francisco CA

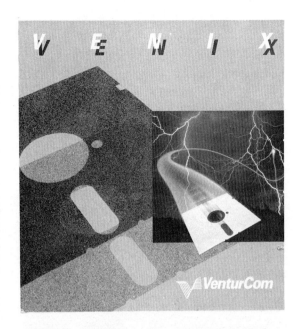

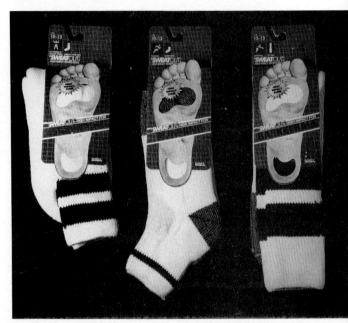

506
Fae E. Druiz Art Director/Designer
Charles Betz Photographer
Regency Graphics Production
Monet Jewelers Client
New York NY

507
Judith Richland, Ellen Weinberger Designers
Paul Dupont, Barry Parker Photographers
United Lithograph Printer
Serif & Sans Typesetter
Richland Design Associates Studio
VenturCom, Inc. Client
Cambridge MA

508
Michael Dweck, Matthew Oscar Art Directors
Alex Isle, Michael Dweck Designers
Michael Dweck & Co. Studio
Socksmith Inc. Client
New York NY

509
Denis Keller Art Director
Guy Olivier Photographer
Design Board, Bahaeghel & Partners Studio
Vandemoortele, Belgium (Resi) Client
Brussels. Belgium

510
Susan Milord Art Director/Designer
Sue Thompson Illustrator
Milord Graphic Design Studio
Forest Foods, Inc. Client
Suffield CT

Calendars

511
Luis Grasso Art Director/Designer
Candido Ortiz Photographer
Pepita Lopez Copywriter
The Colour Group Inc. Production
Puerto Rico Telephone Co. Client
Santurce PR

512
Greg Schuler Art Director/Designer
**Stephen Green-Armytage, Bob Coglanese, Dan Farrell,
  Mark Wyville, Rod Cook** Photographers
Kihm Winship, Kelly Delles Copywriters
Silverman Mower Advertising Agency
Great Lakes Production
New York State Racing Assoc. Client
Syracuse NY

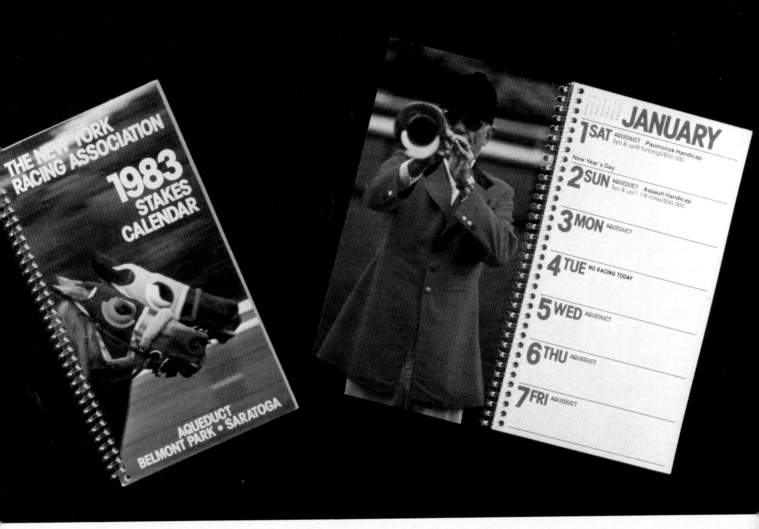

Glundal
Olympic Year
Calendar

513

Connie Maloney Art Director
John Martin Gilbert Designer/Sculptor
Glundal Color Inc. Printer/Client
Syracuse NY

516

Thomas Gass Art Director/Designer
Scott Chaney Photographer
Spectrum Composition Typography
Fox Lithograph Co. Printer
Thomas Gass Ltd Studio
Carnegie Fabrics Client
Brooklyn NY

514

Hoi Ping Law Art Director/Designer
Paramount News Copywriters
Dyer/Kahn Inc. Agency
Paramount Pictures Corp. Client
Los Angeles CA

515

Louis Nelson Art Director
Peter Scavuzzo Designer
**John Carnevale, Clifton Draper, Charles Lewis,
  Phillip Harrington, Robert Woods** Photographers
Louis Nelson Associates Studio
AT & T Technologies Client
New York NY

517

Arthur Beckenstein, Dick Martell Art Directors
Susan Bidel Copywriter
PEOPLE Magazine, Time Inc. Client
New York NY

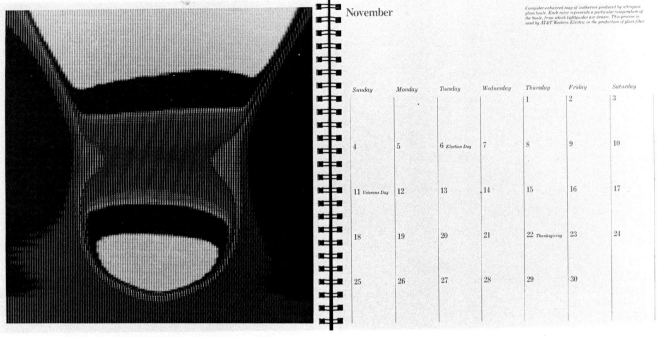

Computer-enhanced map of isotherms produced by nitrogen glass boule. Each color represents a particular temperature of the boule, from which lightguides are drawn. This process is used by AT&T Western Electric in the production of glass fiber.

Sunday	Monday	Tuesday	Wednesday	Thursday	Friday	Saturday
				1	2	3
4	5	6 *Election Day*	7	8	9	10
11 *Veterans Day*	12	13	14	15	16	17
18	19	20	21	22 *Thanksgiving*	23	24
25	26	27	28	29	30	

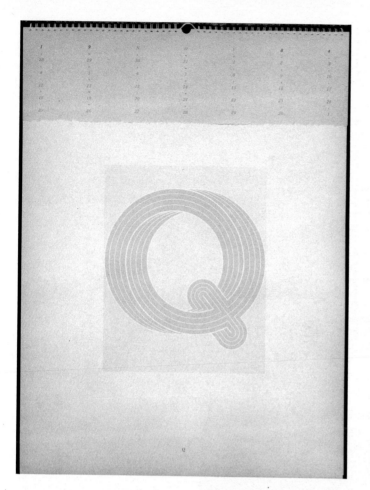

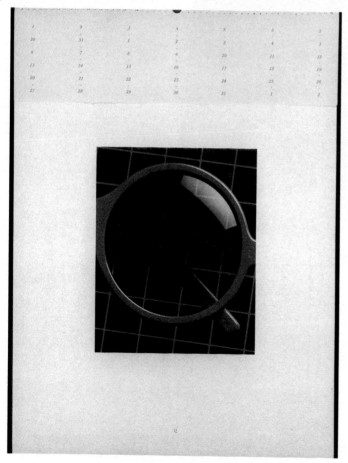

518
McRay Magleby, Paul Boyle, Amanda Onyon Designers
Skip Schmidt, Craig Diamond, Glen Ingles, Ed Bateman
Photographers
**Amanda Onyon, Paul Boyle, Jana Winters, Nathan Gardner,
Don Lambson** Illustrators
Publication Design Studio Class Studio
Quality Press Client
Provo UT

519
Fred Hartson Art Director/Designer
Karl Kohlenberger Copywriter
Donald S. Smith Associates Agency
Electronic Colour/Lester Lithograph Client
Anaheim CA

520
Kit Hinrich, Nancy Koe Designers
Terry Heffernan Photographer
Peterson-Dodge Copywriter
Jonson Pedersen Hinrich & Shakery Agency
Terry Heffernan Inc. Studio
American Presidents Line Client
San Francisco CA

521
Bennett Robinson Art Director
Elaine Isaacson Designer
Bob Day Photographer
Rhoda Weiss Copywriter
Corporate Graphics Inc. Agency
St. Joseph Medical Center Client
New York NY

March

26	27	28	29	1	2	3
4	5	6	7	8	9	10
11	12	13	14	15	16	17
18	19	20	21	22	23	24
25	26	27	28	29	30	31
1	2	3	4	5	6	7

Electronic Colour
Lester Lithograph

LASER SCANNED TONES (714) 835-2188, (213) 724-6222   PRINTING (714) 827-9940

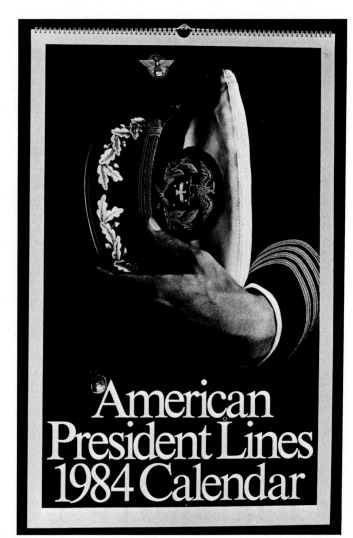

American President Lines 1984 Calendar

Saint Joseph Medical Center
Annual Report/Calendar 1984

522
Hisao Takehana Art Director/Designer
Hiroshige Ando Illustrator
Kobi Graphis Printing
CDP Japan Ltd. Advertising Agency
Matsushita Electric Industrial Co. Ltd. Client
Tokyo, Japan

523
Kyle Neidt Art Director
Calvin Bohner Illustrator
State Economic Opportunity Office, Kansas Client
Fresno CA

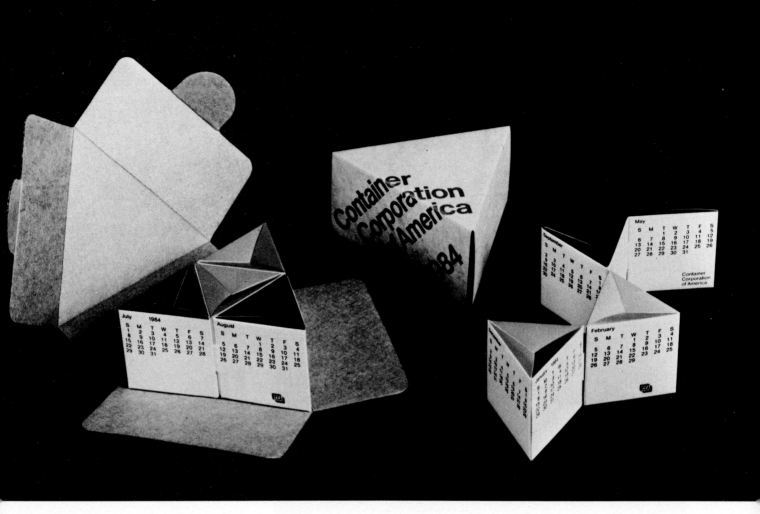

524
J. Hutchcroft, R. Swanson, R. House Designers
R. Patterson Copywriter
CCA Corp. Design Dept. Agency
Container Corporation of America Client
Chicago IL

525
Wayne Pederson Art Director/Designer
Clifton Boutelle, Ann DeLaVergne,
  Focus On Sports Photographers
Group 243 Design Inc. Studio
Domino's Pizza Inc. Client
Ann Arbor MI

526
Mark Greitzer Art Director
Judy Sickle Designer
Michael Alpert Illustrator
Bonni Kogos Copywriter
Millennium Design Communications Agency
American Express Company Client
New York NY

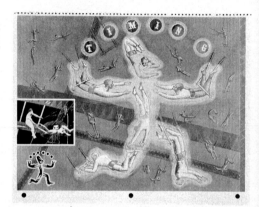

527

Michael K. Frith Art Director
David Kaestle, Michael K. Frith Designers
John E. Barrett Photographer
Henry Beard Copywriter
Henson Associates Agency
Alfred A. Knopf Client
New York NY

528

Shojiro Yanagi Art Director
Toyoo Mori Designer
DYR Agency
Studio Cygnus Inc. Studio
PhotoUnique Client
New York NY

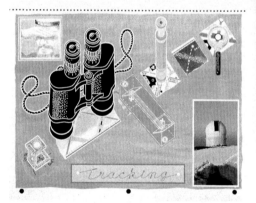

529

Mogens Sorensen Art Director/Designer
Mich Brownfield, Bush Hollyhead, George Hardie Photographers
Bill Riley Copywriter
Bergsøe 3 Agency
ScanDutch L/S Client
Klampenborg, Denmark

530
Jim Camann Art Director/Designer
IBM Charlotte Design Center Studio
Steve Galit Associates Production
IBM Charlotte Client
Charlotte NC

531
Michiteru Taira Art Director/Designer
Nob Fukuda Photographer
Studio Nob Studio
Japan Project Production
Mita Industry Co., Ltd. Client
Osaka. Japan

Logotypes
TRADEMARKS

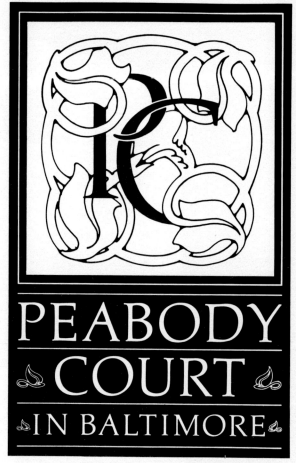

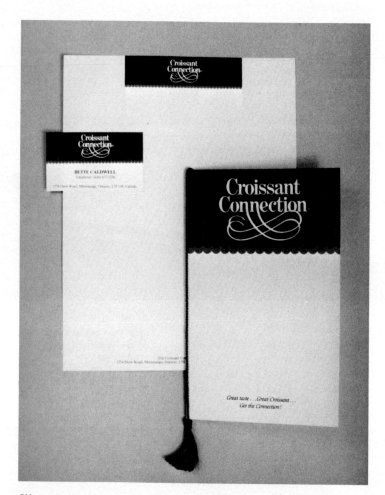

534
Erin Ries Kershner Art Director
Nancy Hart Designer
Rick Parisi Illustrator
Image Dynamics, Inc. Agency
Peabody Court In Baltimore Client
Baltimore MD

532
Israel Fraiman Art Director/Designer
Fraiman Design & Advertising, Inc. Studio
Croissant Connection, Inc. Client
Toronto. Canada

533
Thomas McNulty Designer
John Allen Hull Illustrator
Robert Miles Runyan & Associates Studio/Client
Playa del Rey CA

For all you loafers with bread who want to eat like the upper crust.

Saint Joseph Hospital

535

John Sayles Art Director/Designer
Kragie/Newell Advertising Agency
Saint Joseph Hospital Client
Des Moines IA

536

William Carrig Art Director/Designer
Bozell & Jacobs, Inc. New York Agency
William Carrig Studio
Cathi Stoler Client
New York NY

537

Susan Turner, Clifford Selbert Art Directors
Matt Ralph Designer
Terzis & Company Agency
Europa Design Client
Cambridge MA

538

Lauren Smith Art Director/Designer
Lauren Smith Design Studio
Cine-Graphis Client
Mountain View CA

539

Preston Williamson Art Director/Designer
Preston Williamson Graphic Design Studio
Cafe Nola Bar and Grill Client
Philadelphia PA

540

Jeffrey A. Spear Art Director/Designer
The City Client
Santa Monica CA

541

Bill Smith, Jr., Bob Warkulwiz Art Directors
Michael Rogalski, Joan Walsh Illustrators
Warkulwiz Design Studio
ARA Services Client
Philadelphia PA

PHILABUNDANCE

542
Preston Williamson Art Director/Designer
Preston Williamson Graphic Design Studio
PhilAbundance, Inc. Client
Philadelphia PA

543
Michael Thomas Art Director/Designer
Michael Thomas Art Direction Agency
Maurice Pattengill/Foothills Industrial Mineral
  Consultation Client
Denver CO

544
Terry Lesniewicz, Al Navarre Art Directors/Designers
Lesniewicz/Navarre Agency
The French Bakery Client
Toledo OH

LA CIBOULETTE

545
Meredith G. Bratt Art Director/Illustrator
MGB Designs Studio
La Ciboulette Restaurant Client
Chicago IL

546
Jack Anderson, Ray Terada Art Directors
John Hornall Design Works Studio
Rural Alaska Insurance Agency Client
Seattle WA

547
Michael Hogan Art Director/Designer
Able Advertising, Inc. Agency
Technical Information Services Client
Rochester NY

548
Stavros Cosmopulos Art Director/Illustrator
Arrow Composition/Boston Typesetter
Cosmopulos, Crowley & Daly, Inc./Boston Agency
Waterville Valley, N.H. Client
Boston MA

550
Marvin Berk Art Director/Designer
Creative Images In Inc. Studio
Design-Technics Ceramics, Inc. Client
New York NY

549
John Hornall, Rosie Girasole Designers
Hornall-Anderson Design Works Agency
Intermedia Client
Seattle WA

551
Primo Angeli Art Director/Designer
Charles Schulz, Mark Jones Illustrators
Primo Angeli Graphics Studio
Snoopy's Ice Cream & Cookie Co. Client
San Francisco CA

The Kowloon Club
九龍會

552
Peter Chancellor Art Director
Mark Chan Designer
Chancellor Thomson Ltd. Studio
The Kowloon Club Client
Hong Kong

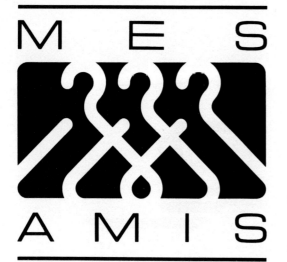

553
Oscar Recalde Art Director/Designer
Or Design Associates Studio
Apparel Management Information Systems Client
Rego Park NY

555
L. Dean Woolever, Donald Lichty Art Directors
L. Dean Woolever Illustrator
NTID Media Production Department Studio
National Technical Institute for the Deaf /RIT Client
Rochester NY

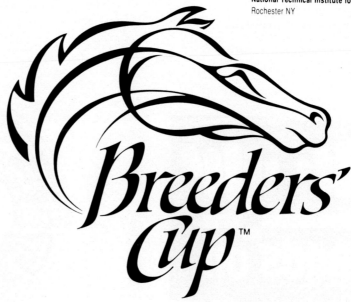

1983 BREEDERS CUP LIMITED

556
Barbara Rosenwach, Rick Barry Designer
Michael A. Letis Creative Director
Robert Landau Associates, Inc. Agency
Breeders' Cup Limited Client
New York NY

554
Elena Gonzalez Art Director/Designer
Elena Gonzalez Diseno Grafico Agency
Fosforera Peruana S.A. Client
Lima. Peru

557
John Coy Art Director
John Coy, John Barr, Kevin Consales Designers
COY, Los Angeles Studio
South Coast Metro Alliance Client
Culver City CA

562
Mark Lichtenstein Art Director
Thomas A. Peters Designer
Lichtenstein Marketing Communications Studio
Stewart/Dean and Associates Client
Rochester NY

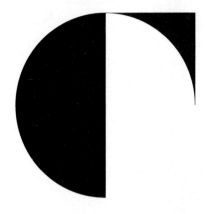

Central Typesetting Company

558
Morava & Oliver Design Office Art Direction
Emmett Morava Designer
Central Typesetting Company
Santa Monica CA

559
Al Luna, Lonnie Whittington Designers
WW3/Papagalos Design & Advertising Agency
Marsh Financial Client
Phoenix AZ

560
Tim Girvin Art Director/Designer
Tim Girvin Design, Inc. Agency
Jim and Randi Gulden Client
Seattle WA

Asian Savings Bank

561
Angel L. Bunag Art Director/Designer
Design Systemat, Inc. Agency
Asian Savings Bank Client
Manile, Philippines

563
Gary Polich Art Director/Designer
Gary Polich Illustrator
Typography Plus, Hoffman Printing Production
Boise Homes Client
Denver CO

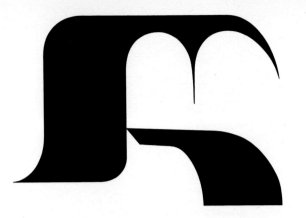

564
Nelu Wolfensohn Art Director/Designer
Graphisme Lavalin Studio
The Bible and the Arts Client
Montreal. Canada

565
Donette Lee Art Director/Illustrator
Lee Design Office Studio
Rancho Mesa Animal Hospital Client
Encinitas CA

566
Heidi Schmeck Art Director/Designer
E.S. McCann & Son, Inc. Client
Greenwich CT

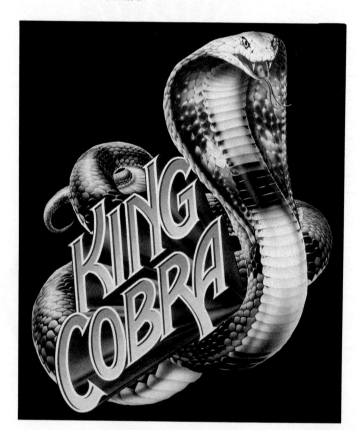

567
Randy Mosher Art Director
Bruce Shaffer Designer
John Maggard Illustrator
Sive Assoc. Agency
The Main Artery Studio
Kings Island Client
Cincinnati OH

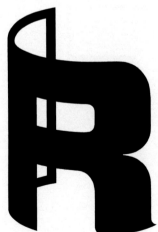

568
Shinzo Saiki & Suniaki Nomura Designers
Saiki Design, Inc. Agency
Renfield Corporation Client
New York NY

569
Ulf Petterson Art Director/Designer
M O R/Malmo Agency
Leif Eriksson Client
Malmo. Sweden

570
Ulf Petterson Art Director/Designer
M O R/Malmo Agency
Investment AB Profectus Client
Malmo. Sweden

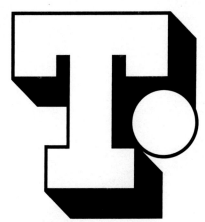

571
Gerd F. Setzke Art Director/Designer
Atelier Setzke Studio
Thalia-Buchhandlung Client
Hamburg. West Germany

572
Clive Gay, Sharon Dowson Designers
Pentagraph (Pty) Ltd. Studio
Rubber and Associated Manufacturers Client
Johannesburg. RSA

573
Susan Jackson Keig Art Director/Designer
Susan Jackson Keig Client
Chicago IL

574
Barbara Redmond Art Director/Designer
Barbara Redmond Design Studio
Media Ventures, Inc. Client
Minneapolis MN

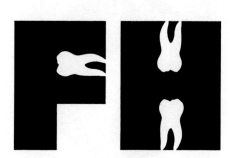

575
Mark P. Freytag Art Director/Designer
The Icon Group Agency
Freeman and Hendricks D.D.S. Client
Dayton OH

576
M. Rouyaee Art Director/Designer
Mikail Creative Director
Marz Graphic Design Client
New York NY

577
Felix Beltran Art Director/Designer
Felix Beltran & Asociados, Mexico Agency
Seldon, Mexico—Carpets Client
Mexico City. Mexico

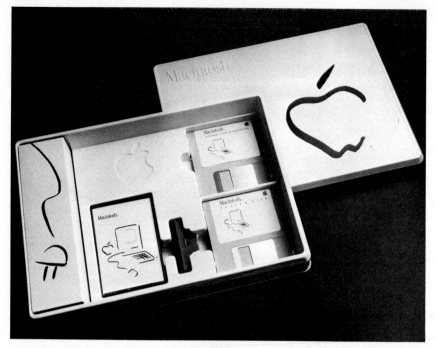

578
Tom Hughes, John Casado Designers
Apple Creative Services Agency
Apple Computer Client
Cupertino CA

579
Fernando Medina Art Director/Designer
Fernando Medina Design Agency
Krmush tis Mykonos Client
Madrid. Spain

P R O M O N T O R Y P O I N T E

RESORT APARTMENTS

OF THE POINTE AT TAPATIO CLIFFS

580
Steve Ditko Art Director/Designer
Thorne, Shepard & Rodgers Agency
SHR Communications, Planning and Design Studio
Promontory Pointe Client
Phoenix AZ

581
Glynn Bell Art Director/Artist
Cooper Bell Limited Studio
Owen Design Consultants Client
Toronto. Canada

IPCO

582
Marshall Harmon Art Director
Ken Higgins Designer
Harmon Kemp Inc. Agency
International Paper Company Client
New York NY

583
Dennis Morabito Art Director/Designer
Burson-Marsteller Agency
Quaker State Client
Pittsburgh PA

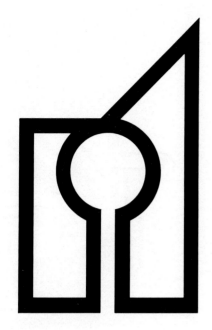

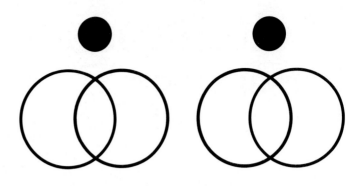

Southwest Wheelchair Athletic Association

584
Lori Bidstrup, Willie Baronet Art Directors/Designers
The Graham Group Agency
Plaza One Client
Lafayette LA

585
William L. Biles Art Director/Designer
Ed Sherrill Copywriter
Technika Agency
Biles Design Studio
Southwest Wheelchair Athletic Association Client
Houston TX

586
Sandra Bluett, Larry Paine Art Directors
Paine Bluett & Paine, Inc. Studio
Kaiser-Georgetown Community Health Plan, Inc. Client
Bethesda MD

587
Peter Jewiss Art Director
Bill Culbert Illustrator
Stadden Hughes Ltd. Agency
Antelope PLC Client
London. England

588
Bev Craig, Michael Kurz Art Directors
John Gallie Designer
Annaline Moag Illustrator
The Ad Co. Agency
Photosepro/Eagle Production
Chain Hardware Merchants Client
Cape Town. RSA

Letterheads

SINGLE UNIT

589
Milie Falcaro & Mary Tiegreen Art Directors/Designers
Falcaro & Tiegreen Ltd. Studio
R.M. Curtis Client
New York NY

590
Rod Dyer Art Director
Clive Piercy Designer
Ann Field Illustrator/Client
Dyer/Kahn, Inc. Agency
Los Angeles CA

591
Steven Sessions Art Director/Designer
Steven Sessions, Inc. Agency
Victoria Best/Body Beautiful Exercise Studio Client
Houston TX

592
Thom Smith Art Director
Greg Holly Designer
SmithGroup Studio
White Light Reproductions Client
Portland OR

593
Stephen S. Quine Art Director/Designer
Eleni Constantopoulos Illustrator
Sparkman & Bartholomew Agency
Mechanix Inc. Production
ADCMW Client
Washington DC

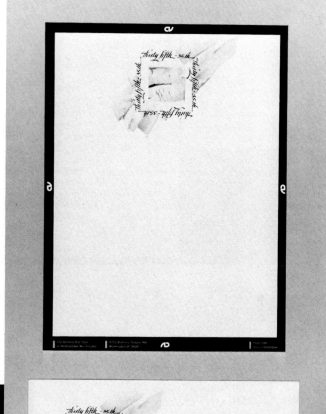

594
Julian Naranjo Art Director/Designer
Julian Naranjo Graphic Design/Design Group West Studio
Custom Touch Draperies Client
Del Mar CA

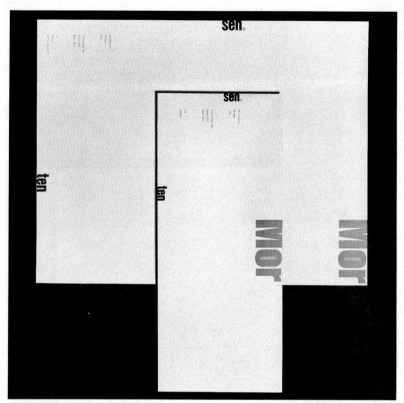

595
Gordon Mortensen Art Director
Jean Larcher Designer
Studio Michel Schmitt Studio/Client
Cergy France

596
Kan Tai-Keung Art Director/Designer
The Group Advertising Ltd. Agency
Gallery A Client
Hong Kong

597
Naava Benyaacov Art Director/Designer
Typecraft Typesetter
Naava Benyaacov Design Studio
John Albano Client
Cranoury NJ

598
Richard Foy Art Director
Patty Van Hook Designer
Knudsen Printing Printer
Communication Arts Incorporated Studio
Realities, Inc. Client
Boulder CO

599
Jim Crouch Art Director
Eve Morris Designer
Julian Naranjo Illustrator
Design Group West Agency
Marte Reavis Client
San Diego CA

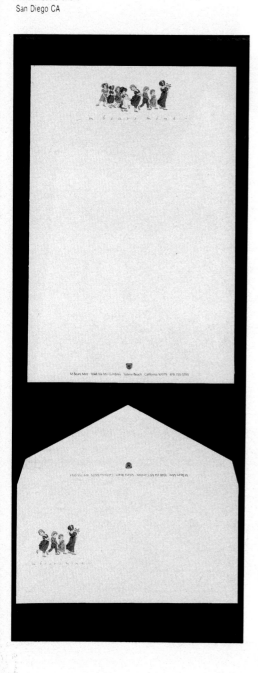

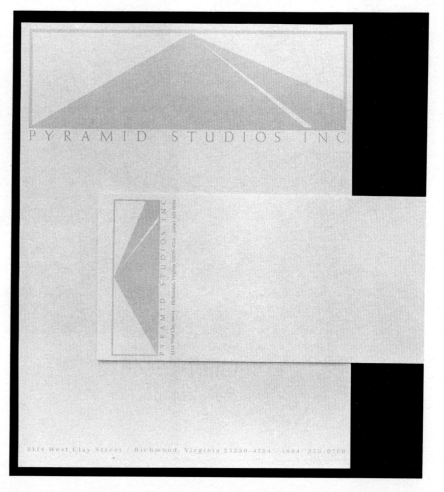

600
Jack Anderson, Cliff Chung Designers
Hornall-Anderson Design Works Agency
Pierce Art Gallery Client
Seattle WA

601
Dixie Merriam Art Director/Designer
Pyramid Studios, Inc. Studio/Client
Richmond VA

602

Sandra Gola Art Director/Designer
Karen L. Mallia Client
Garfield NJ

603

Michel Schmitt Art Director
Jean Larcher Designer
Studio Michel Schmitt Studio/Client
Cergy, France

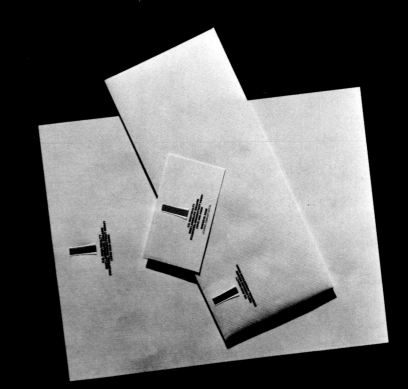

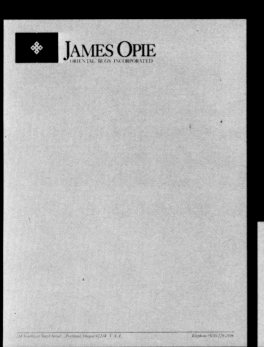

604

Dan Cassel, Bill Backalenick Art Directors
Mike Germakian Designer
Comart Aniforms Agency
Copley Press Production
F.D. Rich Realty Client
Stamford CT

605

Frank DeSantis Art Director/Designer
Mary Rowan Design Assistant
DeSantis Design Studio
Graphic Arts Center, Portland, OR Production
James Opie Oriental Rugs Incorporated Client
Portland OR

606

Kan Tai-keung, Eddy Yu Chi-kong Designers
Fotostudio Limited Photographer
SS Design & Production Agency
Famous Decoration Company Client

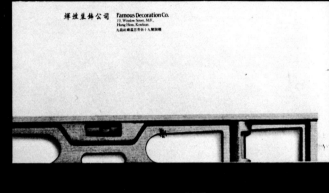

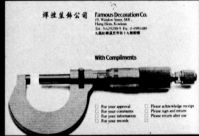

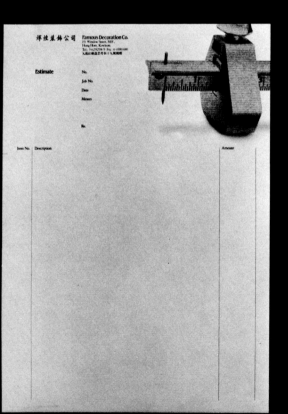

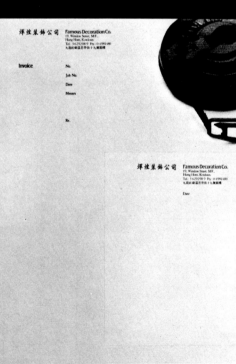

607
Clive Gay Art Director/Designer
Dirk Voornevelt Illustrator
Pentagraph (Pty) Ltd. Studio
I M Lockat Client
Johannesburg, RSA

608
Tibor Kalman Art Director
John Shoptaugh Designer/Illustrator
M&Co. Agency
Music & Co. Client
New York NY

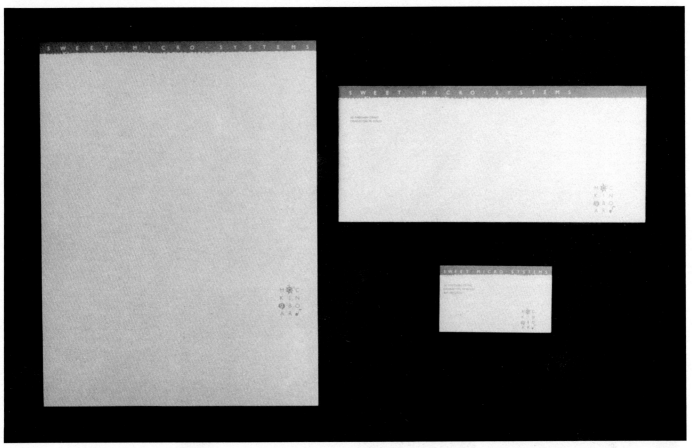

609
Bruce Crocker Art Director/Designer
Altman · Manley Agency
Sweet Micro Systems Client
Cambridge MA

610
George Chadwick, Lauren Smith Art Directors/Designers
Del Tycer Creative Director
Tycer-Fultz-Bellack Agency
The UP Corporation Client
Palo Alto CA

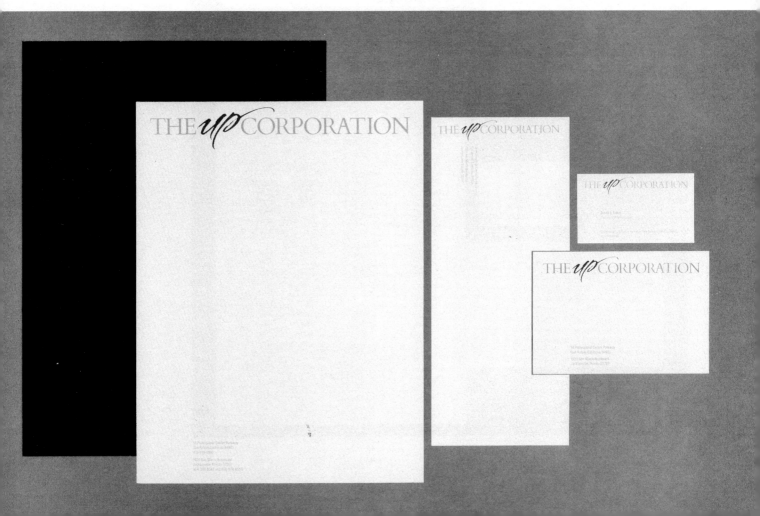

3300 IRVINE AVENUE, SUITE 385, NEWPORT BEACH, CALIFORNIA 92660, (714) 549-3990

JP.Darling

ASSOCIATES/ARCHITECTS

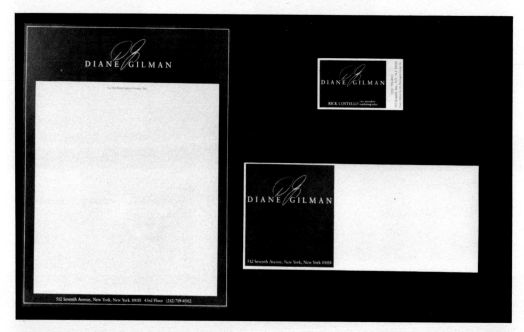

611
JP. Darling & Associates Art Direction/Design
Michael I. Johnson Photographer
JP. Darling & Associates Client
Newport Beach CA

612
Adrienne Y. Carlin Art Director/Designer
AYC Graphics Agency
Lerman Graphics Production
Diane Gilman for The Harrington Group, Inc. Client
New York NY

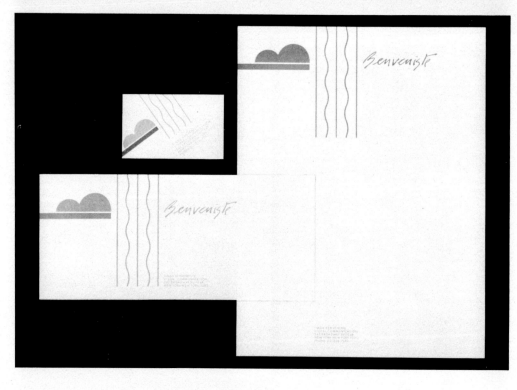

613
Linda Benveniste Art Director/Designer
Linda Benveniste Client
New York NY

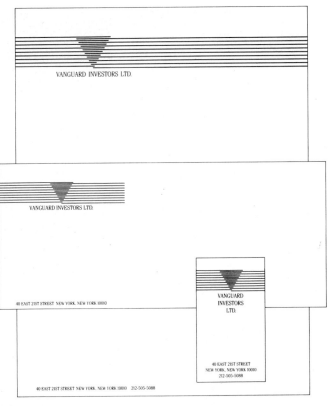

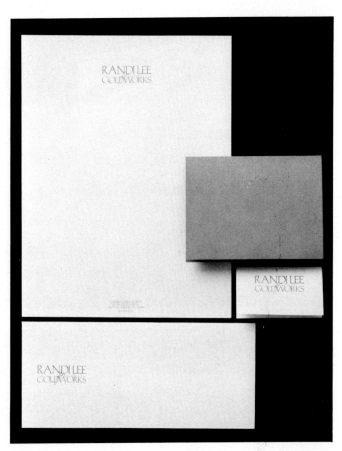

614
June Robinson Nall Art Director
Norico Kanai Designer
Martha Voutas Productions, Inc. Studio
Vanguard Investors Ltd. Client
New York NY

615
Herb Allison, David Schiedt Art Directors
Maelin Levine Designer
Scottie Maxwell Advertising Agency
The Graphics Studio Studio
Randi Lee for Goldworks (Goldsmith) Client
Denver CO

616
Michael Thomas Art Director/Designer
Michael Thomas Art Direction Agency
David Gerbosi Client
Denver CO

617
Eugene Cheltenham Art Director
Eugene Cheltenham Design Studio
Jack Loeb Printing Production Client
Los Angeles CA

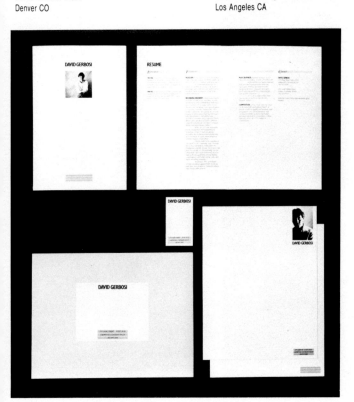

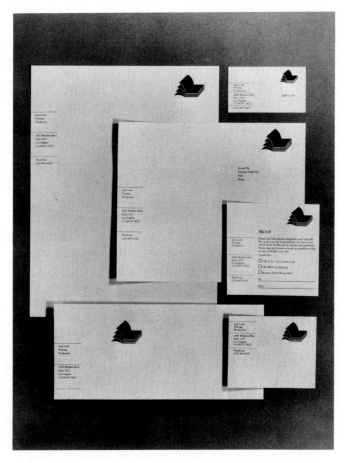

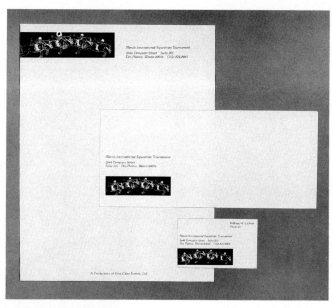

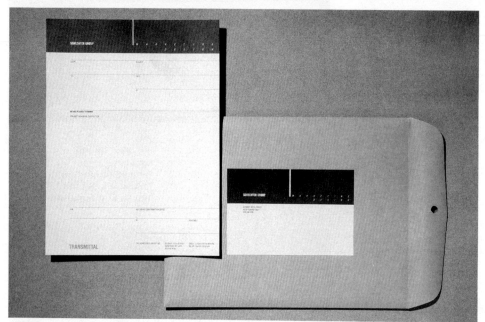

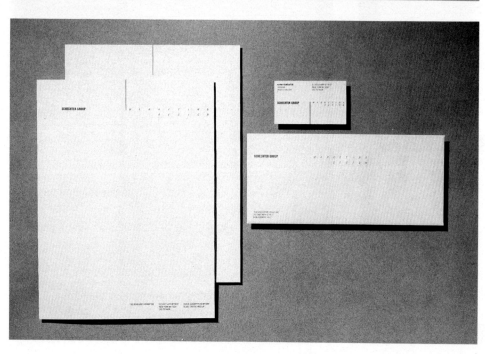

618
David Deahl Art Director
Mike Kelly, Tim Girvin Designers
David Deahl Photography Client
Chicago IL

619
Alan Herman Art Director/Designer
Steve Beland Illustrator
Alan Herman & Assoc., Inc. Agency
First Class Events, Ltd. Client
La Canada CA

620
Alvin H. Schechter Art Director
Ronald Wong Designer
Schechter Group Agency/Client
New York NY

621
Bev Craig, Rachelle Fisher Designer
The Ad Co (Pty) Ltd. Agency
Quickprint Production
Penthouse Travel Client
Cape Town, RSA

622
Mike Smit Art Director/Designer
Smit & Associates, Inc. Agency/Client
Artcraft Lithographers Printer
St. Louis MO

623
Gary Polich Art Director/Designer
The Howard Group, Inc. Agency/Client
Typography Plus, Bruce Hansen Printing Production
Denver CO

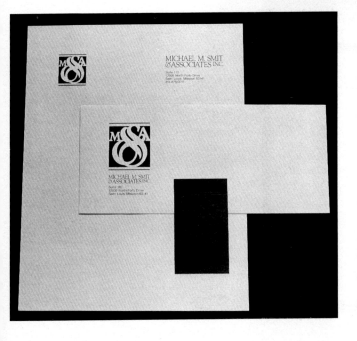

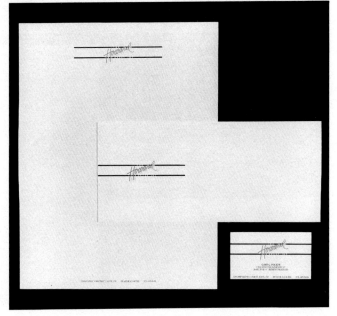

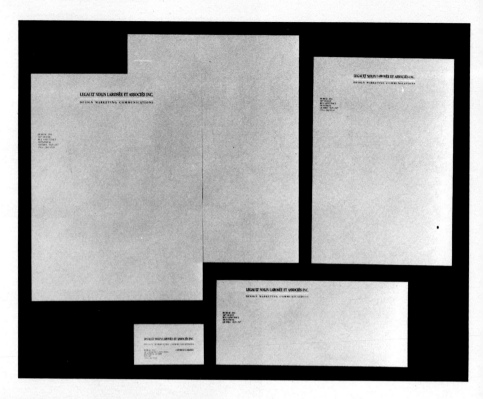

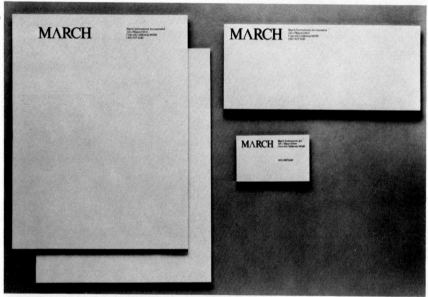

624

Clement Larosee Art Director/Designer
Typographie M&H Itee Typography
Paul Paradis Inc. Printing
Gravure Choquet Inc. Engraving
Legault Nolin Larosee et associes Inc. Agency/Client
Montreal, Canada

625

Andre Nel Art Director
Michael Pearce Designer
Rapid Typographers Type
Wylie Wilson and Munn Agency
March Instruments, Inc. Client
San Francisco CA

626

Harold Burch Art Director/Designer
Harold Burch Design Agency
Jack Freed Photography Client
Fullerton CA

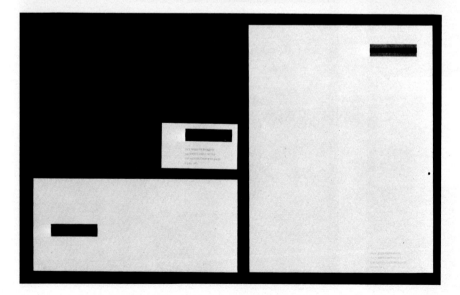

627

Laura Kay Art Director/Designer
Laura Kay Design Studio
Lawrence C. Helms Client
Ashland OR

628

William A. Sloan Art Director/Designer
THREE Studio
Diana Cana Client
New York NY

629

Robert Cipriani, Mark Kent, Janet Ellis Designers
Chadis Printing Printing
Cipriani Advertising Inc. Agency
Carol Lasky
Boston MA

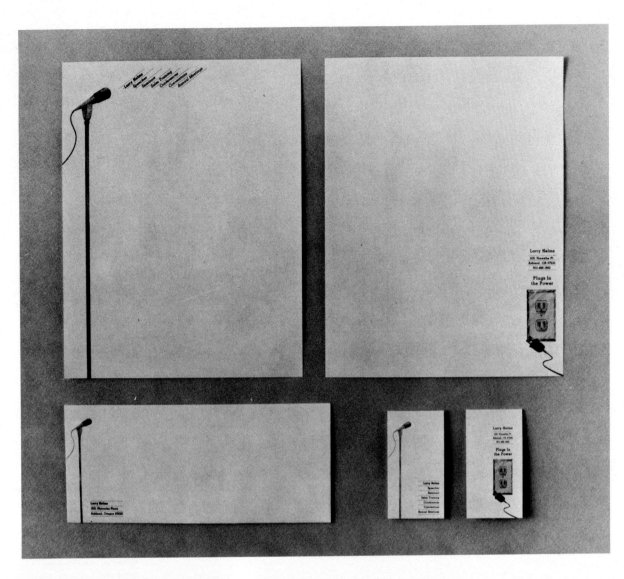

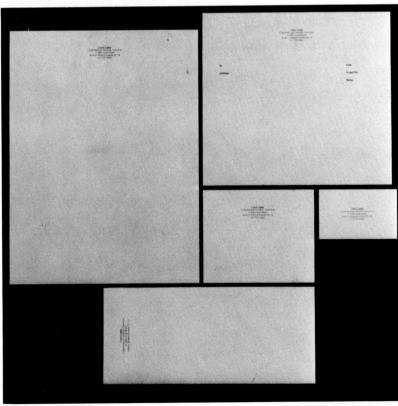

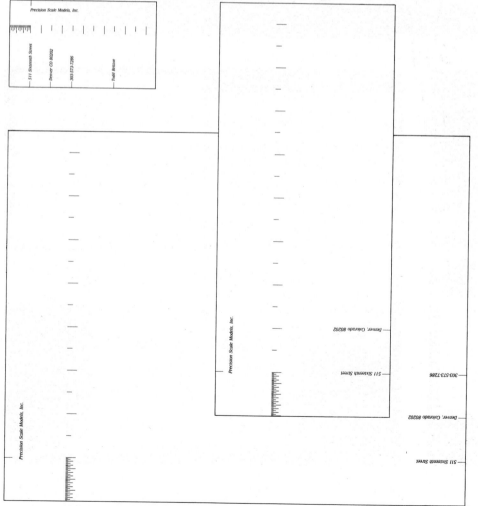

630
Michael Orr Art Director
Robert K. Cassetti Designer
Michael Orr + Associates, Inc. Studio
Ayer & Streb Production
Ken Buschner Studios, Inc. Client
Corning NY

631
Christing Weber Art Director
Victoria Eubanks Designer
Weber Design Studio
Precision Scale Models Inc. Client
Denver CO

632
Bill Ost Art Director/Designer
Triad Productions Inc. Studio/Client
Shawnee Mission KS

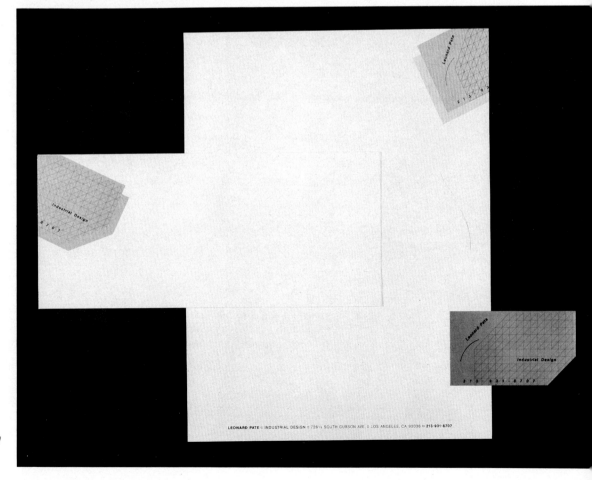

633
Scott Griffiths, Jeff Burne Designers
Jeff Burne Illustrator
Scott Griffiths Design Associates, Inc. Agency
Leonard Pate Industrial Design Client
Studio City CA

Promotion
Pieces

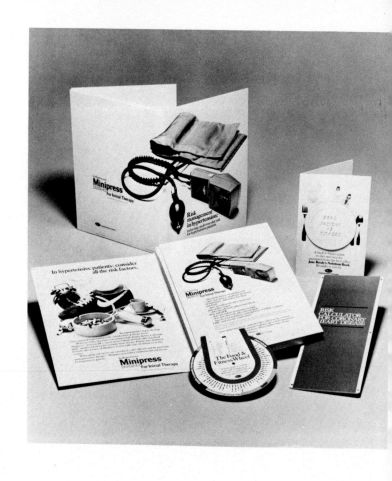

634

Karl H. Steinbrenner Art Director/Designer
Karl Eric Steinbrenner, Rudy Muller Photographers
Health Marketing Systems Agency
Pfizer Laboratories Div. Client
Fleetwood NY

635

Edward K. Korbett Art Director/Designer
Dan Bridy Illustrator
Thomas A. McNulty Copywriter
Marsteller, Inc. Agency
National Intergroup, Inc. Client
Pittsburgh PA

636

Michael Rosen Art Director/Designer
Truman Moore Photographer
Hugh Farrell Copywriter
Hammond Farrell Inc. Agency
American Business Press Client
New York NY

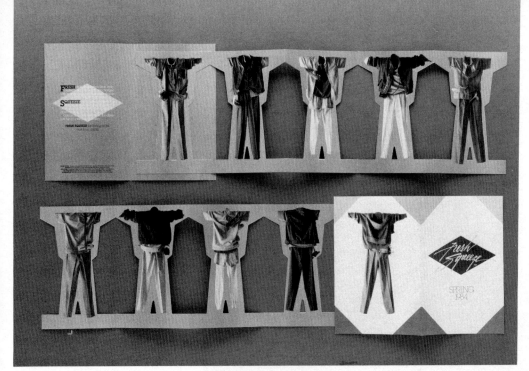

637
Edelstein-Edelstein-French Art Directors/Designers
Jim Cummins Photographer
David Edelstein Copywriter
Edelstein Associates Advertising Agency
Fresh Squeeze Sportswear Client
Seattle WA

638
Andrew Kner Art Director/Designer
Michael George Photographer
Meg Rosoff Copywriter
The New York Times Client
New York NY

639
Lon Foster, Steven Lester Art Directors
Lisa Bell Designer
Cousteau Society, Inc. Photographers
Charlotte Adams Copywriter
Turner Broadcasting System-Design Services Agency
SuperStation WTBS Client
Atlanta GA

640
Peter Belliveau Art Director/Designer
Al Francekevich Photographer
Cari Weisberg Copywriter
Lavey, Wolff, Swift, Inc. Agency
Seamless Hospital Products Company Client
New York NY

641
Don Meyers Art Director/Designer
Bjorn Winter-Fukuhara, Inc. Photographers
Lucia Zampirro Copywriter
Pacificom Agency
Herbert Laboratories Client
Irvine CA

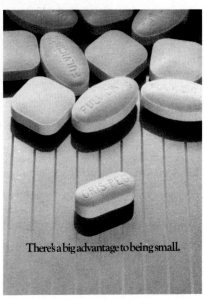

In 1949, three Volkswagen Beetles were sold in the United States. Thirty-five years and five million Beetles later, John Noble has been honored by our industry with more awards for his work on Volkswagen than anyone else.
Executive Vice-President and Creative Director at Doyle Dane Bernbach, John is credited with more than 200 multi-award winning commercials and print campaigns, including

In *Confessions Of An Advertising Man*, David Ogilvy said emotion does not sell. In 1960, Granger Tripp was the Creative Group Head on the first in a long line of Kodak commercials that showed the power of emotion in advertising. Kodak Creative Director for the better part of two decades, Granger has helped develop the use of emotion to its highest level of effectiveness.
How can you make emotion work in advertising? How do you keep from crossing over the fine line into syrupy

In 1981, John McCrosky faced a formidable challenge. Take a faltering snob appeal drink and give it mass appeal by repositioning it against the common soft drink. And that was just for openers. Here's the kicker...maintain its "chic" status among upscale users.
How did Perrier's immense success turn sour? Why was the decision made to compare Perrier to a soft drink? Come join us as John McCrosky, Executive Vice-President of Waring and LaRosa, takes us through this very engaging campaign.

Who says you have to be in New York, Chicago or San Francisco to have national impact? In 1966, Mike Sloan founded an agency in Miami, Florida that created a national presence with such well-known campaigns as "Ryder—the best truck money can rent" and "Florida—when you need it bad, we've got it good".
Even Mike's local accounts have resulted in national attention. His work for Miami's United Way gave birth to "Thanks to you, it's working". And it was

Raymond Rubicam said to "resist the usual".

Here are four who did.

Now you have an opportunity to get inside their heads. To hear about the breakthrough thinking that has resulted in hundreds of first place awards from Andys and Addys to Clios and Cannes.

C R E A T I V E D A Y • J A N U A R Y 2 4

642
Jim Spruell Art Director/Illustrator
Terry Coveny Copywriter
Abramson Associates, Inc. Agency
Washington, D.C. Ad Club Client
Washington DC

643
Nita K. Alvarez Art Director/Designer
Andy Caulfield Photographer
Ramon Alvarez Illustrator
Alvarez Associates Agency
Glendale Adventist Medical Center Client
Los Angeles CA

644
Jody Thompson, Dennis Thompson Art Directors
Dennis Thompson, Elizabeth Berta Designers
Walter Swarthout Photographer
Coming Attractions Communication Service Agency
Callaway Vineyard & Winery Client
San Francisco CA

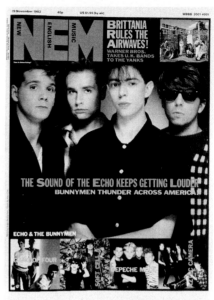

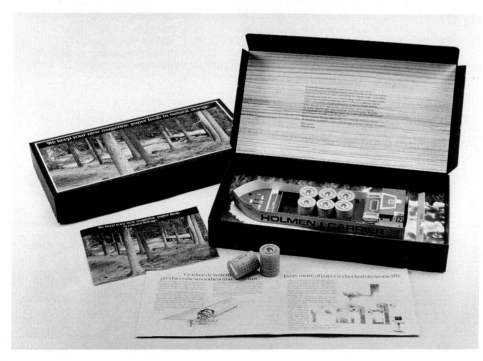

645
Jeffrey Kent Ayeroff Art Director
John Heiden, Michael Hodgson, Laura Lipuma,
 Jeri McManus Designers
Jonas Livingston Copywriter
Warner Bros. Records Client
Burbank CA

646
Dag Heidenberg Art Director
Yvonne Berggren Designer
Claes Annerstedt Photographer
Uno Blaesild Illustrator
Welinder Information AB Agency
Holmens Bruk AB Client
Stockholm. Sweden

647
Jan de Goede Art Director/Designer
De Goede + Others Agency/Client
Chicago IL

Navajo & Fieldstone Cover

SPAR

648
Dick Loomis Art Director/Designer
Mike Evans Copywriter
Glundal Color Printer
Evans Garber & Paige Agency
Mohawk Paper Mills, Inc. Client
Syracuse NY

649
Warren Wilkins, Tommer Peterson Designers
Jim Cummins Photographer
Yun Kon Kim Calligrapher
Wilkins & Peterson Agency
Tommer Peterson & Betty Jo Flett Clients
Seattle WA

Marie (Mimi) Mathilde Benier 1881-1970

Tommer Peterson and Betty Jo Flett
would like you to meet their daughter
Mimi Sang Peterson.
Mimi was born on March 1, 1983
near Seoul, Korea, and came to us on
Northwest Orient Flight #20
at 9:51 AM on June 2, 1983
weighing in at 10 lbs. 15 oz.
without extra baggage.
A small, but exuberant crowd
of two was on hand to meet her.

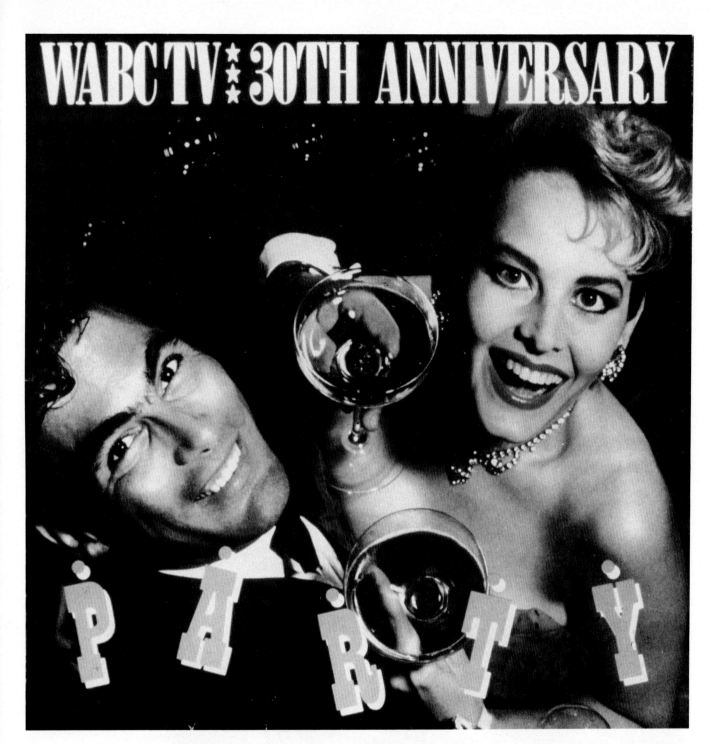

650
Michael Gass Art Director
Izumi Inouye Designer
Abe Selzer Photographer
WABC-TV Studio/Client
New York NY

651
Gavin Patterson Art Director/Designer
Dallas Tomlinson & Associates Agency
BASF SA (Pty) Ltd. Client
Randburg. RSA

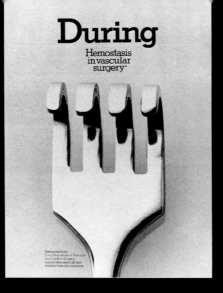
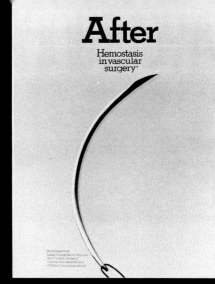

Before

Hemostasis
in vascular
surgery*

During

Hemostasis
in vascular
surgery*

After

Hemostasis
in vascular
surgery*

652

Stephen Brothers Art Director
Carmine Macedonia Photographer
Nina Padukone Copywriter
Sudler & Hennessey, Inc. Agency
Winnebago Corp. Production
Parke-Davis Client
New York NY

653

Robert Weisberg Art Director
Alan Charles Designer
Leon Kuzmanoff Photographer
Sol Korby Illustrator
Alan Charles, Inc. Agency
TIME Magazine Client
New York NY

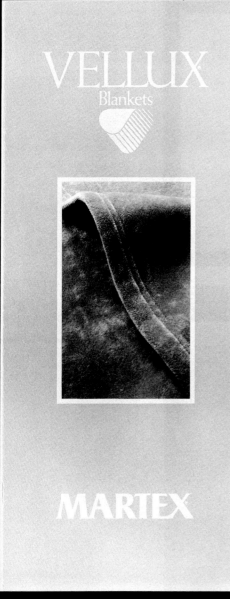

VELLUX
Blankets

MARTEX

RUSSELL REYNOLDS
ASSOCIATES INC.

Serving Organisations
Doing Business in the
Middle East

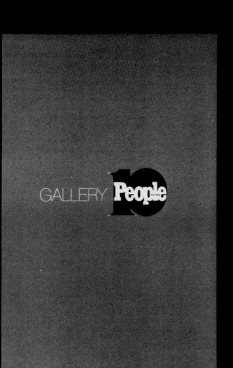

GALLERY **People**

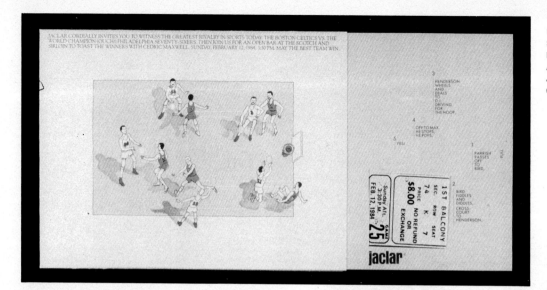

657
Robert Manley, Dick Davis Art Directors
Steven Guarnaccia Illustrator
Rich Binell Copywriter
Altman + Manley Agency
Jaclar Client
Cambridge MA

658
Keith Bright Art Director
Gretchen Goldie, Gregory Berman Designers
Rien Basen Photographer
Doug Johnson, David Kimble, Richard Pietruska,
  Dusty Deyo, Steve Curry Illustrators
Bright & Associates Studio
Holland America Line USA, Inc. Client
Los Angeles CA

659
Karen Gatens Art Director/Designer
Bob Betz, Derrick Chasen, Anne Baker Copywrite
In-House, **Chateau Ste. Michelle** Studio
Chateau Ste. Michelle Client
Woodinville WA

660
Notovitz & Perrault Design Art Direction/Design
Jay Brenner, Joe Marvullo Photographers
Rick Young Copywriter
United States Banknote Corporation Client
New York NY

661
Patricia J. Kelly Art Director/Photographer
James Burton, Julie Gruenhagen Designers
Donna Fowler, Virginia Downing Copywriters
Metropolitan State College, Music Dept. Client
Denver CO

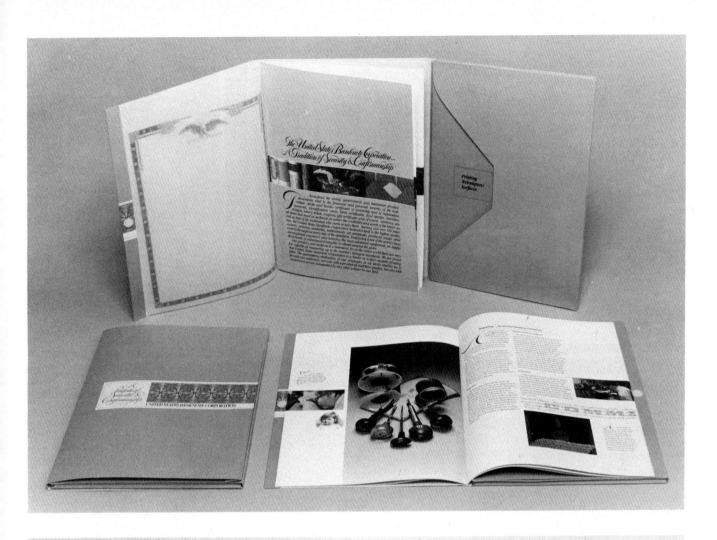

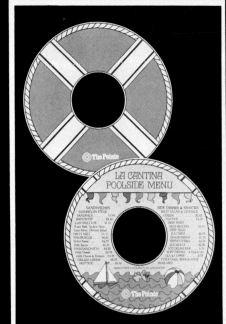

662

Anne Kowalczyk Art Director
Lee Pohlsander Designer
Oliver-McConnel Photographer
Paul Williams Illustrator
Omni Communications Agency
The Ginter Corporation Client
Syracuse NY

663

Warren Wilkins, Tommer Peterson Designers
Dale Windham Photographer
Scott McDougall Illustrator
Wilkins & Peterson Agency
Heath Printers Client
Seattle WA

664

Tim Farrow Designer
Pointe Communications Agency
The Pointe Client
Phoenix AZ

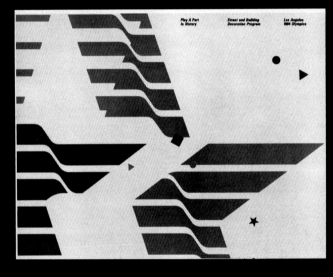

665

Hinsche + Associates Design/Illustration
Hinsche + Associates Studio
Los Angeles Olympic Committee Client
Santa Monica CA

666

Denys Gustafson Art Director
Jan Davis Designer
Apple Computer, Inc. Client
Cupertino CA

667

Schaeffer Boehm Ltd. Art Direction/Design
Richie Williamson Photographer
Susie Phillips Copywriter
Schaeffer Boehm Ltd. Agency
Burlington Mills Client
New York NY

RICKY DAVIS/ST. LOUIS STEAMERS

668
Elizabeth Clark Art Director
North Charles Street Design Organization Studio
University of Pennsylvania Client
Baltimore MD

669
William Kay Art Director
Linda Scuffham Berlinghoff Designer
Arthur J. Klonsky Photographer
Janeart, Ltd. Studio
Puma, USA, Inc. Client

670
Kathy Grubb, Ron Layport Designers
Gray, Baumgarten, Layport Inc. Agency
Gateway Studios Studio
Cox Litho Printing
Maggie Mae's Restaurants Client
Pittsburgh PA

671
Kerry Bierman Art Director
Bill McDowell Designer
**Robert Keeling, Tom Vack, Joe De Natale, Tom Tracy,
   Dick Busher, Michael Mauney** Photographers
Cagney + McDowell Design Office
American Hospital Supply, Equipping and Consulting Client
Evanston IL

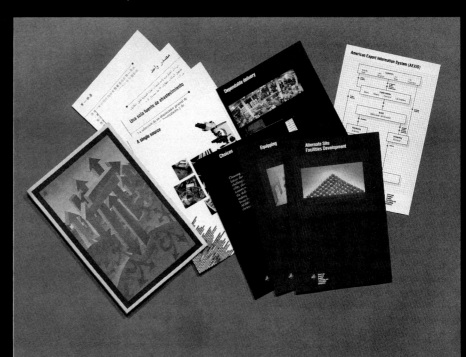

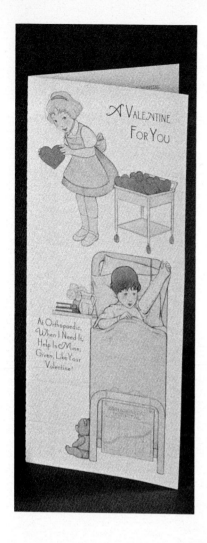

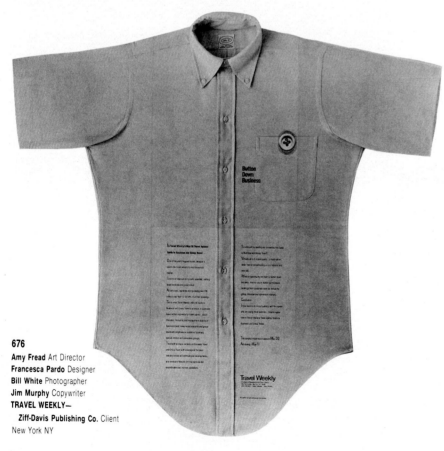

676
Amy Fread Art Director
Francesca Pardo Designer
Bill White Photographer
Jim Murphy Copywriter
TRAVEL WEEKLY—
   Ziff-Davis Publishing Co. Client
New York NY

672
John Coy Art Director
Richard Atkins Designer
Chuck Murphy Illustrator
Lisa Connolly Copywriter
COY, Los Angeles Studio
Culver City CA

673
Henry Beer Art Director
David Shelton Designer
D & K Printing Printer
Communication Arts Incorporated Studio
Trizec Properties, Inc. Client
Boulder CO

674
Tony Sini Designer
Sandage Advertising & Marketing, Inc. Agency
Vermont Ad Club Client
Burlington VT

675
David Bence Art Director
James Iacobucci Designer
James Iacobucci, Peter Delorenzo Copywriters
D'Arcy MacManus Masius Agency
Pontiac Motor Division Client
Bloomfield Hills MI

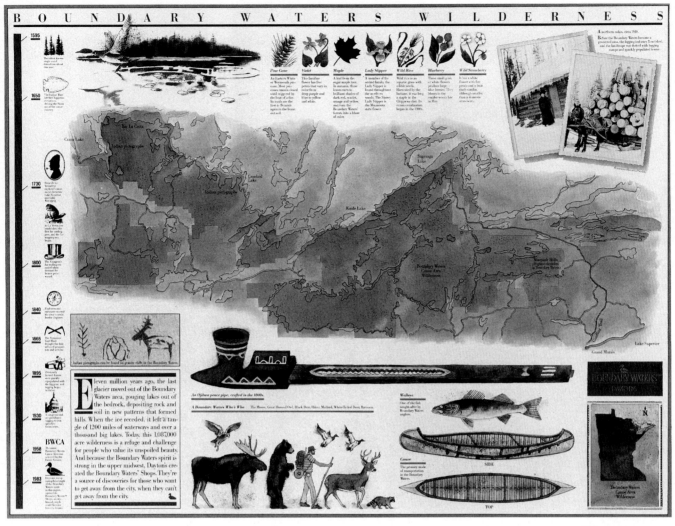

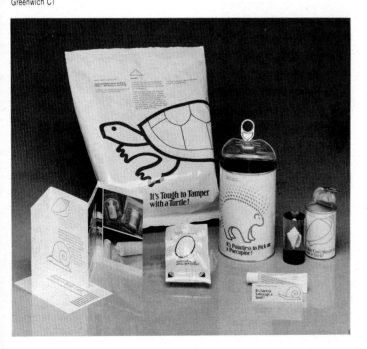

680
Monika Vainius Valys Art Director/Designer
William D. Dowling Copywriter
Impressions—A.B.A. Industries, Inc. Agency
Hertz Penske Truck Leasing, Inc. Client
Roslyn Heights NY

681
Tibor Kalman Art Director/Designer
M&Co. Agency/Client
New York NY

682
Carol A. Peligian Art Director/Designer
Helayne Spivak Copywriter
Karastan Rug Mills, A Division of Fieldcrest Mills Client
New York NY

683
John Waters Art Director
Linda Grimm Designer
Michael Meyers Photographer
John Waters Associates, Inc. Agency
The Gunlocke Company Client
New York NY

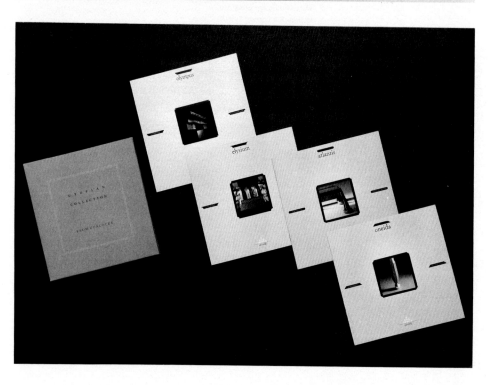

684
Santoro Design Designer
Faculty Press, Inc. Production
St. Lukes/Roosevelt Hospital Center Clie
Brooklyn NY

685
Victor Liebert Art Director
Lesley Teitelbaum Copywriter
Trevira In-House Agency Agency
Trevira Client
New York NY

686
David Gauger, Jeanne Kimmel Art Directors
Jeanne Kimmel Illustrator
Gauger Sparks Silva, Inc. Agency
Dicor Community Developers Client
San Francisco CA

687
Linda Powell Art Director/Designer
William Sharpe Photographer
James Johnson Illustrator
Debra Wierenga Copywriter
Herman Miller, Inc. Agency
Miltech, Inc. Client
Zeeland MI

688
Mark Huie, Gail Rigelhaupt Designer
Mark L. Handler Creative Director
George Feldman, William Schrank, Carol Mayberry Copywriters
Handler Group, Inc. Agency
Katz Communications, Inc. Client
New York NY

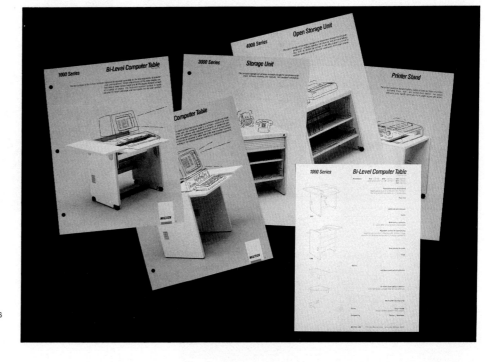

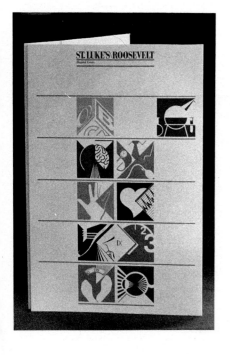

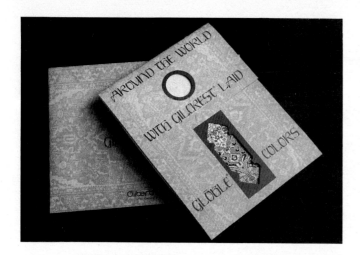

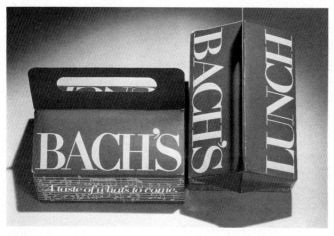

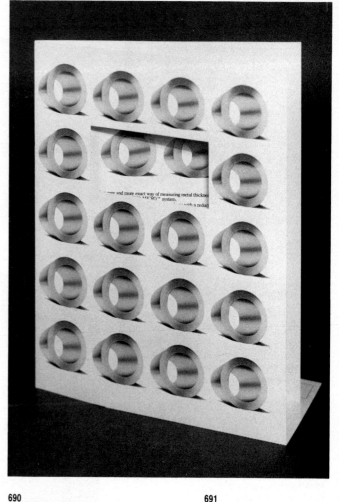

689
R.E. Jelinski Art Director/Designer
Jelinski Design Associates Copywriter
Castel-Pierce Print Production
Gilbert Paper Client
Menasha WI

690
Raymond Lee Art Director/Designer
J.S. Bach Illustrator
Graziano Palumbo Copywriter
Raymond Lee + Associates Agency
CentreStage Music Client
Toronto. Canada

691
Tom Roth Art Director
Daphne Geismar Designer
Sally Anderson Bruce Photographer
Steve Trygg Copywriter
Anderson, Lembke, Welinder Agency
AccuRay Corporation Client
Stamford CT

693
Steven Voorhees Art Director/Designer
Judith Friedmann Illustrator
Theodore L. Horne Copywriter
Sieber & McIntyre Agency
Pharmaceutical Div., Sandoz Inc. Client
Chicago IL

692
Sandy Nelms Art Director/Designer
Claire Maddox Creative Director/Copywriter
The Maddox Agency Agency/Client
Roanoke VA

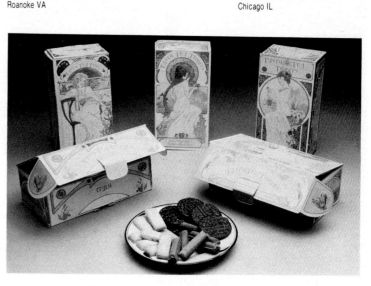

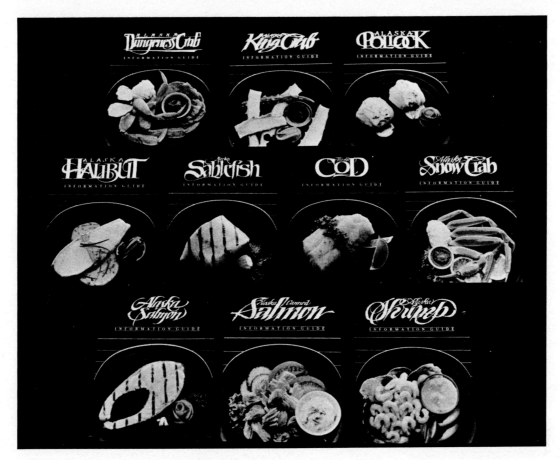

694

James Paquet Art Director/Designer
George Mattei Photographer
Skip Watts Copywriter
Fletcher-Walker-Gessell Agency
Bobst Group, Inc. Client
Midland Park NJ

695

Jan Lipetz Art Director/Designer
Aaron Jones, Lis DeMarco Photographers
Tim Girvin Calligrapher
Anita Carmin-Tomisser Copywriter
Evans/Kraft, Inc. Agency
Alaska Seafood Marketing Institute Client
Seattle WA

696

Gail N. Strong Art Director
Claire E. Lukacs Designer
Ted Horowitz, Peter B. Kaplan, Jeff Kellner, Steve Krongard,
   Tom Leighton, Jay Maisel, Cheryl Rossum Photographers
J.P. Lohman Agency
EQK Partners Client
New York NY

The *Car*

The Domino's Pizza Hot One™ wears number 30 in the PPG Indy Car World Series. The Hot One™ is an evolved version of the March Indy car, the English-built machine that is the most popular car on the Indy circuit. The four-camshaft, aluminum V-8 Cosworth DFX engine delivers 750 horsepower, at over 10,000 rpms. That translates into 200 miles per hour on the oval track. *This machine is built for speed.*

The Hot One™ is equipped with independent suspension, rack and pinion steering, A.P. Lockheed vented brakes, and carries 40 gallons of methanol for fuel, burned at a rate of 1.8 miles per gallon. The Hot One™, like most Indy Cars, uses giant Goodyear racing slicks for tires, which provide tremendous traction for the automobile.

*N*umber 30 got its name, the Hot One™, from Domino's Pizza, the company that sponsors the Indy car in the PPG Indy Car World Series. Domino's Pizza Delivers™ pizza in thirty minutes or less, all across the nation, making them the number one pizza delivery company in the world. Watch for the Domino's Pizza Team Shierson Hot One™, with driver Howdy Holmes, in the PPG Indy Car World Series.

*C*ar *S*tatistics	
Length:	14.6'
Weight:	1500 lbs.
Wheelbase:	111"
Track: front	66"
rear	65"

The *Team*

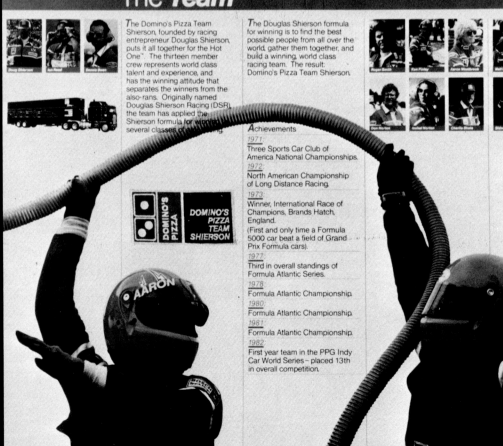

The Domino's Pizza Team Shierson, founded by racing entrepreneur Douglas Shierson, puts it all together for the Hot One™. The thirteen member crew represents world class talent and experience, and has the winning attitude that separates the winners from the also-rans. Originally named Douglas Shierson Racing (DSR), the team has applied the Shierson formula for winning several classes of auto racing.

The Douglas Shierson formula for winning is to find the best possible people from all over the world, gather them together, and build a winning, world class racing team. The result: Domino's Pizza Team Shierson.

*A*chievements

1971:
Three Sports Car Club of America National Championships.

1972:
North American Championship of Long Distance Racing.

1973:
Winner, International Race of Champions, Brands Hatch, England.
(First and only time a Formula 5000 car beat a field of Grand Prix Formula cars).

1977:
Third in overall standings of Formula Atlantic Series.

1978:
Formula Atlantic Championship.

1980:
Formula Atlantic Championship.

1981:
Formula Atlantic Championship.

1982:
First year team in the PPG Indy Car World Series – placed 13th in overall competition.

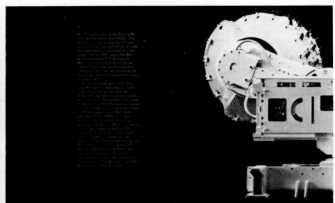

697
Ernie Perich Art Director/Designer
Ann DeLaVergne Photographer
Group 243 Design, Inc. Agency
Village Graphics Production
Domino's Pizza, Inc. Client
Ann Arbor MI

698
Dennis Moran, Robert Adam, Dennis Morabito Designers
John W. Wiater, Neil McGlone Copywriters/Editors
Burson-Marsteller Agency
Adam Filippo + Moran, Inc. Studio
Eickhoff Corporation Client
Pittsburgh PA

699
Carolyn McIntyre Art Director
North Charles Street Design Organization Studio
Mount Vernon College Client
Baltimore MD

Self-Promotion

700
Bob Taylor Art Director/Designer
Pat Dypold Illustrator
Arnold Grisman Copywriter
J. Walter Thompson Agency/Client
Chicago IL

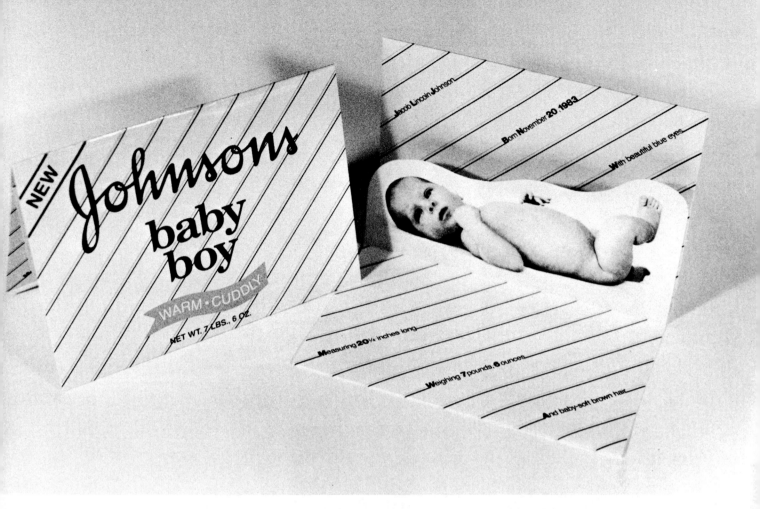

701
Craig Lynn Johnson Art Director
Carla Carwile Copywriter
Bradford/Will Graphics Typography
Craig & Joleen Johnson Clients
Sacramento CA

702
Jorge Alonso Art Director/Designer
Mary Weikert, Roger Marshutz Photographers
Fotouhi Alonso Agency
Mary Weikert Client
Los Angeles CA

703
Bruce Blackburn Art Director/Designer
Tom Mann Copywriter
Danne & Blackburn Agency
George Haling Photographer/Client
New York NY

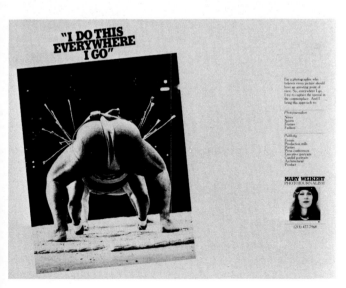

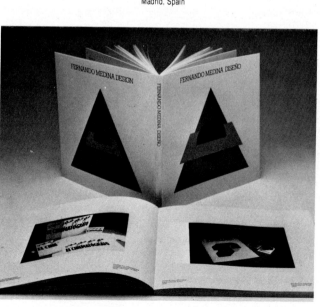

704
Gene Bradford Art Director/Designer
Gaby Rona Photographer
A & L Graphico Printer
Gene Bradford Client
Studio City CA

705
Jack Murphy Art Director/Designer
Mike Condon Copywriter
Alingh Design Assoc. Inc Studio/Client
Des Moines IA

706
Ron Layport Art Director/Designer
Chuck Fuhrer Photographer
Sundown Studios Studio
Gray, Baumgarten, Layport Inc. Agency/Client
Pittsburgh PA

707
Ilene Wagner Art Director/Designer
S. Gourevitch Printer
Graphics/Graphique Studio/Client
San Diego CA

708
Joel Goldstein Art Director
Mike DeLesseps Designer
Dick Durrance II Photographer/Client
New York NY

709
Fernando Medina Designer
Fernando Medina Client
Madrid. Spain

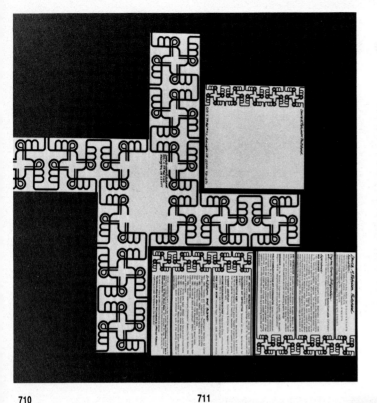

710
Laura M. Robinson Pritchard Designer/Client
Arlington VA

711
Charles Hively Art Director/Designer
Jerry Jeanmard Illustrator
Julie Harrigan Copywriter
Metzdorf-Marschalk Agency/Client
Houston TX

712
Stuart M. Berni Art Director
Larry Edlavitch Designer
Laurie N. Yarnell Copywriter
The Berni Corporation Agency/Client
Greenwich CT

713
Larney Walker Designer
Ron Brueckner Copywriter
Gordon Meyer Photographer/Client
Chicago IL

714
Barbara Lehman Art Director/Designer
Jakki Savan, Barbara Lehman Copywriters
Lehman Design Client
Denver CO

715
Paul Tanck Designer/Copywriter
Marcia Stone Photographer
Paul Tanck Design Client
Venice CA

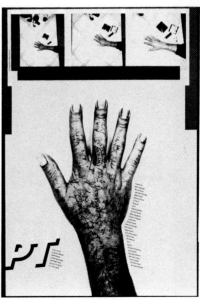

716
Anthony Russell Art Director
Casey Clark Designer
Anthony Russell Inc. Studio/Client
New York NY

717
Gerd Hiepler Art Director
Lou Myers Illustrator
GGK International Agency
Dieter Weber Production
IBM Client
New York NY

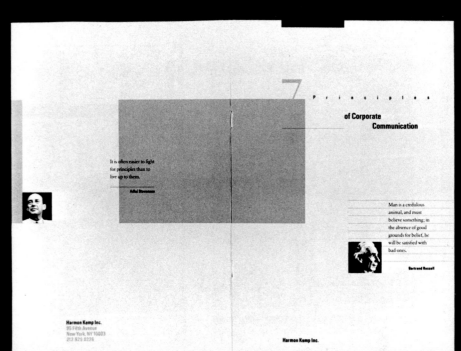

718
Marshall Harmon, Karen Keenan Designers
Susan Wides Photographer
Dave Kemp Copywriter
Lee Daniels Printing Production
Harmon Kemp Inc. Agency/Client
New York NY

719
John Katz Art Director/Photographer
Woody Pirtle Copywriter
John Katz Client
Dallas TX

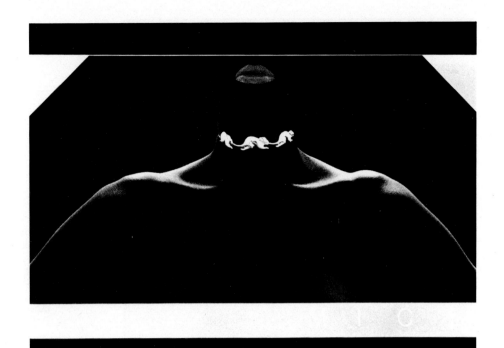

720
Ellie Malavis Art Director/Designer
Harvey Marks Copywriter
Metzdorf-Marschalk Co. Agency
Hotel Inter-Continental Client
Houston TX

721
Richard M. Kontir Art Director/Designer
Robert E. Lee Copywriter
S.D. Scott Printing Production
Lee & Young Communications Inc. Agency/Client
New York NY

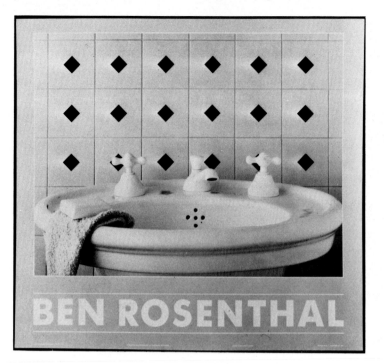

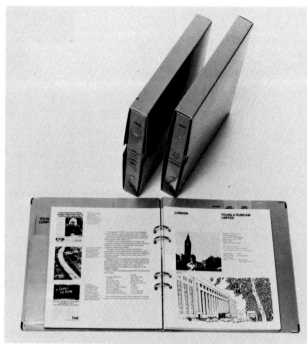

722
Cheryl Lewin Art Director/Designer
Ben Rosenthal Photographer
Cheryl Lewin Design Studio
Graphique de France Client
New York NY

723
Jan Robert Soderstrom Designer
Joan Hafey Editor
Roy Zucca Type Director
Soderstrom Reklame & Design, Oslo Agency
Sarpsborg Papp A.S., Moltzau Trykkerier A.S. Production
Young & Rubicam Inc. Client
New York NY

724
Sally Oelschlager Art Director/Designer
Rick Dublin Photographer
Nancy Shafer Copywriter
Colle McVoy Advertising Agency/Client
Minneapolis MN

725
John Vitro Art Director/Designer
Marshall Harrington Photographer
Cheryl Bailey Copywriter
Franklin & Associates Agency
Commercial Press Client
San Diego CA

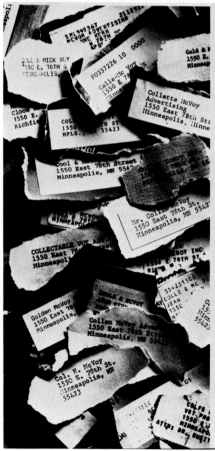

726
Joyce Fitzpaterick Hartley Designer
Kristen Drechsler Henderson Copywriter
Peabody Communications Agency
Camercon Davidson Photographer/Client
Washington DC

727
Tom Styrkowicz Art Director/Designer
Alan Kaplan Photographer
Jim Friedland Copywriter
Groups of One or More Client
New York NY

728
Chris Cotter Art Director
Camille Julianna Copywriter
Chris Cotter, Camille Julianna Designers/Clients
Baltimore MD

729
Fritz Haase Art Director/Designer
Anselm Dworak Typographer
Drukerei Asendorf/Atelier Haase & Knels Client
Bremen. West Germany

730
Michael Donovan, Nancye Green Art Directors
Jennifer Barry Designer
Ken Collins Photographer
Donovan and Green Client
New York NY

731
Carol Marsh Art Director/Designer
Tom Casalini Photographer
Jack O'Hara Copywriter
Casalini Photography Inc. Client
Zionsville IN

732
David Daniels Designer/Client
Jamaic Plain MA

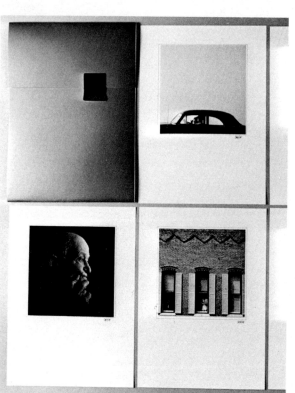

GOUGH COOPER COMPANIES

733
Gavin Patterson Art Director
Riki Klopper Designer
Donald Dallas Copywriter
Dallas Tomlinson & Associates Agency
Gough Cooper Group Client
Randburg. RSA

CORPORATE IDENTITY

The purpose of this manual is to define the concepts
of a Corporate identity for the Gough Cooper Companies
and outline the procedures for its implementation.
This manual is intended to serve as a guide for all
persons responsible for the implementation of the
programme as it relates to all phases of visual
communications. Our goal is to develop a cohesive
communications system that will constantly build
towards maximum recognition and awareness of the
Gough Cooper Companies.
Any situation that might arise that
is not covered in this manual or is of an exceptional
nature should be discussed with head office in
Randburg before its implementation.

page 1

CORPORATE EMBLEM

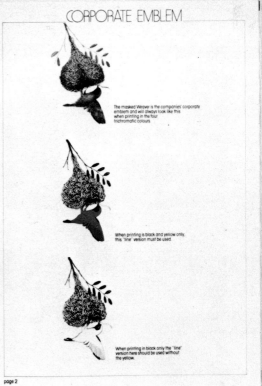

The masked Weaver is the companies' corporate
emblem and will always look like this
when printing in the four
trichromatic colours.

When printing is black and yellow only,
this "line" version must be used.

When printing in black only the "line"
version here should be used without
the yellow.

page 2

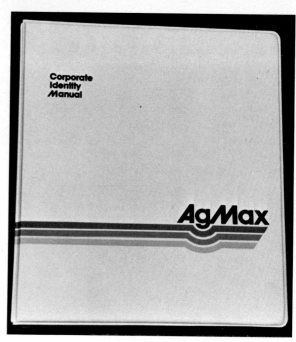

734

James Selak Art Director
Mark Lichtenstein Designer
Pete Steiner Photographer
Ann Miller Copywriter
Lichtenstein Marketing Communications Studio
Xerox Corporation Client
Rochester NY

735

Gregory A. Bauer Art Director/Designer
David E. Carter Copywriter
Denise Spaulding Logo
David E. Carter Corporate Communications, Inc. Agency
AgMax, Inc. Client
Ashland KY

736

Nardy Henigan Art Director/Designer
Mark Levine Copywriter
University Publications Agency
Northern Illinois University Client
DeKalb IL

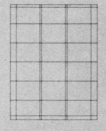
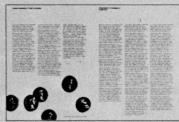

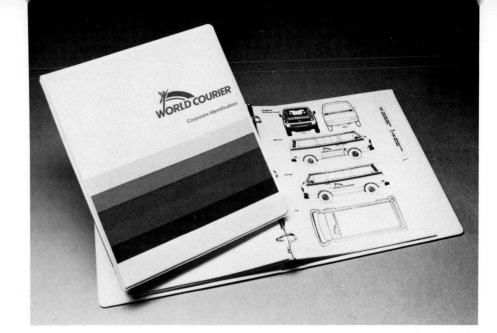

737
Robert B. Hufsmith Art Director/Designer
Thomas N. Kelly Copywriter
2 in 10, Inc. Agency
Allied Printing Services Production
World Courier, Inc. Client
Hartford CT

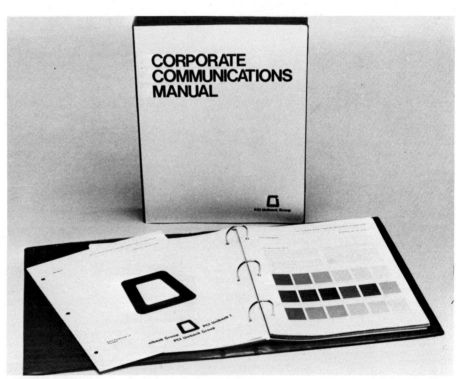

738
Angel L. Bunag Art Director/Designer
Eddie Go Photographer
Lino Maderazo Illustrator
Design Systemat, Inc. Agency
Philippine Commercial International Bank Client
Manila. Philippines

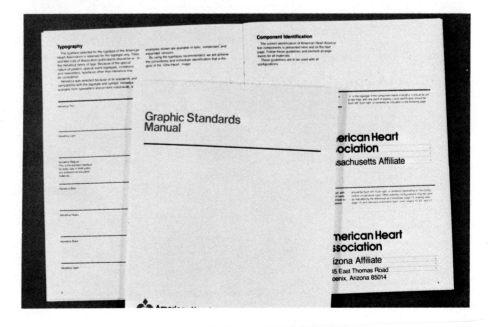

739
Gary L. Hackney Art Director/Designer
Lou Welch Creative Services Director
American Heart Association Design Studio Agency/Client
Dallas TX

740

Brian D. Fox Art Director
Mili Smythe Designer
Cathy Pavia Illustrator
Matt Foster Logo Designer
B.D. Fox & Friends Advertising Agency
Starlight Foundation Client
Los Angeles CA

Starlight Foundation

"Starlight, Starbright
first star
I see tonight,
wish I may,
wish I might,
have the wish
I wish tonight."

A non-profit charity organization dedicated to fulfilling wishes of chronically and terminally ill children.

T H I S   I S   S T A R L I G H T

The story of Starlight began when president Peter Samuelson and his cousin, Emma Samms, brought Sean, a desperately ill 12-year-old boy, and his mother from London to Los Angeles for a holiday. The wonderful 10-day stay included all the wonders of Southern California including Disneyland and a helicopter ride. It was a marvelous gift of carefree fun for this family who had been through very sad and painful times, but especially for Sean who, unfortunately, had little time left to him.

Providing this last bit of happiness to Sean, away from despair and stress, was such a meaningful experience for the host and hostess that it was a very natural development to begin the formation of what is now the "STARLIGHT FOUNDATION." With Renee Missel, Mr. Samuelson and a group of Los Angeles executives joined forces to dedicate their efforts to making the wishes of these special children come true. During the past year Starlight has fulfilled over 150 wishes.

ANNA
Age: 10
Disease: Acute Lymphatic Leukemia
Wish: To own a pink bicycle with a basket.
Starlight's Response: Anna had the best birthday ever. She was the proudest little girl on the block.

TONI
Age: 18
Disease: Brain Tumor
Wish: Toni wanted to drive on a race track in a race car.
Starlight's Response: Starlight arranged for a well-known race driver and a race car to take Toni around the Riverside Track. Her story was featured on Eyewitness News.

LEONARD
Age: 11
Disease: Resection Medullo Blastoma
Wish: To own a color television
Starlight's Response: Leonard had never had his own t.v. However, his happiness lasted only 3 weeks. He died in August.

ELENA
Age: 18
Disease: Acute Lymphoblastic Leukemia
Wish: To go to Lourdes, France.
Starlight's Response: Starlight sent Elena and her mother to Lourdes for the most meaningful week of their lives. Elena's cane mysteriously disappeared on arrival there, and she has not used one since.

MILDRED
Age: 12
Disease: Leukemia
Wish: To come to the United States from Holland to visit her terminally ill grandmother.
Starlight's Response: Starlight brought the family of four over from Holland. But a wonderful reunion was interrupted when Mildred was found in relapse and had to return to Europe after two weeks. She died in December.

WILLY
Age: 11
Disease: Hodgkin's Disease
Wish: To own a race car.
Starlight's Response: Starlight delivered a Malibu-style car, "The Flame," to Willy. He could hardly believe his eyes! To find a real mini race car in his driveway was a miracle. A dream come true.

DEBBIE
Age: 18
Disease: Down's Syndrome/Severe Lung Disease
Wish: To meet "The Fonz."
Starlight's Response: Henry Winkler called Debbie many times. Her family and doctor credit Debbie's brighter spirit and her willingness to take her medication directly to these phone conversations.

MARK
Age: 9
Disease: Bone Cancer
Wish: To go to an Angel's baseball game.
Starlight's Response: Starlight arranged for a box at the game as well as plans for dinner to be served and a visit to the dugout to meet the team. Unfortunately, Mark died 3 days before the game.

ANGELIQUE
Age: 14
Disease: Renal Failure
Wish: To meet Michael Jackson.
Starlight's Response: Michael Jackson entertained Angelique on his estate, showing her his collection of animals. Angelique had a sprained ankle on the day of the visit, but said she would crawl, if necessary, to be there. She is a very grateful girl.

TROY
Age: 12
Disease: Renal Failure
Wish: To go fishing for a week in Yuma, and to go there in a motorhome.
Starlight's Response: Troy's family was very excited that they could visit their relatives in Yuma and share the fishing experience with some favorite uncles.

There are others and there will be many more. Your help is needed in this very important and meaningful program. Please use the enclosed donation form and help us help these very special children.

We will be grateful for your generosity.

All donations are tax deductible. Please call our office for further information:
(213)276-6331

SPECIAL THANKS TO:
Webber Engineering; TWA Airlines; Air France Airlines; Magic Mountain Park; KLM Airlines; Deelin, Inc.; Howard Klein; Disneyland Park; Century City Rotary Club; Henry Winkler; Michael Jackson; Disneyland Hotel; Ranch House Inn; Bob Thomas Public Relations; Holiday Inn, Anaheim; Imperial Airlines; B.D. Fox & Friends, Inc.; Cathy Pavia; Matt Foster; Peter Greco; Anderson Printing and Embossing; Valley Film Services.

Designed by B.D. Fox & Friends, Inc.; Color Illustration by Cathy Pavia; Logo Design by Matt Foster; Type Design by Peter Greco; Printing by Anderson Printing & Embossing; Color Separation by Valley Film Service.

741
Michael Richards Art Director
Bill Swensen Designer/Illustrator
Univ. of Utah Graphic Design Group Studio
Univ. of Utah Student Health Group Client
Salt Lake City UT

742
Julius Friedman, Charles Byrne Designers
Bichsel, Morris Photographers
Images Studio
Taft Museum, Images Client
Louisville KY

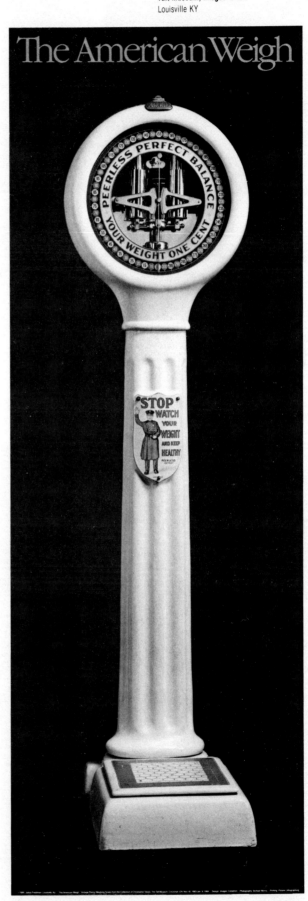

I HAVE A VERY LOW TOLERANCE FOR DRINKING AND DRIVING.

THOUSANDS OF DRUNK DRIVERS GET GROUNDED EVERY YEAR.

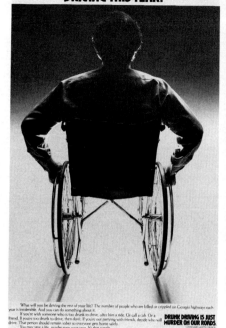

WHAT WILL YOU BE DRIVING THIS YEAR?

743

Dan Scarlotto, Mark Ashley Art Directors
Mike Granberry, Marty Clark Photographers
Daniel Russ Copywriter
Pringle Dixon Pringle Agency
Governor's Safety Council Client
Atlanta GA

745

Dave Martin Art Director/Designer
James McLoughlin Photographer
Peter Faulkner Copywriter
Doyle Dane Bernbach, Inc. Agency
American Diabetes Association Client
New York NY

746

Jerry Prestomburgo Art Director/Designer
Arthur Peck Photographer
Jerry Prestomburgo Copywriter
Warwick Advertising Inc. Agency
Seagram Distillers Co. Client
New York NY

744

Gail Kennedy Art Director/Designer
Carl Fischer Photographer
Charles Silbert Copywriter
Hy Zazula Retoucher
Young & Rubicam Agency
American Cancer Society Client
New York NY

Diabetes can appear right under your nose.

Overweight, especially if you're over forty, is a risk factor of diabetes. And it's not a sign to ignore.
Diabetes is a very serious disease that can lead to blindness. Heart attacks. And kidney failure.
Diabetes can also lead to death. In fact, it's the third largest killer disease in the United States.
The American Diabetes Association is trying to change all this. We offer programs to help people understand this complex disease. And deal with it effectively.
We also support vital research dedicated to discovering better treatment. And at reducing diabetes to a disease of the past.
To learn more, please contact your local chapter of the American Diabetes Association.

△ American Diabetes Association.
Help for today. Hope for tomorrow.

These one oz. jiggers of 80 proof spirits, 10 oz. glasses of beer, and 3 oz. glasses of wine are equal in alcohol content.

Surprised?

We can understand if you are.
It seems hard to believe that the alcohol content in the three groups of glasses above is, in fact, equal.
And so it's true that sometimes when you think you're drinking less, you may actually be drinking more. Because any alcoholic beverage should be used only in moderation, it's important that you know what you're drinking as well as how much. Remember, even though it may look light, it shouldn't be taken lightly.

THE HOUSE OF SEAGRAM

FOR REPRINTS PLEASE WRITE ADVERTISING DEPT. CU-184, THE HOUSE OF SEAGRAM, 375 PARK AVE., N.Y. N.Y. 10152

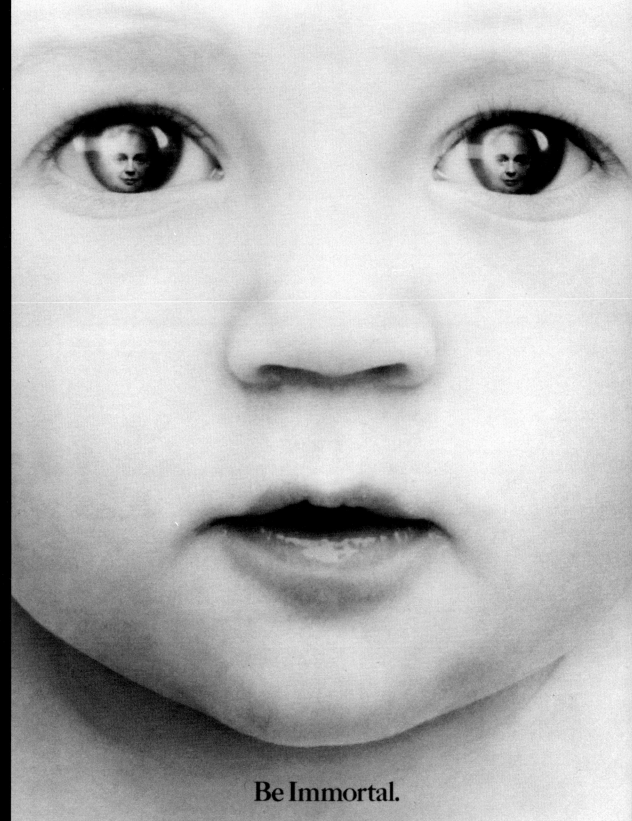

Be Immortal.

If you could look into the eyes of generations yet to come, you would be there.

Immortality lies not in the things we leave behind, but in the people our lives have touched, for good or bad.

By including the American Cancer Society in your will, you can have a powerful effect on those who come after you.

You see, cancer *is* beatable. The survival rate for all cancers is already approaching 50% in the United States.

But helping to beat cancer costs money. For approximately 30% of our annual income, we depend on bequests. To help us save lives and diminish suffering. And help achieve the Society's long-range goal: to eliminate cancer entirely.

So after you have remembered those close to you in your will, we ask that you remember the American Cancer Society.

You'll be leaving behind a legacy of life for others. And that is a beautiful way of living forever yourself.

AMERICAN CANCER SOCIETY

For more information, call your local ACS unit or write to the American Cancer Society, 4 West 35th Street, New York, NY 10001.

747

Pieter van Velsen Art Director/Designer
Michael Steenmeyer Photographer
Ben Verkaaik Illustrator
Peter Zeehandelaar Copywriter
Hettinga, De Lang, Possel, DeBoers Agency
Revalidatiecentrum "De Trappenberg" Client
Amsterdam. Holland

748

Jac Coverdale Art Director/Designer
Jim Arndt Photographer
Jerry Fury Copywriter
Clarity Coverdale Advertising Agency
YMCA/USA Client
Minneapolis MN

749

Charles Hively Art Director/Designer
Fred Housel Photographer
Julie Harrigan Copywriter
The Metzdorf-Marschalk Company Agency
KPRC-TV/Houston Client
Houston TX

750

Bill Heinrich Art Director/Designer
Mimi Reichert, Brian Mullaney, Margo Azen Copywriters
Young & Rubicam Agency
Lighthouse for the Blind Client
New York NY

751

Richard Brown Art Director/Designer
Tony Garcia Photographer
Roger Levinsohn, John van den Houten Copywriters
Richard Brown Assoc. Agency
Herpes Information Council Client
Monsey NJ

752

Lisa Levy, Patrick Kelly Art Directors
Duane Michals Photographer
Barry Biederman, Bill McCullam Copywriters
Biederman & Co. Agency
John Jay College / ITT Corp. Client
New York NY

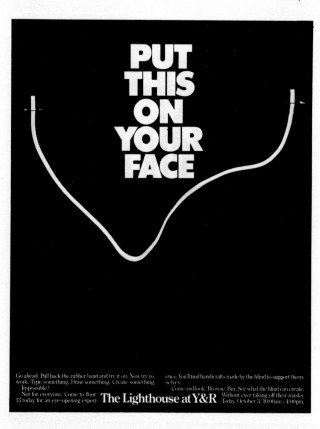

Everybody starts at the bottom.

Real winning comes in not staying there. In United States Diving, young people learn that it's okay to be afraid, that there's no shame in failing. And as they learn to dazzle the air and knife the water, they learn something much more important. That the most soaring triumphs are in simply trying again.

Stretch.

It's the only way to see how far there really is. For thousands of young people, one place to stretch is in local swim clubs and the novice programs of United States Swimming. They get coaching, fun, encouragement, a little taste of competitive swimming and a big lesson that we can all afford to remember. They're learning that nothing is too new to try. And that's a lesson that reaches a long way past the edge of the pool.

Frank Rizzo Art Director/Designer
David Lyday Copywriter
Tracy-Locke/BBDO Agency
Phillips Petroleum Company Client
Dallas TX

754

Mike Huntley Designer
Anne Wilson Mechanical Art
Philip Morris Design Group Studio
Philip Morris USA Client
Richmond VA

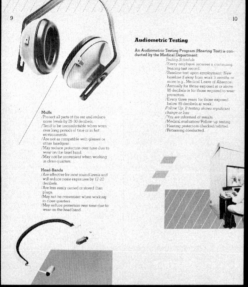

NOISE
and You

Hearing Conservation Program

PHILIP MORRIS USA

9

10

Audiometric Testing

An Audiometric Testing Program (Hearing Test) is conducted by the Medical Department.

Muffs

Head-Bands

G O O D H E A L T H

755

McRay Magleby Art Director/Illustrator
Graphic Communications Studio
Brigham Young University Client
Provo UT

PANCAKE DAY
MAR. 3

7 am - 4 pm
BACON
SAUSAGE

BERING MEMORIAL UNITED METHODIST CHURCH

PRINTING—SAN JACINTO GRAPHICS

756

David B. Waller Jr. Art Director/Designer
Charles W. Orton Photographer
Identity Inc. Agency
Graphic Design Associates Production
Bering Memorial United Methodist Church Client
Houston TX

Editorial Design

SINGLE UNIT

757
Michael Grossman, Marianne Gaffney Designers
Kinuko Craft Illustrator
Sean Kelly Author
NATIONAL LAMPOON Magazine Client
New York NY

758
Lee Walker Art Director/Designer
Duffy Stowers Photographer
Lee Walker Copywriter
City Publishing, Inc.—CITYTIMES Magazine Client
Knoxville TN

A L L E L U I A !

PON THE OCCASION OF THIS YEAR'S VERNAL EQUINOX, WHEN WE COMMEM-orate the Mystery of the Resurrection, the most basic tenet of what is (if the word of the president of the United States is anything to go by) our state religion, it behooves each of us, Fundamentalist and un-American alike, to doff our Easter bonnets and contemplate that age-old question: Are you washed in the blood of the Lamb? the Rabbit? the Baby Chick? a Druse? a Nicaraguan? a Grenadian? What this nation, under God, needs is a good old-fashioned Christian bloodbath! Say Amen, somebody!

ILLUSTRATION BY KINUKO CRAFT

DUFFY STOWERS

SPREE!

One bright sunny day in the city, enjoying lunch with your friends, you suddenly spot a magnificent jet black dress with hot white polka dots—just like the one you'd have if money allowed—worn stunningly along the sidewalk in front of you.

That's when it strikes. The Urge to Splurge. *I really do need a new dress. I've worn mine 50 times. I only have three black dresses (maybe four, but none of them have that inexplicable, metropolitan pizzaz). And I'd really like something new to sustain me during budget abuse pains.* Startled, then shamed, you

wonder if you really have an urge to splurge, or just the Green Plague, an advanced state of bank accountlessness.

But before you join Budget Abusers Anonymous (BAA), make certain of the disease. How? By tearing off an an All-Out Splurge. The true

TO PAGE 42

WRITER
ON THE ROOF

GOD'S COUNTRY
A is for America, B is for Bible,
C is for Civil Liberties.

Story by John Calderazzo
Photos by Jay Paris

KNOTS
The Only 7 You'll
Ever Need to Know
By DAN FALES

Street
smart!

C asual luggage is
picking up great
speed on the fashion
front. The category is
turning new corners as a
product of great style and
practicality. It's chic; it
gives an air of confidence;
it shows individuality;
it's for the here and now.
Take a look at casual
luggage as it spans new
horizons.

LUGGAGE ON THE MOVE

759
Bryan L. Peterson Art Director/Designer
Mark Robinson Illustrator
Ken Shelton Editor
Graphic Communications Studio
Brigham Young University Client
Provo UT

760
Thomas E. Hawley Art Director/Designer
Jay Paris Photographer
John Fleischman Copywriter
OHIO Magazine Client
Columbus OH

761
Al Braverman Art Director/Designer
Philip Gottheil Photographer
MOTOR BOATING & SAILING Magazine Client
New York NY

762
Hans Gschliesser Art Director
Leland Bobbe Photographer
LUGGAGE & TRAVELWARE Magazine Client
Norwalk CT

763
David Carson Art Director/Designer
Bill Cottle Photographer
Carson Design Agency
CIF SPORTS Magazine Client
Cardiff CA

764
James T. Walsh Art Director/Designer
Frank Riccio Illustrator
**EMERGENCY MEDICINE Magazine—
Fischer Medical Publications** Client
New York NY

765
Barbara Savinar Art Director/Designer
Tom McCarthy Photographer
Susan Ochshorn Editor
Diners Club Media Services Publication Office
Amoco Enterprises, Inc., THE AMOCO TRAVELER Client
New York NY

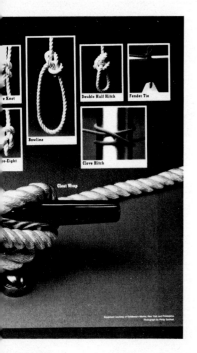

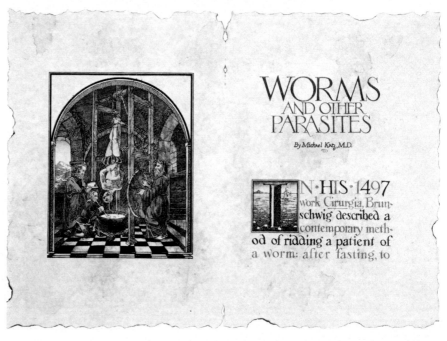

ESKIMOS

THE LAST AND FIRST

As one way of life
passes, another arrives.

Text by Robert Coles
Photographs by Alex Harris

One of the "last" Eskimos
was photographed
in Shungnak, Alaska.

THE WILD BIRDS

"Where have they gone?" Wheeler thinks. But he knows. Gone to the cities, forever or for the day. Gone to the shopping center. Gone to the golf course. Gone to the grave.

He can remember Saturday afternoons when you could hardly find space in Hargrave to hitch a horse, and later ones when an automobile could not move through the crowd on Front Street as fast as a man could walk.

Wheeler is standing at his office window, whose lower pane announces Wheeler Catlett & Son, Attorneys at Law; he is looking out diagonally across the courthouse square and the roofs of the stores along Front Street at the shining reach of the Ohio, where a white towboat is shoving an island of coal barges against the current, its screws roiling the water in a long fan behind it. The barges are empty, coming up from the power plant at Jefferson, whose dark plume of smoke Wheeler can also see, stretching out eastward, upriver, under the gray sky.

Below him, the square and the streets around it are deserted. Even the loafers are gone from the courthouse, where, the offices shut, they are barred from the weekday diversions of the public interest, and it is too cold to sit on the benches under the social security trees, now leafless, in

Fiction by Wendell Berry
ILLUSTRATION BY BRAD HOLLAND

STREET CHIC

The old-fashioned
schoolgirl look
in a modern
mode, right: a
loose-fitting
middy blouse
over a sheer,
tiered skirt.

A billowy,
drop-waist jumper,
left, gets a gutsy
finish with
a gang of chains.

Instant impact, right:
layers of relaxed,
roomy pieces paired
with layered
legs, rugged boots.

766
Al Foti, Merrill Cason Art Directors
Al Foti Designer
Alex Harris Photographer
MD Publications Client
New York NY

768
Mitch Shostak, Mary Zisk Art Directors
Rosaly Migdal Designer
Tom Leonard Illustrator
Barbara Krasnoff Copywriter
PC Magazine—Ziff-Davis Publishing Co. Client
New York NY

767

Stanley Braverman Art Director/Designer
Stephanie Stokes Photographer
SIGNATURE Magazine Client
New York NY

769

Louise Kollenbaum Art Director
Dian-Aziza Ooka Designer
Brad Holland Illustrator
Mark Twain Behrens Calligrapher
MOTHER JONES Magazine Client
San Francisco CA

770

Paula Greif Art Director
Laurie Rosenwald Designer
Laurie Sagalyn Photographer
MADEMOISELLE Magazine, Conde Nast Client
New York NY

771

David Armario Art Director/Designer
David Febland Illustrator
Robert McCarthy Copywriter
CONSUMER ELECTRONICS MONTHLY Publication—
    CES Publications Client
New York NY

772

Nina Scerbo Art Director
Paul Yalowitz Illustrator
WORKING MOTHER Magazine Client
New York NY

773

Carla Barr Art Director
Stephanie Phelan Designer
Daniel Aubry Photographer
CONNOISSEUR Magazine Client
New York NY

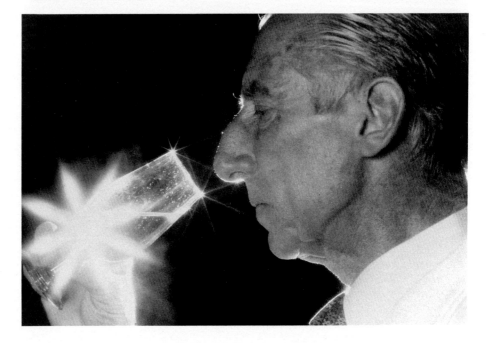

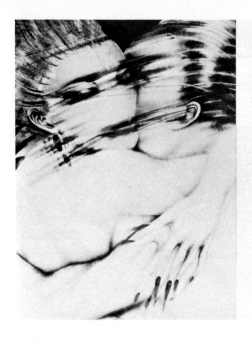

NORMAN'S DATE

he was the best bullshitter around, but his story about the blonde? man, i knew that wasn't a lie

fiction
BY AMIRI BARAKA

IN PRAISE OF CANADIAN MEN

FOR THE MODERN WOMAN,
THERE IS NO LOVER BETTER
BY SUSAN SWAN

He had on jeans and a thin yellow shell that winter afternoon. It was early February and so cold that our ski boots made squeaking sounds on the snow as we walked through the woods looking for a solitary spot. The trees were coated in ice, and when the wind blew the icicles made a clanking sound. It was like being underwater in a world of frozen white coral. He spread his ski jacket and mine on the ground and the nervous look on his face as he contemplated what had to be done next made me think he was going to be like some of the other boys who took you into the great outdoors to make love and backed down at the last moment

Into the MAINSTREAM

A Rainbow revolution is in the making. MS-DOS opens a whole new world of compatibility and performance.

BY JONATHAN COHLER

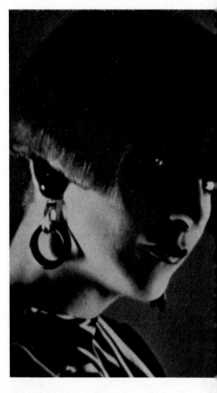

By Robert S. Peck

When George Orwell's book was first published 34 years ago, the year he chose as its title seemed far away. Yet now, 1984 is upon us.

1984 gave life to Orwell's dark vision of a world divided into three constantly warring totalitarian states. Citizens of Oceania, the post-nuclear war successor of western civilization, lead a frightening existence, where independent thought is treated as a criminal act. Oceania's citizens are all members of the Party and must maintain a worshipful attitude toward Big Brother, their all-seeing leader. Through omnipresent two-way telescreens, the Party pushes its propaganda while also spying on the populace.

1984

Who is Big Brother?

zinski

777

Barbara Solowan Art Director
Bernadette Gillen Designer
Theo Dimson Illustrator
Karen Hanley Editor
CITY WOMAN Magazine—Comac Communications Ltd. Client
Toronto. Canada

778

Richard Schemm Art Director
Steve Phillips Designer
Harold Naideau Photographer
Harold Naideau Studio Studio
Service Publications Client
New York NY

779

Peter Deutsch Art Director
Bob Day Photographer
Beverly Russell Editor
Anthony Russell, Inc. Agency
INTERIORS Magazine Client
New York NY

POLISHING THE FASHION
IMAGE

Today's fashion-aware client expects and demands more than just a becoming hairstyle or pretty makeup. All the salon services must come into play to complement today's total fashion look.

In this special fashion section you will find the latest news from the couture and unlimited ideas to help expand your Menu of Professional Services. You can use these tips to help your clients achieve and complement the look of fashion that the leading designers have decreed.

We are bringing you the spring news early, so you can be prepared to give your clients all the up-to-date services to get them ready for spring.

The fashion silhouette influences every service you offer, so we've included tips on haircolor with the newest shades and techniques; how to apply the newest makeup shades to coordinate with spring's softer mood; ways to prepare your client's skin for the brighter hues by thorough cleansing and gentle conditioning. And don't overlook all the other services you should be offering to complete the 1984 look: hair removal, diet, exercise, nutrition and the special ways you can serve your male client for the spring season.

You as a professional are in the unique position of being able to offer your client services that she or he can get nowhere else but in your salon. So make the most of it!

Here is what the experts have to say to guide you in pulling together the spring '84 total look of fashion.

FOR HAIR:
COSMETIC COLORS SPELL GLAMOUR

Dazzling haircolor is a "must" to carry off the new, more feminine look of fashion so prevalent this spring.

Leland Hirsch, director of haircoloring at Nubest & Co. Salon, predicts a strong trend to intense, bright shades infused into browns and blondes.

"There is a retro, more glamorous feeling going on right now. The Marilyn Monroe 'really blonde' look is in. Reds are very red. We are doing a lot of cosmetic coloring using shades of red, wine, plum and fuchsia to add brightness and intense tonal values to the hair.

"Many women want to keep their own natural shade and just spark it up a bit. They don't want heavy colors. So these cosmetic tints which are non-peroxide, non-ammonia and color only the hair's cuticle, are quite popular.

"I don't believe in haircolor being a fashion statement; it's a very individual situation. You must take into consideration a client's skin tone, lifestyle and ultimately what is going to be best for her. So you can't say reds are in or blondes are in – they're all in, but it's a question of degree."
continued on page 64

January 63

776

Robert Woolley Art Director
John Zielinski Illustrator
Jack J. Podell Director. ABA Press
Donna Tashjian Staff Director Creative Services
**STUDENT LAWYER Magazine—American Bar Association
Press** Client
Chicago IL

NEUROSCIENCE

THE MIND WITHIN THE BRAIN

By showing that the mind is a consequence of electrical and chemical activity in the brain, neuroscientists may profoundly affect both the treatment of mental illness and the foundations of philosophy

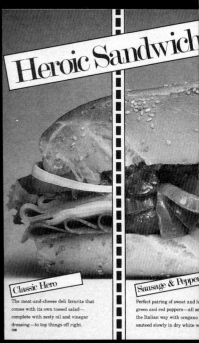

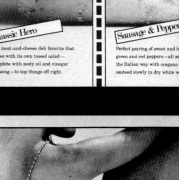

Heroic Sandwich

Classic Hero
The meat-and-cheese deli favorite that comes with its own tossed salad—complete with zesty oil and vinegar dressing—to top things off right.

Sausage & Peppers
Perfect pairing of sweet and hot green and red peppers—all served the Italian way with oregano and sauteed slowly in dry white wine.

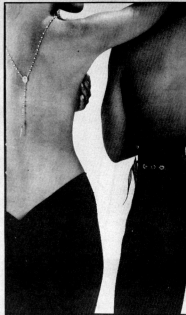

Photograph by Steven Klein

Café Seiyoken, in Manhattan, blends East and West in decor and menu.

UPSCALE

Some of the hot ideas of recent years—pasta, mesquite, and exhibition kitchens—have spread far beyond their origins, and the sophisticated consumer welcomes these new fashionable restaurants.

by Joan Lang

The restaurateurs at the cutting edge of the upscale segment are the haute couturiers of the restaurant world. While they provide something that is affordable to a relative few, they set the styles that are adapted throughout the industry. And just as the world's best dressed eagerly await the designer's new collections, the newly sophisticated upscale American consumer is enthusiastically greeting the opening of scores of fashionable new restaurants.

American restaurateurs and chefs are moving into the public eye, attracting attention and followings. The phenomenon of the culinary celebrity is relatively new in this country, but it is fostering a rapid spread of ideas. A new generation of restaurateurs is creating food that is more inventive and less bound to tradition, and restaurant concepts that are new and very exciting.

Modern American cuisine

One of the hottest trends to hit the upscale segment is the development of a new style of indigenous cooking.

RESTAURANT BUSINESS 5/20/84

783
Tamara Schneider Art Director
Jane Wilson Designer
Irwin Horowitz Photographer
LADIES' HOME JOURNAL Client
New York NY

784
Edwin Torres Art Director/Designer
Steven Klein Photographer
ISLAND Magazine Client
New York NY

780
Howard E. Paine Art Director
Jean-Leon Huens Artist
W.E. Garrett Editor
NATIONAL GEOGRAPHIC Magazine Client
Washington DC

781
Eric Seidman Art Director
Theodore Kalomirakis Designer
Jean-Michel Folon Illustrator
DISCOVER Magazine—Time, Inc. Client
New York NY

782
Joan Dworkin Art Director/Designer
RESTAURANT BUSINESS Magazine Client
New York NY

785

Peter Chancellor Art Director
Barry Aldridge Photographer
Chancellor Thomson Ltd. Studio
The Hongkong Bank Client
Hong Kong

The World's Longest Tea Party

by Jacki Passmore

Hearty, piled high . . . anything but humdrum, these all-American champions are built to feed a family, with lofty layers of tender meat, cheese, seafood and sausage. They're just four of the great recipes stuffed into our Super Sandwich Cookbook, page 110. From eat-with-knife-and-fork combos to regional specialties.

New Orleans, a sandwich
 only sliced salami, provolone,
zzarella are layered with
pings of tangy olive salad.

Lobster Roll

Down-East seafood salad special—chunks of meaty lobster, slices of crunchy celery tossed with mayonnaise, lemon juice and a dash of pepper for zip.

109

PHO·to·GRA·phs: HU·man BE·ings BO·dy TeXt: anne HOL·land·ER

Island recently paid a call on Anne Hollander, the noted art historian and costume historian whose 1978 book, *Seeing Through Clothes*, has yet to be surpassed in its provocative, perceptive, and all-inclusive examination of art, costume, cloth, the body, and how it's all intertwined. If you haven't read her book, you should. It's available in paperback from Avon Books. You've probably read her other writings in *The New York Times Magazine* and *Gentleman's Quarterly* as well as many other places, or heard one of her enthralling lectures around the world.

Interviewed by Alfred Sturtevant

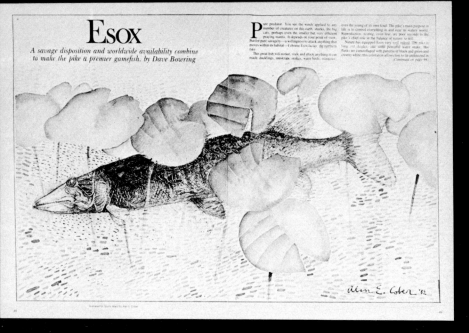

Esox

A savage disposition and worldwide availability combine to make the pike a premier gamefish. by Dave Bowring

786
Gary Gretter Art Director/Designer
Alan E. Cober Illustrator
SPORTS AFIELD Magazine Client
New York NY

787
Kan Tai-keung, Ben Lai Designers
Illustration Workshop Illustrator
The Group Advertising Limited Agency
Sing Tao Newspaper Ltd. Client
Hong Kong

Fiction by B. H. Friedman

DUPLEX

WINNER OF THE NELSON ALGREN AWARD

788
Robert J. Post Art Director/Designer
John Craig Illustrator
CHICAGO Magazine, WFMT, Inc. Client
Chicago IL

789
Anthony T. Mazzola Editor-In-Chief
Jerold Smokler Designer
Bill Silano Photographer
HARPER'S BAZAAR Magazine Client
New York NY

Editorial Design

MULTIPLE UNIT

A cube of tobacco-colored cork becomes the most daring bangle bracelet, *opposite page, upper left,* from Rodolfo Contreras at Judith Feldman. The 3"-wide, laminated bracelet, about $54. At Breakaway Fashions, NYC; De Zanella, Detroit, MI; Mary McCauley, Ft. Worth. Triple strands of tinted twine—in brown, blue and ochre—are studded with natural woods for a slinky summer belt, *opposite page, center.* From Yves Saint Laurent Rive Gauche. Available at Saint Laurent Rive Gauche Boutiques. Skin as smooth as this doesn't come naturally. Neutrogena's Rainbath Shower Gel softens as it cleanses, so your skin looks and feels moist, always. Bangles in wood—ebony, maple—plus ivory take shape as rounded squares, sculptural crescents or strong faceted cuffs, on *the wrist at right.* The four hinged bracelets by James I. Murphy, from $125 to $205. At Henri Bendel; Jere Scott Ltd. at Stanley Korshak, Chicago. Natural fir wood becomes a one-of-a-kind hand-carved cuff, *above, right.* From Virginia Estrada, NYC, about $165. The newest necklace now—the choker—gets all-natural treatment from Saint Laurent Rive Gauche, *below, far right.* The layers of differing shaped beads are all in wood. At Saint Laurent Rive Gauche Boutiques. Here and on the following two pages: body makeup, Jan Pittman; manicures, Christiana and Carmen Skin Care Salon, NYC. See Fashion Guide for details, next to last page.

ACCESSORIES NOW NATURAL WONDERS
WOOD

All manner of polished and raw woods—ebony, maple, fir and cork—are bringing out the best in the season's boldly-shaped cuffs, belts, necklaces.

An armful of smooth stone sculptures, *left,* makes today's all-natural point. These one-of-a-kind cuffs in green serpentine, smoky gray quartz and a jade-toned quartz, from Stephen Dweck, about $765 to $980. At Bergdorf Goodman; Divino, Boston; Ultimo, Chicago; Etc. at Village Sportswear, Mountain Brook, AL; Polly Adams, Laredo, TX (special order); Amen Wardy, Newport Beach, CA. Natural-look nail lacquer is new now, too: Baby Love is a next-to-no-color shade of High Resilience Nail Enamel by Coty. Mineral shades of green make for a marvelous two-piece belt buckle, *below,* in glimmering fluorite and tourmaline. It's the closing for a wide spandex belt, handpainted in multi, coordinated tones. From Alex & Lee, about $1,375. At Bergdorf Goodman; Frost Bros.; Abbraccio, Honolulu. Natural-fissure shaped pieces of reflective pyrite are set in sterling silver, *opposite page,* for some of the gutsiest (new-season) wrist accents going. Cuffs from Victor Carranza, about $225 to $325. At Bergdorf Goodman; Hattie, Birmingham, MI; Palm Beach, Scottsdale.

ACCESSORIES NOW NATURAL WONDERS
STONE

Raw or refined, direct-to-you-from-the-earth stones—quartz and others with exotic names like serpentine, tourmaline—are now the most sensational belts and bracelets you can wear.

THE BIG FALL

GREAT NEW LOOKS TO FALL FOR THIS YEAR

A SNEAK PREVIEW OF THE BEST OF FALL FASHION

COORDINATION by Shirley Gregory
PHOTOGRAPHY by Myron Zabol
MAKE-UP by Steve Marino using Prescriptives
HAIR by Stephen Corbett at Devah
MODELS by Bookings

THE SECOND TIME AROUND

Fashionable approaches for brides with a past

FALLING FOR **RYKIEL**

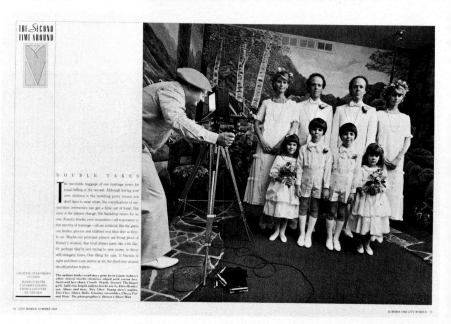

FALLING FOR **FIDANI**

FALLING FOR **SUNG**

790
Jonathan Rogers Art Director/Designer
Myron Zabol Photographer
Eugen Groh Illustrator
Shirley Gregory Coordinator/Producer
AVENUE Magazine Client
Toronto Canada

791
Barbara Solowan Art Director/Designer
Nigel Dickson Photographer
Shirley Gregory Fashion Editor
CITY WOMAN Magazine—Comac Communications Ltd. Client
Toronto. Canada

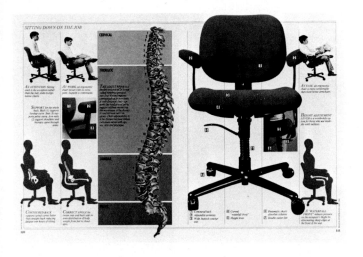

792

Bill Jensen Art Director/Designer
Seth Joel, A.A. Murphy, Robert Lorenz,
  Bettmann Archive Photographers
James Jones Sculptor
DIGITAL REVIEW—Ziff-Davis Publishing Client
New York NY

793

Kimberly Zarley Art Director/Designer
Geoffrey Wheeler Photographer
CLUB TIES Magazine—The Lovelace Corporation Client
Denver CO

794

Joanna Hudgens Art Director/Designer
Stephen H. Taylor Photographer
Hub Mail Advertising Services, Inc. Agency
Communication Consultants, Inc. Client
Boston MA

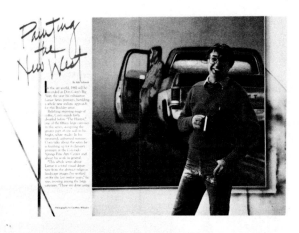

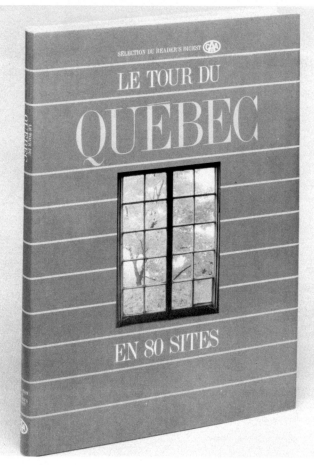

795

Lauren M. Weinberger Art Director/Designer
Stephen Anderson Photographer
Mats Gustavson Illustrator
VOGUE PATTERNS Magazine Client
New York NY

796

Val Mitrofanow Art Director
Andree Payette Designer
Mia & Klaus Photographers
Reader's Digest Association (Canada) Ltd. Client
Westmount, Canada

797

Michael Grossman, Timothy McCarthy Designers
Ron Hauge Illustrator
NATIONAL LAMPOON Magazine Client
New York NY

798

Georges Haroutiun, Joanna Bain Art Directors
Dyan Parro Designer
Tim Saunders Photographer
Ashley Harvey Publisher
M.A.G. Graphics Ltd. Studio
IMAGES Magazine Client
Toronto, Canada

UNDERSTANDING JAPANESE

THE OCCI-
DENTAL JUMP-
SUIT GOES
ORIENTAL IN
THIS INTER-
PRETATION
WORN WITH
SLEEVELESS
KIMONO
WRAP
— LINDA
LUNDSTROM,
TORONTO.

PHOTO-
GRAPHY: TIM
SAUNDERS.
MAKEUP:
KATHRYN.
HAIR: BILL
ROWLEY
(MONROE
HAIRSTYLING,
TORONTO).

FASHION CO-
ORDINATION:
LOUISA MAIN
AND
ROBERTA
SEIDMAN.
HOSIERY:
PHANTOM,
TORONTO.
SHOES:
BROWN'S
AND QUINTO,
TORONTO
AND
MONTREAL.
JEWELLERY:
ART GALLERY
OF ONTARIO
SHOP AND
ESPTORONTO.

KIMONO
WITH A SYM-
METRICAL
HEMLINE,
PANTS AND
TANK TOP,
A VERSATILE
ENSEMBLE IN
COTTON
CHIKARA,
MONTREAL.

THE MIKADO
COAT AND
COORDINAT-
ING, SLENDER
SKIRT IN
COTTON
BROCADE,
CORAL
FAILLE
BLOUSE
— MARILYN
BROOKS,
TORONTO.

INFLUENCED
BY THE
SAMURAI
WARRIOR'S
COSTUME

THE SHOGUN
JACKET WITH
EXTENDED
SHOULDERS
IN A STRIPED
SILK BLEND
THAT
EMPHASIZES
THE DESIGN.
JACKET AND
COORDINAT-
ING SKIRT
— SIMON
CHANG.

Dark Visions~The Art Of Sue Coe

THE ISSUE IS LIFE AND death, nothing less. The last-minute stay that spared J. D. Autry dramatized the dilemma of the death penalty and raised again the question of whether Autry and the 1,230 other residents now on death row would ever be executed.

TO DIE OR NOT TO DIE

THE GURNEY IN THE DEATH CHAMBER. Out of commission in Texas—at least temporarily

799

Louise Kollenbaum Art Director
Dian-Aziza Ooka Designer
Sue Coe Illustrator
Dian-Aziza Ooka Handlettering
Mackenzie & Harris Typesetting
MOTHER JONES Magazine Client
San Francisco CA

800

Margaret Joskow Art Director
Wally McNamee Photographer
NEWSWEEK Magazine Client
New York NY

801

Terry Lesniewicz, Al Navarre Art Directors/Designers
Richard Campen, John Garner, Robert Benton Photographers
Lee Comer, Ted Ligibel Copywriters
Lesniewicz/Navarre Agency
Landmarks Committee of the Maumee Valley Historical Society Client
Toledo OH

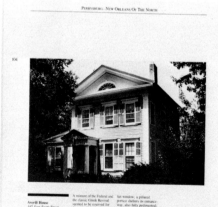

BY LEE COMER AND TED LIGIBEL

LIGHTS ALONG THE RIVER.

LANDMARK ARCHITECTURE OF THE MAUMEE RIVER VALLEY.

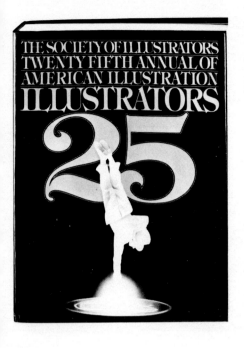

The World According To Mother Goose

There is sense as well as nonsense in nursery rhymes—even the silliest story can amaze, delight, and, in fact, teach.

Not long ago I dropped in on a friend and found her engrossed in a game with her little boy. "Pat-a-cake, pat-a-cake, baker's man, / Bake me a cake as fast as you can; / Pat it and prick it, and mark it with a B, / Put it in the oven for baby and me," she sang, clapping the child's hands together in time to the words and finally embracing him with a bear hug. Watching her took me back in memory to the time when the man-sized sons I have today gurgled on my lap with equal delight. I did not learn the nursery rhymes I sang from any baby-care manual—rather, I called them up spontaneously, word perfect, from the warm memories of my own childhood.

By Moyra Bremner

Illustrated by Winslow Pinney Pels

Charming concept This Christmas rhyme not only expresses the charitable spirit of the holiday. It also introduces a small child to the notion that a whole can be divided in half.

802

Robert Anthony Designer
James E. Tennison Illustrator
Art Weithas Editor
Madison Square Press Publisher
Society of Illustrators Client
New York NY

803

Deirdre Costa Major Art Director
Winslow Pinney Pels Illustrator
PARENTS Magazine—Gruner & Jahr Client
New York NY

804

Sylvain Michaelis Art Director/Designer
Michaelis/Carpelis Design Assoc. Studio
Fred Dodnick Production
Ballantyne Books Client
New York NY

The World According to Mother Goose (Continued)

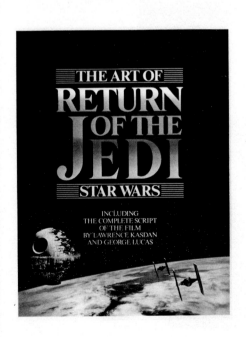

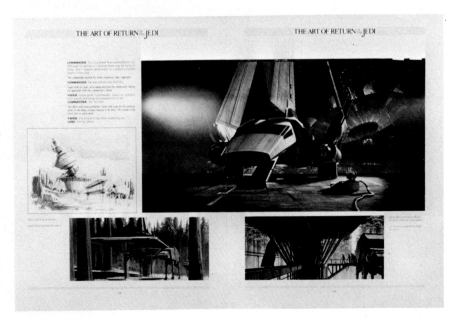

THE LOOKS OF LOVING

Seven Stories of Passion (and Fashion)

RIGHT TIME, RIGHT PLACE, RIGHT MAN. I'm dying to fix my underpants. Why does this always happen to me when I'm out with a new guy? I can feel the little elastic strip riding up my left buttock. I can't believe I'm in this idiotic situation *again*. If I knew this guy better — and I wish I did — I could just give them a good tug. Meanwhile, he's asking me, Do I like baseball? Well, I had a boyfriend in college who was mad for baseball. Our dates consisted of watch-

Proof that opposites attract: the tough and tender pair up of a short and slim black leather skirt, a soft as can be ivory colored sweater set. Maglia leather skirt, Marie France Picard cardigan, 172; and pullover, 148. Rjmn, Astaspe Lani Designs earrings. For stores, see SHOP.

ing baseball on TV. Truthfully, I prefer dinner in French restaurants. Aloud, I say, "I love baseball." Do I like jazz? Jazz tends to depress me. Not all jazz, no. I like bebop that you can dance to, but not the kind where you sit in a smoky room with all these bearded guys doing their Bob Dylan imitations. "Yes, I like jazz. I like almost everything." Smile. Laugh. I'm an enthusiastic person. Full of beans. Ah. There. The old hand-in-the-pocket trick. One little yank down and all is well. I hope I look okay — maybe I should've worn a skirt. Actually we must look like the type of young lovers that people write songs about. I mean, this fellow is gorgeous. Okay, I'll admit it: He's terrific. Now, if only my undies stay put....

— Jennifer Moses

DEAR JANE: IT'S 5 A.M. I'M WRITING THIS in an all-night diner. Just wait till you hear.... Derek slept with Wren—while I was in L.A. last week. After I found out, I considered: slitting my wrists, slitting his throat, slitting Wren's throat, slitting their throats and my wrists. Trooper that I am, I regained my sanity soon thereafter. I called to ask Derek to meet me for sup-per—Jane, I was homicidal. Well, he saunters in wearing the famous petulant pout. "Why did you sleep with Wren?" I ask him calmly. "What are you talking about?" he replies pathologically. "Wren confessed...." I mutter through clenched teeth. "I see," he says, lighting a cigarette, heaving it into his lungs, spewing it out his nostrils. "Derek, you realize this is the end. I'm returning your tape deck, mixing board and VCR." He kisses my neck, whispers in my ear, "Baby, I'm such a moron. I really love you. I just got that restless feeling...." Jane, at that point, I wept exactly four tears. He seemed contrite, squirming in his chair, chain-smoking, staring into space. He said, "Please, let's have some food and talk. I want to work it out, Maude. Really." Well,

Some enchanted evening! The daring — baring! — spaghetti-strapped dress has a dropped waist and a skirt that falls to mid-calf in soft gathers. By Saint Originals of cotton velveteen, from Compton, 186. Scooter, Paris necklace. For stores, see SHOP.

FEET FIRST

The bottom line on your lower extremities
BY SHIRLEY GREGORY

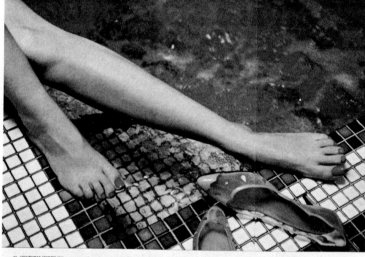

LEONARDO DA VINCI CONSIDERED THE HUMAN FOOT "A MASTERPIECE OF ENGINEERING AND A WORK OF ART." FEET ARE THE FOUNDATIONS OF THE BODY; HOW WE WALK REFLECTS OUR SENSE OF WELL-BEING, OUR SELF-CONFIDENCE, PRESENCE AND POWER. BUT CARE OF THE FEET IS OFTEN OVERLOOKED BECAUSE, UNLIKE HANDS, THEY ARE NOT ON CONSTANT DISPLAY. YET OUR FEET ARE THE PART OF THE BODY WE USE MOST — THE AVERAGE NORTH AMERICAN WOMAN WALKS AROUND THE WORLD THREE TIMES DURING HER LIFETIME. FEET CAN BE BEAUTIFUL — TAKE CARE OF THEM AND THEY'LL TAKE CARE OF YOU

LOCATION: THE McGILL CLUB
PINK LEATHER AND NET SHOES WITH TEARDROP TRIM
RED LEATHER AND WHITE MESH SHOES WITH BLUE AND PINK BANDS
FROM BOUTIQUE QUINTO

PHOTOGRAPHY BY MYRON ZABOL

805
Paula Greif Art Director
Wynn Dan Designer
Steven Meisel Photographer
MADEMOISELLE Magazine—Conde Nast Client
New York NY

JAPAN
As the West First Saw It

Not only were the people and situations strange to Occidental eyes, so was the highly stylized look of early photographs

By Rainer Fabian and Hans-Christian Adam

sweater with the V-neck down the back—he said he was going to draw a lipstick mouth on the back of my neck. Then he kissed me there to show just where the mouth would be and another few kisses for the eyes and nose. He asked me to wear all my sweaters that way from now on and the way I was feeling made it very easy to say yes or, rather, *oui*. —Gwenda Blair

SHE: YOU SAID YOU WERE

sure you knew how to get there. —I was sure. The Coach House should be right here. —She: So what happened? —He: Well, if you hadn't made me so hysterical over the story about the Polish pizza parlor, I would have watched the street signs. —She: Oh, sure. I bet you tell that to all the girls you go out with. Invite them to a fancy restaurant, then *accidentally* end up on the waterfront where you just happen to know a great little diner. I know a smooth operator when I see one. —He: *What!* Actually, I was *only* planning to kidnap you. Even now, a speedboat is waiting down at pier 83 to whisk you away to a remote island compound somewhere in the Great Lakes region. But I can't go through with it. Five minutes ago, I thought: What kind of ransom would anyone pay for this girl, anyway? I'd be lucky if I got $39 and that gorgeous gold bag of yours out of this caper. —She: Oh, come on. I'm worth my weight in gold. You'd probably keep me up there and make me be your slave. —He: Well, you'd have a steady job anyway, which is more than you can say for yourself now. —She: Right, so the least you could have done for a poor, starving dancer is feed her a hot meal, preferably a pricey one. —He: So, what time is it, 7:20? They may still have our table if we run back. —She: No, never mind. Actually, I don't notice hunger when I'm this happy. —He: Happy? You mean you're not annoyed? —She: The only thing that bothers me is my feet. —He: So, let's sit down. —She: What about my dress? —He: I'll buy you a hundred dresses. —She: Darling! That's so romantic ... even if your father *is* the mogul of Seventh Avenue.... —Ann Armbruster

806

Barbara Solowan Art Director
Bernadette Gillen Designer
Myron Zabol Photographer
Shirley Gregory Fashion Editor
CITY WOMAN Magazine—Comac Communications Client
Toronto, Canada

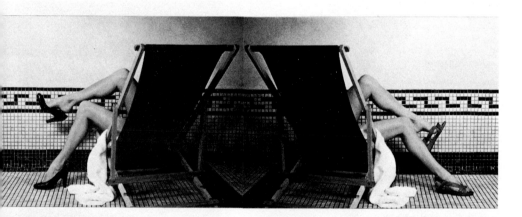

A pedicure can be a luxurious experience, soothing away the tensions of the day. Start by wiping off old polish with a cotton ball soaked in remover—Dior makes one that contains no acetone. Then relax your feet and soften tough, dry skin in warm water and Saltzy foot-bath salts, made of chamomile, currant leaves and other herbs. A rub with Scholl's Feet Beauty Stone or Hard Skin Reducer will remove softened skin; for especially rough areas try Estée Lauder's European Smoothing Body Buffer, a cream containing particle-size scrubbing beads. Clip nails straight across in a square shape the perfect length is nail tip matching toe tips) and smooth with a fine emery board. Cuticle remover is next. Brush on Dior's remover and gently push cuticles back with an orangewood stick. Soak feet again and towel dry. Lavish on a rich moisturizer such as Clinique's Quick Improvement Foot Cream, taking the time to massage it into your feet, thus stimulating and relaxing your whole body. A fresh coat of polish provides the finishing touch. Separate the toes with twisted tissue and apply a clear base coat; let dry, then add two coats of polish.

Finish with a protective topcoat. Shown here, Juvena nail lacquers; the color, a rich fuchsia quartz.

Only if the shoe fits should you wear it. Improperly fitted shoes cause problems such as corns, callouses, blisters and bunions. When buying new shoes choose leather or a porous fabric that will allow air to reach your feet. Make sure your heel fits the back of the shoe snugly but without pinching, with the top of the shoe curving in to the top of your heel. Walk and stand in the new shoes to be sure your feet don't slide and that the widest part of your foot fits the widest part of the shoe. Linings should be smooth and wrinkle free. If you are considering open-toed shoes or sandals, make sure all toes are supported by the soles of the shoes. Have your feet remeasured occasionally; changes in weight can alter the size of your feet. And remember that shoe sizes may vary according to style or manufacturer; the same size might not always be right for you. Most important, throw away uncomfortable shoes. You can always find another pair of shoes but your feet are irreplaceable. FOR PRODUCT INFORMATION SEE SHOPPER'S GUIDE, PAGE 109.

BRIGHT ROYAL BLUE ROUND-TOE PUMPS, CHARLES JOURDAN; RED WEDGE-HEEL ANKLE-STRAP SANDALS, MIGNASI

RED WEDGE-HEEL SANDALS WITH BACK BOW, MIGNASI
BLUE-AND-YELLOW STRAP SANDALS, ENZO DI ROMA/MULTICOLOR
ANKLE-TIED STRAP SANDAL, MAUD FRIZON

807

Al Foti, Merrill Cason Art Directors
Al Foti Designer
MD Publications Client
New York NY

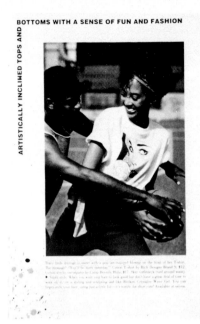

ARTIST AT PLAY

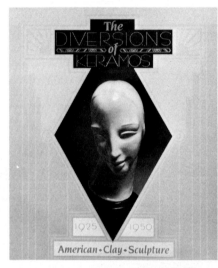

808
Bill Feeney Designer
Karen Heerlein Photographer
Nancy DeFelice Copywriter
Beauvais Printing, Inc. Production
Doubleday/Dolphin Book Client
Guilford CT

809
Victoria Peslak Art Director
Dania Martinez Designer
Rudy Molacek Photographer
SEVENTEEN Magazine Client
New York NY

810
C.W. Pike Art Director/Designer
Courtney Frisse, Bob Pike & Others Photographers
Ross Anderson, Dr. Barbara Perry Editors
The Great Northern Pikes Studio
Everson Museum of Art Client
Fayetteville NY

811
John Coy Art Director
Laurie Handler Designer
Donald Hull, Penelope Potter Photographers
COY, Los Angeles Studio
Alan Lithograph Printer
The J. Paul Getty Museum Client
Culver City CA

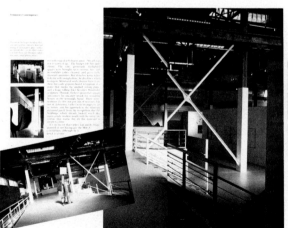

812
Ken Windsor Art Director/Designer
Tim Street Porter Photographer

PROGRESSIVE ARCHITECTURE—Reinhold Publishing
Company Client
Stamford CT

TV Graphics

813

Brian M. Robertson Designer/Illustrator
WMAR TV 2 Graphics Department Studio
News Department Client
Baltimore MD

814

Brian M. Robertson Designer/Illustrator
WMAR TV Graphics Department Studio
News Graphics—Sports Client
Baltimore MD

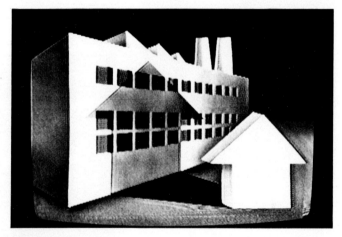

815

Mona MacDonald, Sue Hughes Art Directors
Sue Hughes Designer/Illustrator
George Coppola Photographer
WPGH-TV 53 Client
Pittsburgh PA

816

Ben Blank Art Director
Mark Trudell Designer
ABC News Graphics Agency
ABC News Client
New York NY

817

Francois Bota, Beverly Littlewood Art Directors
Francois Bota Illustrator
WNBC-TV News 4 Client
New York NY

818

Beverly Littlewood, Turk Winterrowd Art Directors
Turk Winterrowd Designer/Illustrator
WNBC-TV News 4 Client
New York NY

819
Jack Flechsig Art Director/Designer
WXYZ-TV Client
Detroit MI

820
Gwen Gipson Art Director/Designer
WXYZ-TV Client
Detroit MI

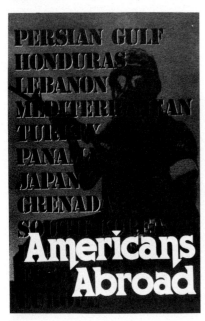

821
Beverly Littlewood, Francois Bota Art Directors
Francois Bota Illustrator/Designer
WNBC-TV News 4 Client
New York NY

822
Ken Dyball Art Director
Kelly Lee Designer
ABC News Inc. Client
Washington DC

823
Ken Dyball Art Director
Al Kamajian Designer
ABC News Inc. Client
Washington DC

824
Percy Powers Art Director/Illustrator
KXAS-TV News Client
Fort Worth TX

825
Jack Flechsig Art Director/Designer
WXYZ-TV Client
Detroit MI

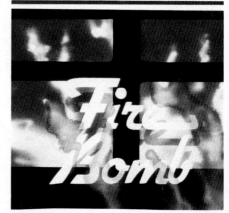

826
Bari Gilbert Art Director
Jerome W. Bailey, Bari Gilbert Designers
WNBC-TV Client
New York NY

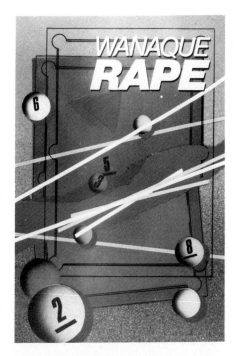

827
Beverly Littlewood, Turk Winterrowd Art Directors
Turk Winterrowd Designer/Illustrator
WNBC-TV News 4 Client
New York NY

828
Beverly Littlewood, Paula Goldstein Art Directors
Paula Goldstein Illustrator
WNBC-TV News 4 Client
New York NY

829
Beverly Littlewood, Francois Bota Art Directors
Francois Bota Illustrator
WNBC-TV News 4 Client
New York NY

830
Ben Blank Art Director
David Millman Designer
ABC News Graphics Agency
ABC News Client
New York NY

831
Ken Dyball Art Director
Alice Kreit Designer
ABC News Inc. Client
Washington DC

832
Beverly Littlewood, Burton Kravitz Art Directors
Burton Kravitz Illustrator
WNBC-TV News 4 Client
New York NY

833
Ken Dyball Art Director
Earl C. Bateman III Designer
ABC News Inc. Client
Washington DC

Consumer
SINGLE UNIT

835

John Speakman Art Director
George Anketell Creative Director
Hal Kanter, Bill Durnan Copywriters
MacLaren Advertising Agency
Chamberlain & Associates Production
Molson Ontario Breweries Ltd. Client
Toronto, Canada

WARNING.
ALTHOUGH IN THE BEST POSSIBLE TASTE WHAT YOU ARE ABOUT TO SEE IS FOR ADULTS ONLY.

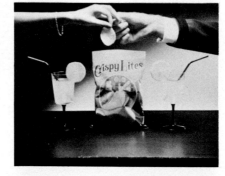
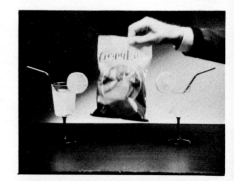

837

Johann Hoekstra Art Director
Anthony Makin Copywriter
Grey Phillips, Bunton, Mundel & Blake Agency
James Garrett and Partners Production
BMW S.A. Client
Johannesburg. RSA

834
Ralph Price Art Director/Designer
Bill Werts Photographer
Michael Wagman Copywriter
Foot, Cone, & Belding Agency
California Milk Advisory Board Client
Los Angeles CA

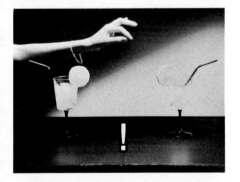

836
Mike Graham Art Director
Andy Edwards Creative Director
Basil Mina Copywriter
BBDO S.A. Agency
Feldman Cornell Film Company
Willards Foods Client
Johannesburg. RSA

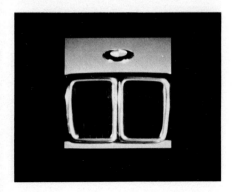
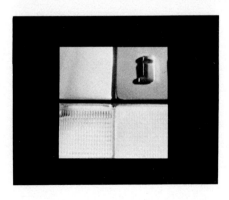

839
Bob Santangelo Art Director
Loretta Wakuya Creative Director
Dan Lombardi Copywriter
Johnston Films Production
Dancer Fitzgerald Sample Agency
Nabisco/Chips Ahoy! Client
New York NY

  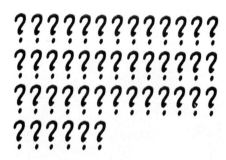

IBM

841
Howard Benson Art Director
Barry Biederman Copywriter
Biederman & Co. Agency
Bill Fertik & Co. Production
Israel Ministry of Tourism, N.A. Client
New York NY

838
H. Brian O'Neill Art Director/Copywriter
Dennis O'Keefe Photographer
Larry Chernoff, Filmcore, Los Angeles Editor
KYW-TV Client
Philadelphia PA

840
Hans Peter. Weiss Art Director/Designer
GGK New York Agency
Gunther Maier Studio
IBM Client
New York NY

842
Joe Genova Art Director
Richie Kahn Copywriter
Campbell-Ewald Company Agency
Eastern Air Lines, Inc. Client
New York NY

844
Tony Dick Art Director
Graeme Lind Photographer
Alan Morris, Allan Johnston Copywriters
MOJO Australia Agency
Ross Wood Productions Studio
Australian Tourist Commission Client
Los Angeles CA

846
Gary Alfredson, Bob Taylor Art Directors
Jim Voss-Grumish Designer
Ralph Rydholm Copywriter
J. Walter Thompson Agency
Rick Levine Productions Production
Pepsi Client
Chicago IL

843

Stu Rosenwasser Art Director
Larry Spector Copywriter
Campbell-Ewald Company Agency
National Car Rental Client
New York NY

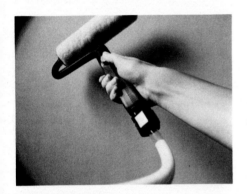 

845

Cary Cochrane Art Director
Tom McConnaughy Group Creative Director
Ron Hawkins Creative Director
Jerry Fields Copywriter
Ogilvy & Mather Agency
Wagner Spray Tech Client
Chicago IL

847

Marty Neumeier Art Director
Mark Oliver Creative Director
Sandra Higashi Designer
Mark Oliver, Inc. Agency
Educational Video Production
Stubbies Ltd. Client
Santa Barbara CA

849
Donald Boehme, George Kase Creative Directors
Lou Beres & Assoc. Agency
Ron Finley Films Studio
Chapman Industries Corporation Client
Chicago IL

851
Cyril Vickers Art Director
Terry Howard Copywriter
Ayer Barker Ltd. Agency
James Garrett & Partners Production
Sharp Electronics (UK) Ltd. Client
London. England

848
Denis Hagen Art Director
Lee King Creative Director
Judy Gerstein Copywriter
Bozell & Jacobs, Inc. Agency
Killiam Productions Production
Illinois State Lottery Client
Chicago-IL

850
David DeVary Art Director
John Scott Creative Director
Sandy Stern Copywriter
J. Walter Thompson/Chicago Agency
Pfeifer Story Productions Studio
Kraft—Miracle Whip Client
Chicago IL

 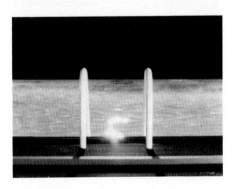

852
Audrey Nizen Creative Director
Ian Leech Director
Harry Lake Director of Photography
Shop 34, In-house Agency
Ian Leech & Assoc. Production
Macy's NY Client
New York NY

 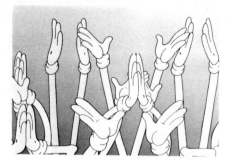 

854
Richard Sabean Art Director
Tom Nathan Copywriter
Michael Pollock Producer
TBWA Agency
John St. Clair Production
Evian Client
New York NY

856
Rhonda Gainer Art Director/Creative Director
Feliz Limardo Cameraman
Hank Corwin Editor
Hechter In-House Agency
Daniel Hechter Menswear Client
New York NY

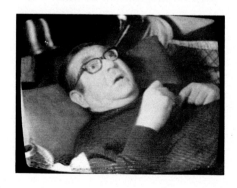  

853
Ken Eustace Art Director
Jill Taffet Designer
Joan Roach Copywriter
Taffetdesign, Inc. Production
McCann-Erickson Worldwide Agency
Fernleaf Milk Client
New York NY

855
Bill Wurtzel Art Director/Designer
Ron Wagner Copywriter
Hicks & Greist, Inc. Agency
Gemini Productions Studio
Greek National Tourist Organization Client
New York NY

857
Michael Grasso Art Director
Angie Gordon Copywriter
Tim Miller, Kimball Howell Producers
Kathy Soifer Production Supervisor
Grasso Productions, Inc. Agency
WABC-TV Client
New York NY

859

Joe Puhy Art Director/Producer
Mark Fenske Copywriter
Manny Perez Director
Young & Rubicam Agency
Filmfair Production House
Lincoln-Mercury Client
New York NY

861

Lila Sternglass Art Director
Bill Hamilton Copywriter
Stew Birbrower Director
Rumrill Hoyt New York Agency
Griner Cuesta Films Production
New York State Lottery Client
New York NY

 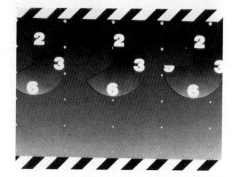 

858
Doros, Frank Arcuri Designers
Jack Silverman Creative Director
Peter Heath Director
Film Fair, Harold Friedman Consortium Production
Leber Katz Partners Advertising Agency
U.S. Shoe—Capezio Client
New York NY

860
Andy DeSantis Art Director
Klaus Lucka Director
Hal Silverman Copywriter
Doyle, Dane, Bernbach Agency
Klaus Lucka Productions Production Company
Volkswagen Jetta Client
New York NY

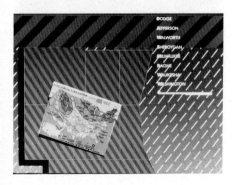

862
John Constable Art Director
Nancy Laurence, Larry Lamb Designers
Paul Churchill Photographer
Frankenberry, Laughlin & Constable, Inc. Agency
Lamb & Comapny, Inc. Production
MILWAUKEE JOURNAL Client
Minneapolis MN

864

Bill Yip Director/Designer
Ron Stannett Cameraman
Denise Chevrefils, Ruby Deziel, Penny Cadrain Copywriters
MacLaren Advertising (Montreal) Agency
McWaters Vanlint & Associates Production
Via Rail Canada, Inc. Client
Toronto, Canada

866

Herb Gross Producer/Director/Copywriter
Mark Foggetti Cinematographer
Rik Morden Editor
Mamouth Pictures Special Effects
Herb Gross & Company Production
Empire Vision Client
Rochester NY

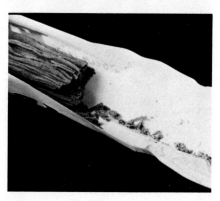

FOR NUT NUTS.

NUTCHO'S NUTCHO'S

863

Brent Wickes Art Director
Pam Freir Creative Director/Copywriter
Hayhurst Advertising Limited Agency
Owl Films Production
Laura Secord Limited Client
Toronto. Canada

865

Bob McGrath Art Director
Allen Jones Cinematographer
Rob Showell Copywriter
Simons Advertising Limited Agency
Allen Jones Productions Production
Sun-Rype Products Limited Client
Vancouver, Canada

Gatorade

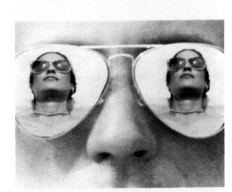

empire vision

Cadbury's **Flake**
Cadbury's **Flake**
Cadbury's **Flake**
Cadbury's **Flake**

867

Terrance Iles Art Director
William Martin Copywriter
Ousama Rawi Director/Cameraman
Scali, McCabe, Sloves (Canada) Ltd. Agency
Rawifilm Canada, Inc. Studio
Cadbury, Schweppes, Powell, Inc. Client
Toronto. Canada

868
Jim Greenwood Art Director
Joey Reiman, B.A. Albert Creative Directors
David Marinaccio Copywriter
D'Arcy MacManus Masius, Atlanta Agency
CHARLEX, New York Production
Dairmen, Inc. Client
Atlanta GA

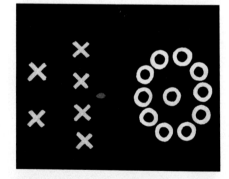

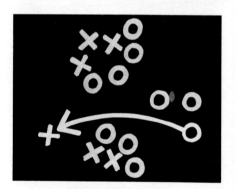

869
Bill Hoo Art Director
Charles McAleer Copywriter
ClarkeGowardFitts Agency
Kim & Gifford Production
Health Stop Client
Boston MA

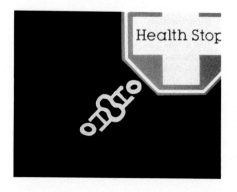

870
Mike Faems Creative Director
Don Guy Director
Terrye Rutherford, Pat McNaney Producers
Dennis, Guy & Hirsch Production Company
Young & Rubicam Agency
Pabst Blue Ribbon Client
New York NY

Pabst LIGHT

"SURF GIRL"
:30 SECOND COMMERCIAL

And now some of the best beer bellies in America.

MUSIC UP THROUGHOUT

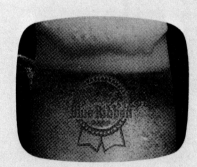

These beer bellies are brought to you

by new Pabst Light. Just 96

great tasting calories that won't fill you up. Or out.

Consumer
CAMPAIGN

872
Jeff Vetter, Greg Sullentrup Art Directors
Gerry Mandel Creative Director
Gary Rom, Peter Serchuk, Roland Harris Copywriters
D'Arcy MacManus Masius, St. Louis Agency
Craig MacGowan, John Seaton Production
Anheuser-Busch, Inc.—Budweiser Client
St. Louis MO

871

Patrick Fanelli Creative Director
Tony Jaffe Copywriter
Woody Walters Producer
Wiliam Esty Company, Inc. Agency
MasterCard International, Inc Client
New York NY

874
Tom Fichter Art Director
P. Kip Anderson Director of Photography
Mickey Lonchar Copywriter
Northstar Productions, Inc. Production
Mogelgaard & Associates Agency
Pietro's Corporation Client
Seattle WA

 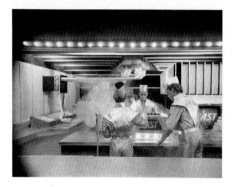

873
Jim Consor, Scott Pollack, Jim Trippler Art Directors
Richard Greenberg Director
Robert Greenberg Producer
Grey Advertising Agency
R/Greenberg Associates, Inc. Production
AMC Renault Client
New York NY

875
Marien de Goffau Art Director
Frits Leentvaar Creative Director
Arie Kleijn Copywriter
McCann-Erickson Nederland B.V. Agency
Koedijk Film B.V. Production Company
Aegon N.V. Client
Amsterdam. Holland

876

Tom Peck Art Director
Debby Stern Copywriter
Gerald Hamline Director
Young & Rubicam Agency
Michael Daniels Production House
Richardson—Vicks—Oil of Olay Client
New York NY

878

Les Sharpe Art Director
Graham De Lacy Designer
Wyn Crane Copywriter
Preller Sharpe Rice (Pty) Ltd. Agency
Wave Two Production
IGI Insurance Client
Johannesburg. RSA

880

Jorma Kosunen Art Director
Carl-Gustav Nykvist Photographer
Sven Melander Copywriter
MK, Marknaskommunikation AB Agency
Europa Film AB Production
AB Pripps Bryggerier Client
Stockholm. Sweden

Corporate

882
Jack Havey Art Director
Carol Gillette Designer
Dan Osgood, Video Productions Photographer
Ad-Media, Inc. Agency
Robert Gilmore Associates Production
Central Maine Power Company Client
Augusta ME

884
Jack Schatz Art Director/Copywriter
Jack Riedel Photographer
Corporate Concepts Agency
Hoechst Fibers Industries Client
New York NY

881
Joan Lerman Art Director/Copywriter
Norm Grey Creative Director
Bernie Walker Producer
BDA/BBDO Agency
HISK Productions Production
Delta Air Lines Client
Atlanta GA

DELTA IS READY WHEN YOU ARE®

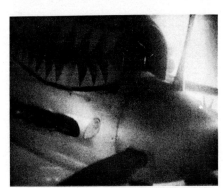

883
Mike Rizzo Art Director
Jim Hyman Creative Director
Cindy Duffy Producer
Chuck Rudnick Copywriter
Marsteller, Inc. Agency
Gould Client
Chicago. IL

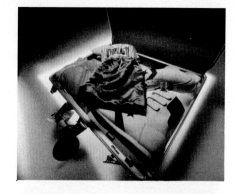

885
Caron Perkal Art Director
Louis Newman Copywriter
Grey Advertising, Los Angeles Agency
Ian Leech & Associates Production
Vons Grocery Co. Client
Los Angeles CA

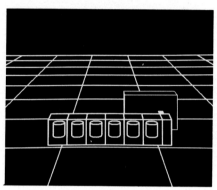
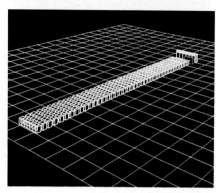
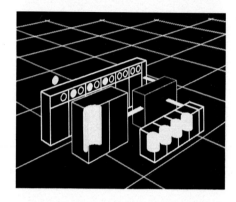

887
Lennart Soderqvist Art Director/Designer
Kent Person Photographer
Urban Falkmarken Account Supervisor
Welinder Information AB Agency
Video Produktion AB Production
HIAB-FOCO AB Client
Stockholm. Sweden

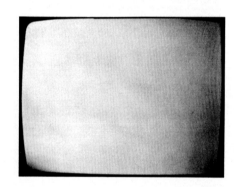

Political

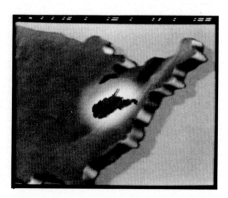

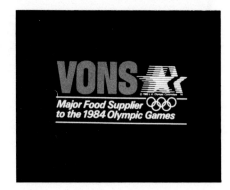

886
Michael Godfrey Art Director
Steve Hug Artist/Animator
Tom Anderson Producer
Sanburn Godfrey Advertising, Inc. Agency
Goldon Graphics Studio
Masstor Systems Corporation Client
Palo Alto CA

888
Judith Press Brenner Art Director/Copywriter
Mark Oberthaler Editor
Barry Rebo Cameraman
Press Brenner Communications Agency
Broadway Video Studio
Friends of Jay Rockefeller Client
New York NY

Public Service

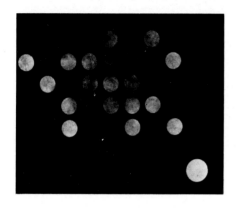

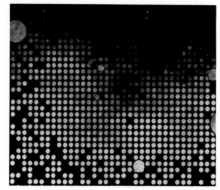

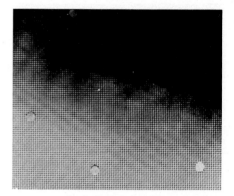

890
Chuck Mumah Art Director
Dick Harrison Copywriter
Tucker Wayne & Company Agency
Jayan Films Production
United Way of Metropolitan Atlanta Client
Atlanta GA

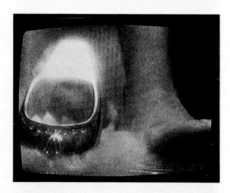

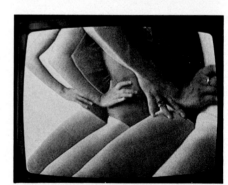

892
Jac Coverdale Art Director/Designer
Jerry Fury Copywriter
Clarity Coverdale Advertising AgencyProducer
Wy Spano Client
Minneapolis MN

889

Ken Morrison Art Director
Larry Lamb, Jerry Stenback Designers
Paul Churchill, Tom Berthiaume Photographer
Martin William Advertising, Inc. Agency
Lamb & Comapny, Inc. Production
Archer Daniels Midland Client
Minneapolis MN

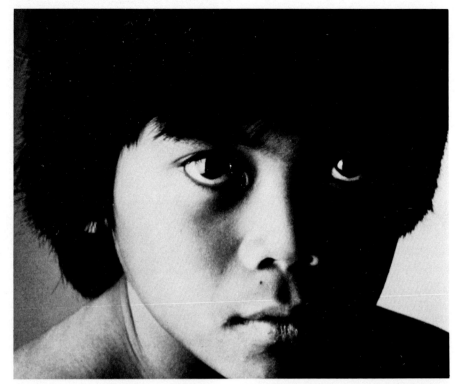

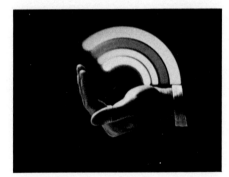

891

Jac Coverdale Art Director
Jerry Fury Copywriter
Clarity Coverdale Advertising Agency
James Productions Production
YMCA/USA Client
Minneapolis MN

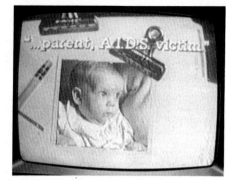

893
Michael Grasso Art Director
Angie Gordon Copywriter
Tim Miller, Kimball Howell Producers
Kathy Soifer Production Supervisor
Grasso Productions, Inc. Agency
WABC-TV Client
New York NY

895
Gene Powers Art Director
Robert Peluce Designer
Dave Nelson Copywriter
Cargill Wilson & Acree Agency
Kurtz & Friends Studio
Alabama Power Company Client
Burbank CA

897
Tony Kerr Art Director
Colin McLaren Director
Pam Frostad Copywriter
McKim Advertising Agency
T.D.F. Films Ltd. Studio
The Canadian Red Cross Society Client
Toronto. Canada

896
Ann King Art Director
Elbert Budin Photographer
Heather Choate Copywriter
Foot, Cone, & Belding Agency
Ampersand Productions Studio
United States Forest Service Client
Los Angeles CA

894
Lila Sternglass Art Director
Bill Hamilton Copywriter
Chuck East Director
Rumrill Hoyt New York Agency
Iris Films Production
Church of the Nazarene Client
New York NY

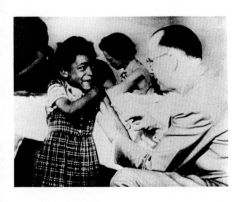  

898
Paul Schupanitz Art Director/Producer
Dick Stevens Still Photographer
Ed Des Lauriers Copywriter
Campbell-Mithun, Inc. Agency
Wilson-Griak Studio
National Mental Health Assoc. Client
Minneapolis MN

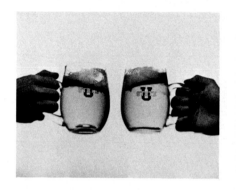

900
Jim Fitts Art Director
Jon Goward Copywriter
ClarkeGowardFitts Agency
September Productions Production
Massachusetts Society for Prevention of Cruelty to Children Client
Boston MA

899
Len Fink Art Director
Jack Silverman Creative Director
Herb Millr Agency Producer
Leber Katz Partners Advertising Agency
Lovinger, Tardio, & Melsky Production
The Ad Council, Dept. of Transportation Client
New York NY

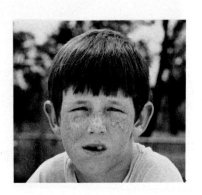

901
John R. Wagner Art Director
Victor Haboush Photographer
Irene Wilson Copywriter
Zwiren & Wagner Advertising Agency
The Haboush Company Studio
Illinois Department of Children & Family Services Client
Chicago IL

Show Openings

902
Michael Collery, Ron Tsang, Paul Sidlo, Bruce Soloway Art Directors
Ron Tsang Designer
Michael Collery Animator
Cranston/Csuri Productions, Inc. Production
ABC News Client
Columbus OH

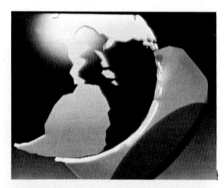

904
C.R. Russell Art Director/Illustrator
Bill Mandel Creative Director
Neil Sandstad Design Director
Michael Taylor, Linda Martin Copywriters
Metropolitan Museum of Art Production
WNET: Arts and Sciences Client
New York NY

903
Orest Woronewych Art Director of Design
Paul Fuentes Designer
Cranston/Csuri Productions, Inc. Production
Cinemax Client
New York NY

905
Bob Blansky Art Director/Designer
Benton & Bowles, Inc. Agency
Dolphin Productions Production
Edge of Night for Proctoer & Gamble Client
New York NY

Special Creative Achievement

Art Illustration

906
Bob Novak Illustrator
Greg Paul Art Director
Bob Novak Studio
THE PLAIN DEALER Sunday Magazine Client
Lyndhurst OH

908
Hubert Kretzschmar Computer Illustrator/Designer
Fiorucci Client
New York NY

907
Liz Kathman Grubow Illustrator
Summerfair Inc. Client
Cincinnati OH

909
Leo and Diane Dillon Illustrators
Victor Liebert Art Director
Joshua Taylor Production
Caswell-Massey Co., Ltd. Client
New York NY

910
Ken Walker Illustrator/Designer
Triad Productions Inc. Studio/Client
Shawnee Mission KS

911
Allen Weinberg Art Director/Designer
**T.J. Martell Memorial Foundation for Leukemia
  and Cancer Research** Client
New York NY

912
Glenn Batkin Illustrator/Designer
Lord, Geller, Federico, Einstein, Inc. Agency/Client
New York NY

913
Bud Huntoon Illustrator
Jon Cornwell Art Director/Designer
**Provident Corporate Communications (In-House
  Design Unit)** Agency
Provident Insurance Co. Client
Chattanooga TN

914
Ramon Gonzalez Teja Art Director
Pladur Client
Madrid. Spain

915
Michael Hampshire Illustrator
J. Robert Teringo Art Director
National Geographic Society Client
Washington DC

916
Lorna Balian Illustrator/Designer
John Balian Technical Illustrator & Creative Advisor
Abingdon Press Client
Nashville TN

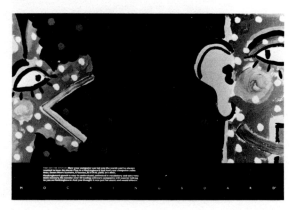

917
Matthew Imperiale Illustrator
Bruce Crocker Art Director/Designer
Altman + Manley Agency
Sweet Micro Systems Client
Cambridge MA

918
Denise Hilton-Putnam Illustrator
Richard Salzman Artist's Representative Client
San Diego CA

919
Heather Cooper Illustrator
Heather Cooper Illustration & Design Ltd. Agency
Lowell Williams Design Client
Toronto, Canada

920
Barbara J. Kelley Illustrator
Steve MacDonald Art Director
THE WALL STREET JOURNAL Client
New York NY

921
Alain Gauthier, Greg MacNair Illustrators
David Bartels Art Director/Designer
Bartels & Company, Inc. Agency
Gordon Restaurant Client
St. Louis MO

922
Ron Mazur Illustrator
East House Enterprises, Inc. Agency
Parfums Stern for Oscar De La Renta Client
New York NY

923
Paul Leibow Illustrator
Leibow Inc. Studio
ORACLE Newspaper Client
Englewood NJ

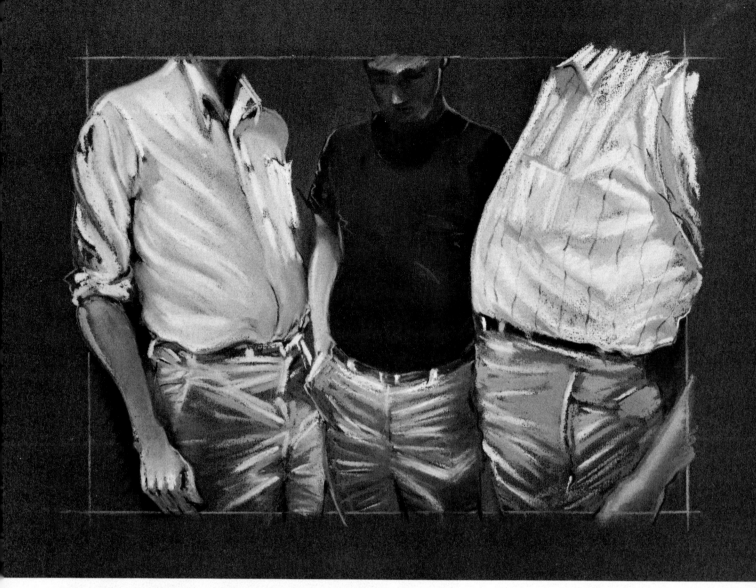

924
Barbara Maslen Illustrator/Client
New York NY

925

Richard Hess Illustrator
Hans Peter Weiss Art Director
GGK New York Agency
Gunther Maier Studio
IBM Client
New York NY

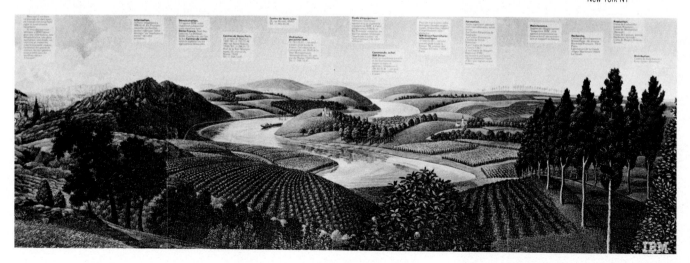

926
Bryan Honkawa Illustrator
Scott A. Mednick, Lisa Pogue Designers
Douglas Boyd Design Studio
Gore Graphics Client
Pacific Palisades CA

927
Javier Romero Illustrator
Javier Atela Art Director
Periscope Studio, Inc. Studio
Monet Jewelry Client
New York NY

928

Liam Roberts Illustrator
J. Bruce Haag Art Director/Designer
33 METAL PRODUCING Client
New York NY

929

Marie Buckley Illustrator
Louise Hutchison Art Director/Designer
National Technical Institute for the Deaf/RIT Client
Rochester NY

9 BIG CITIES, AND HOW THEY COMPETE

by Dina Eliash

930

Seymour Chwast Illustrator
Tom Staebler Art Director
Theo Kouvatsos Designer
PLAYBOY Magazine—Playboy Enterprises, Inc. Client
Chicago IL

931

Laura Smith Illustrator
Lee Ann Jaffee Art Director
MEETINGS & CONVENTIONS Magazine—Ziff Davis Publishing Co. Client
New York NY

932

John Berkey Illustrator
Bryan Canniff Art Director
POPULAR MECHANICS Magazine Client
New York NY

933

Al Brandtner Illustrator
Roseann Hebeler Brown Art Director
Michael J. Walsh Designer
MONTHLY DETROIT Magazine Client
Birmingham MI

934

Brad Holland Illustrator
Robert Priest Art Director
NEWSWEEK Magazine Client
New York NY

935

Vivienne Flescher Illustrator
Tony Iannotta Petrella Art Director/Designer
WORKING WOMAN Magazine Client
New York NY

Winter, Spring, Summer, Fall...make this the healthiest year of all.

New York State Health Department

936
Winslow Pinney Pels Illustrator
Penelope Murphy Art Director
New York State Health Department Client
Albany NY

937
John Stadler Illustrator
The Long Acre Press, Inc. Client
New York NY

938
Sandra Higashi Illustrator
Marty Neumeier Art Director/Designer
Neumeier Design Team Studio
Chroma Lith Client
Santa Barbara CA

939
Henrik Drescher Illustrator
Louise Kollenbaum Art Director
Dian-Aziza Ooka Designer
MOTHER JONES Magazine Client
San Francisco CA

940
Birney Lettick Illustrator
Jim Clarke Art Director
Stuart Bresner Creative Director
The Bloom Agency Agency
All Brand Importers Client
New York NY

941
R.J. Shay Illustrator
Shay Productions Agency
Sell, Inc. Client
St. Louis MO

942
Kevin McPhee Illustrator/Designer
Anthony Russell Art Director
Anthony Russell, Inc. Studio
Squibb Corporation Client
New York NY

943
Steve Berman Illustrator
Robert J. Post Art Director
CHICAGO Magazine Client
Chicago IL

944
Javier Romero Illustrator/Art Director
Periscope Studio, Inc. Studio
Telefon Records Client
New York NY

945
Gary Meyer Illustrator
Rick Albert & Gary Meyer Designers
Design Projects Studio
Film Ventures International Client
Santa Monica CA

946
David Coulson Illustrator
James T. Walsh Art Director/Designer
EMERGENCY MEDICINE Magazine—
Fischer Medical Publications Client
New York NY

947
McRay Magleby Illustrator
Graphic Communications Studio
Brigham Young University Client
Provo UT

FIDELITY PRINTS JULY

1 2 3 4 5 6 7 8 9 10 11 12 13 14 15 16 17 18 19 20 21 22 23 24 25 26 27 28 29 30 31

948
Steven Guarnaccia Illustrator
Robert Manley Art Director
Altman + Manley Agency
Multigroup Health Plan Client
Cambridge MA

949
Regan Dunnick Illustrator
Steven Sessions Art Director
Steven Sessions, Inc. Studio
Fidelity Printing Company Client
Houston TX

951
Jean-Christian Knaff Illustrator
Danielle Roy Designer
Legault Nolin Larosee et associes inc. Agency
Christopher Robin Client
Montreal Canada

950
Brad Holland Illustrator
David Bartels Art Director
Bill Kumke Designer
Bartels & Company, Inc. Client
St. Louis. MO

Photography

January

Sun	Mon	Tues	Wed	Thurs	Fri	Sat
1	2	3	4	5	6	7
8	9	10	11	12	13	14
15	16	17	18	19	20	21
22	23	24	25	26	27	28
29	30	31				

952
Dennis Gottlieb Photographer
Glenn Staada, Joe Merlo Designers
Design I Studio
L.P. Thebault Company Client
Parsippany NJ

953
Suzanne Szasz Photographer/Client
New York NY

954
Tim Bush Photographer/Client
Cleveland OH

955
Marshall Harrington Photographer
John F. Vitro Art Director/Designer
Franklin and Associates Agency
National Decision Systems Client
San Diego CA

956
Walter Iooss Jr. Photographer
Mike Rizzo Art Director/Designer
Jim Hyman Creative Director
Marsteller, Inc. Agency
Westinghouse Client
Chicago Il

957
Casey Sills Photographer
Bob Post Art Director
Alfredo S. Lanier Senior Editor
CHICAGO Magazine Client
Chicago IL

Expanding the limits of human performance.

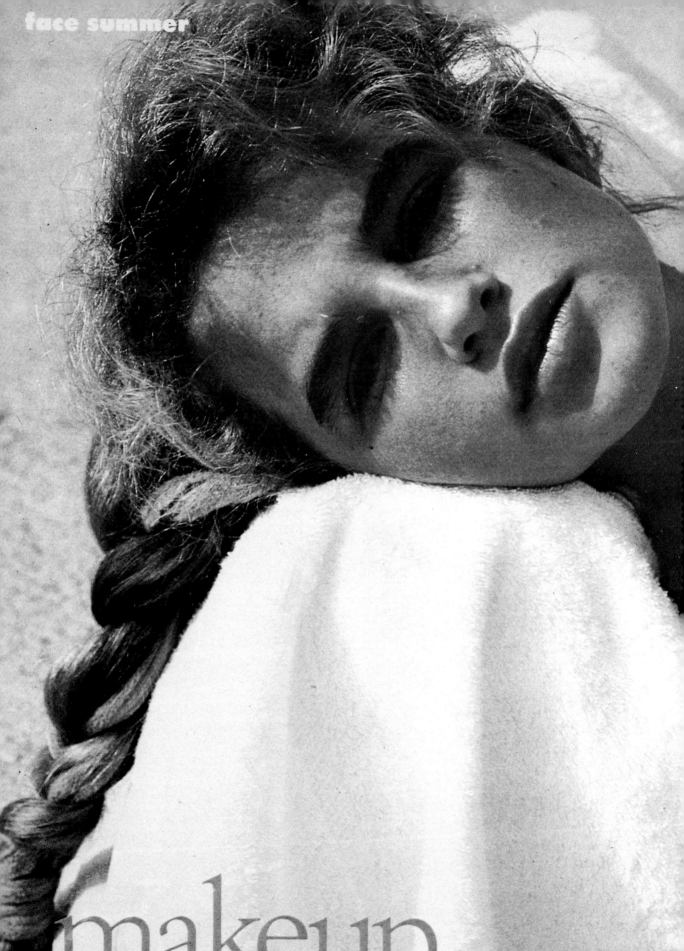

makeup
that's sheer, soft,

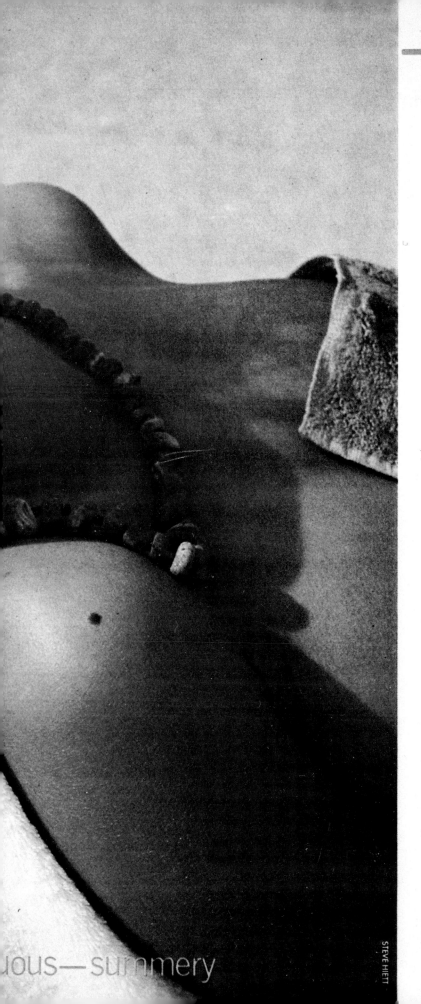

uous—summery

STEVE HIETT

959

Phil Porcella Photographer
Janet Ellis Art Director/Designer
Cipriani Advertising, Inc. Agency
Honeywell Information Systems Client
Boston MA

960

Dennis Manarchy Photographer
David DeVary Art Director/Designer
John Scott Creative Director
J. Walter THompson/Chicago Agency
Kraft Client
Chicago IL

961

Kirk S. Zutell Photographer
Ron Redding Art Director
Jan Rosenfeld Designer
brt Photographic Illustrations Studio
York Wallcovering, Inc. Client
Lancaster PA

1983 Annual Report   33

RON WU STUDIOS 179 ST. PAUL ST., ROCHESTER, NEW YORK 14604 716-454-3600

962
Michel Tcherevkoff Photographer
James Talarico Art Director/Designer
Mary Lee Cato Creative Director
Hallways Advertising, Inc. Agency
Comtempra Communications, Inc. Production
Frank B. Hall and Co., Inc. Client
New York NY

963
Ron Wu Photographer/Client
Robert Petrick Designer
Rochester NY

964
Chris Steele-Perkins/Magnum
  Photographer
Louise Kollenbaum Art Director
Martha Geering Designer
MOTHER JONES Magazine Client
San Francisco CA

This unusual view of the Peninsula Hotel captures its architectural splendour.

此圖充份表現出半島酒店堂皇華麗之建築特色。

"The suspension bridge seems eternal like the hills that ring the central city or the Ohio River itself."

965
Barry Aldridge Photographer
Peter Chancellor Art Director
Chancellor Thomson Ltd. Studio
The Hongkong & Shanghai Hotels Ltd. Client
Hong Kong

966
Roger Lantaff Photographer/Client
Langley WA

967
Gregory Thorp Photographer
Thomas E. Hawley Art Director/Designer
OHIO Magazine Client
Columbus OH

968
Gabe Palmer Photographer
Bob Newman Art Director/Designer
Newman Design Agency
Palmer/Kane Inc. Studio
Multibank Client
W. Redding CT

969
David Burnett Photographer
Diana Graham Art Director/Designer
Gips + Balkind + Associates Agency
Lebanon Valley Offset, Inc. Production
Johnson & Higgins, Inc. Client
New York NY

JOHNSON & HIGGINS
ANNUAL REVIEW
1983

970
Bruno J. Zehnder Photographer
M. Christian Guillon Art Director
ZOOM Magazine, Paris Client
New York NY

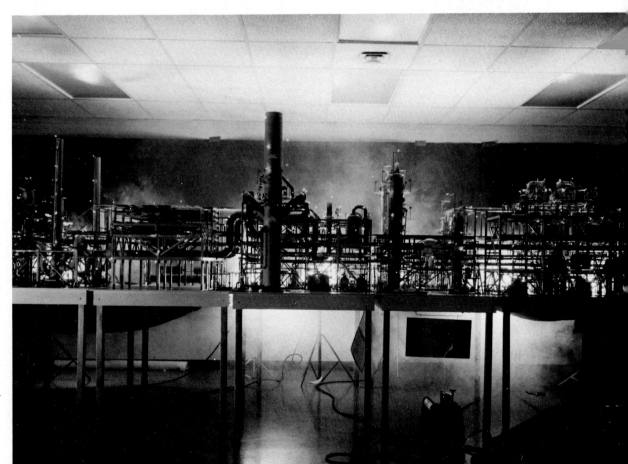

971
Walt Seng Photographer
John J. Brady Art Director/Designer
John Brady Design Consultants, Inc.
  Agency
 Dravo Engineers, Inc. Client
Pittsburgh PA

972
Gary Braasch Photographer
Joe Rattan Art Director
Chris Hill Designer
HILL/A Graphic Design Group Agency
Superb Litho, Inc. Client/Printer
Portland OR

973
Bret Lopez Photographer
Hoi Ping Law Art Director/Designer
Dyer/Kahn, Inc. Agency
Malibu Art & Design Client
Los Angeles CA

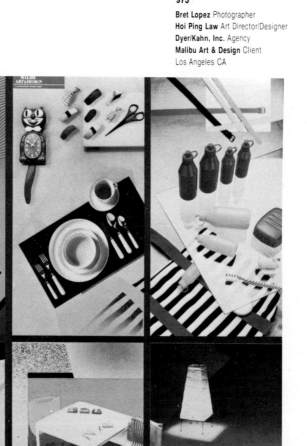

974
Ted Kawalerski Photographer
Robert Meyer, Frank Jepson Art Director
Robert Meyer Design, Inc. Studio
Bausch & Lomb Client
Rochester NY

975
NASA Photographer
Richard McMillan Art Director/Designer
COGENERATION WORLD Magazine Client
La Verne CA

976
Peter Ward, Bruce Coleman, Inc. Photographers
Al Braverman Art Director
MOTOR BOATING & SAILING Magazine Client
New York NY

977
Corson Hirschfeld Photographer
Lance Vander Hye Art Director
D'Arcy, MacManus & Masius Agency
Anheuser-Busch, Inc. Client
Cincinnati OH

978
John Katz Photographer
Linda Eissler Art Director/Designer
Eisenberg, Inc. Agency
Uncle Tai's Restaurant Client
Dallas TX

979
Fritz Haase Photographer/Designer
Atelier Haase & Knels Agency
Buro Bremerhaven Werbung Client
Bremen. Germany

980
Susan Cushner Photographer
Susan Turner, Clifford Selbert Art Directors
Terzis & Company Agency
Clifford Selbert Design Studio
Europa Design Client
Cambridge MA

981
ABC—In-House Photographers
Frederick H. Myers Art Director/Designer
Grey Advertising, Inc. Agency
ABC Movies For Television Client
New York NY

She wanted a future for her family.
To breathe the mountain air. To watch life grow.

But all she had was courage. Love.
And a dream of a place called home.

JANE FONDA in THE DOLLMAKER

abc An ABC Theater Presentation

982

Alain Evrard Photographer
Kan Tai-keung, Freeman Lau Siu-hong Designers
SS Design & Production Agency
The Mandarin International Hotels Limited Client
Hong Kong

983

Steen Svensson Photographer
Ina Kahn Art Director
Victor Liebert Designer
Trevira-In-House Agency
Mary McFadden Client
New York NY

984

Christopher Gould Photographer
Jeff Barnes Designer
Barnes Design Office Studio
Kieffer-Nolde, Inc. Client
Chicago IL

FOOD FOR THOUGHT

985

Barbara Bordnick Photographer
Irwin Goldberg Art Director/Designer
Nadler & Larimer, Inc. Agency
Faberge Client
New York NY

986

Laurie Simmons Photographer
Paula Greif Art Director
Julia Gorton Designer
MADEMOISELLE Magazine—Conde Nast Client
New York NY

Typography

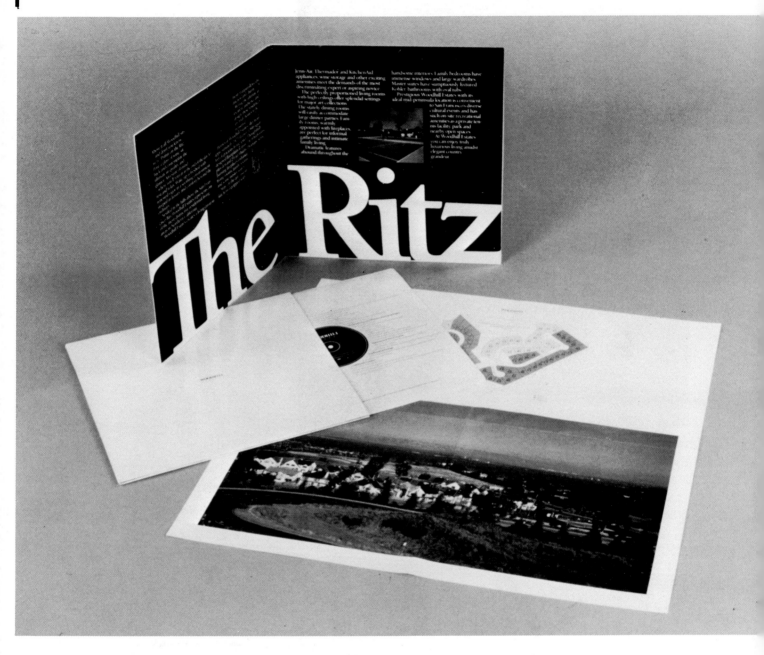

75 Grove Street / Rochester, NY 14605 / (716) 232-1610

987
David Gauger/Robert Ankers Art Directors
Jeanne Kimmel Designer
John Horvers Photographer
Susan Goldstein Copywriter
Gauger Sparks Silva, Inc. Agency
Dividend Development Corporation Client
San Francisco CA

988
Joe LaMay, William McElveney Art Directors/Designers
McElveney & LaMay Studio
Preptech Client
Rochester NY

989
Michael Tedesco Art Director
Executone Inc. Client
New York NY

990
Sharon L. Occhipinti Art Director/Designer
Bob Lapides Copywriter
Doyle Dane Bernbach Agency
Celanese Client
New York NY

991
Jerry Coward Art Director/Designer
Dana Viers Calligraphy
Jerry Cowart-Designers Studio
Inventive Minds Client
Los Angeles CA

if you're flying to London this fall, fly the world's favourite airline, round trip, for as little as $498.

and British Airways can also save you money on your hotel, car rental, entertainment and sightseeing.

but book now to reserve your seat. And ask your travel agent about British Airways' hotel, car rental, "London Showtime" and other packages.

Make your departure any Sunday to Thursday— October 16 to December 14, or December 25 to January 31. Return any Monday to Friday— October 23 to January 1, or January 7 to February 29.

It's only $25 more for a Friday or Saturday departure. And $25 more for a Saturday or Sunday return.

Stay 7 days to 1 month. Pay in full within 7 days of booking, but no later than 21 days prior to your departure. And consider your fare guaranteed, as long as you don't change your reservations.

Then, no ifs, ands or buts. Just enjoy.

British airways
The world's favourite airline.

FARE FOR CHILDREN 2-11 YEARS $448. ACCOMPANIED CHILDREN UNDER 2 YEARS FLY FREE. FARES AND CONDITIONS SUBJECT TO CHANGE WITHOUT NOTICE. FARES SUBJECT TO GOVERNMENT APPROVAL. BRITISH AIRWAYS ONTARIO TOUR OPERATOR LICENCE #1508998 *Subject to schedules in conjunction with Air Canada

People weekly

IT ADDS UP IN

25 MOST INTRIGUING PEOPLE OF 1983

SPECIAL YEAR-END DOUBLE ISSUE

4,000,000 CIRCULATION RATE BASE

33,000,000 TOTAL ADULT READERS

20%* COVERAGE OF U.S. ADULTS

CONSISTENT BONUS CIRCULATION

P4C $2.18* CPM

4C:11/7

CLOSING DATES BW:12/5

ON SALE FROM: 12/26/83 THRU 1/2/84

PAGE COST 4C:$72,075 BW:$55,925

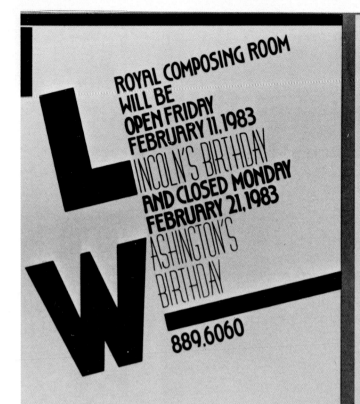

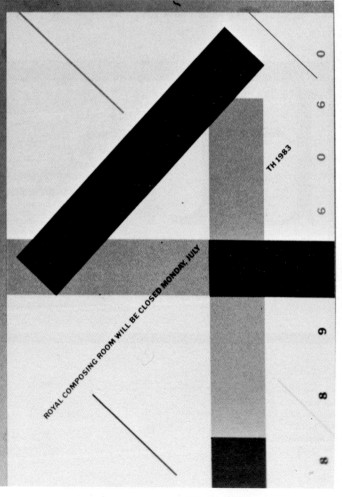

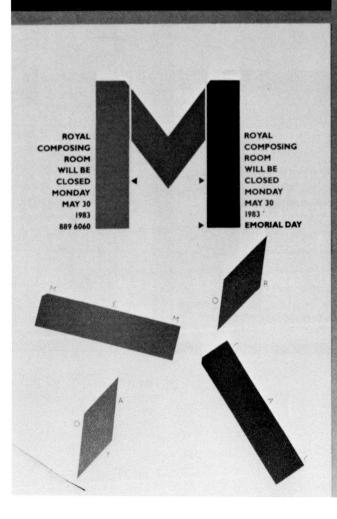

994
Martin Solomon Art Director/Designer
Royal Composing Room, Inc. Production/Client
New York NY

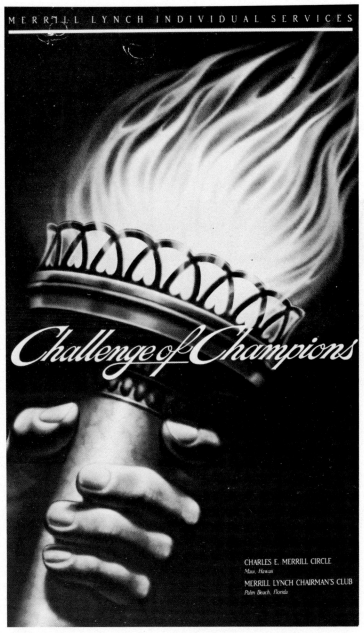

MERRILL LYNCH INDIVIDUAL SERVICES

Challenge of Champions

CHARLES E. MERRILL CIRCLE
Maui, Hawaii

MERRILL LYNCH CHAIRMAN'S CLUB
Palm Beach, Florida

995
Dydee M. Koin Art Director
Thom Gleason Designer/Creative Director
Impressions-A.B.A. Industries Inc. Agency
Merrill Lynch Client
Roslyn Heights NY

REED
SMITH

996
Dennis Morabito Art Director/Designer
Burson-Marsteller Agency
Reed Smith Shaw + McClay Client
Pittsburgh PA

In the beginning, a multitude of voices rang out across the wires and rumbled: "Locations!" *A*nd out of the darkness sprang forth a land filled with cities great and small. Farms and forests. River towns. Southern settings. Urban lights. Industrial sites. Shores and harbors. All heavenly. *A*nd so the producers saw Illinois and said that it was good. *T*hen the voices sought casting directors. And talent begotten in the images and likenesses of the script. *A*nd lo, casting was fruitful. And extras multiplied. *Y*et the voices coveted crews of great strength. State of the art equipment. Post-Production. And were fearful of the cost. *B*ut Illinois calmed the voices. And the producers read the bottom line and saw that it was good. Very good. *C*aterers and hotel rooms were found. And the voices made a joyful noise. *S*till they desired a covenant with those most high. And it came to pass that city and state officials were perfect angels. *T*he sea of red tape parted. *A*nd the producers looked upon all that had gone before them in Illinois, gave thanks and said: "*L*et there be 'Lights! Camera! Action!'" *W*ord has it that Illinois is a divine place to shoot. *Contact Lucy Salenger, Managing Director, Illinois Film Office, Department of Commerce and Community Affairs, 310 South Michigan Avenue, Chicago, Illinois 60604. (312) 793-3600. She'll make a believer out of you.*

Illinois

997
Robert Qually Art Director/Designer
Stephanie Ross Copywriter
Qually & Company Inc. Agency
IL Film Office Client
Chicago IL

998
David Reneric Art Director
Tim Girvin Designer
Seiniger and Associates, Inc. Agency
Tim Girvin Design, Inc. Studio
Universal—RKO—Studios, Inc. Client
Seattle WA

OBERL!N

1000
Anne Twomey Art Director/Designer
A + Design Studio
Anne Twomey Client
New York NY

999
Domenica A. Genovese Art Director
The North Charles St. Design Organization Agency
Oberlin College Client
Baltimore MD

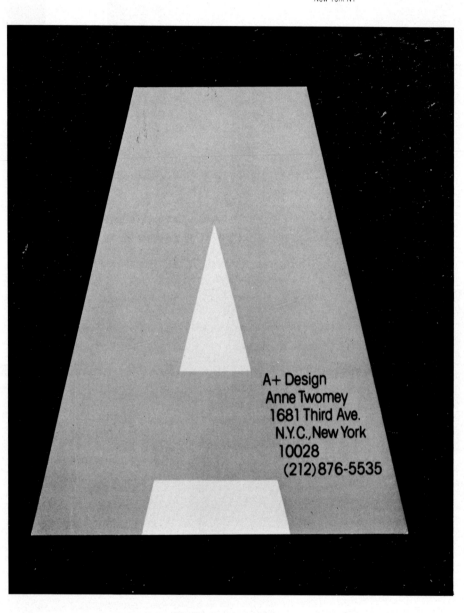

A+ Design
Anne Twomey
1681 Third Ave.
N.Y.C., New York
10028
(212)876-5535

1001
Lee Ann Jaffee Art Director
Tim Girvin Illustrator
MEETINGS & CONVENTIONS Magazine
Ziff-Davis Publishing Company Client
New York NY

1002
Rimo Angeli, Eric Read, Ray Honda Designers
Eric Read Illustrator
Primo Angeli Graphics Studio
Lucca Delicatessens, Inc. Client
San Francisco CA

1003
Paula Greif Art Director
Wynn Dan Designer
Eric Boman Photographer
MADEMOISELLE, Conde Nast Client
New York NY

THE LIGHT touch

How to be a better blonde, a more beautiful brunette—a really ravishing redhead

What to do when you want your hair to look a little lighter? Go a bit brighter! "Anyone, from the palest blonde to the darkest brunette can go brighter as long as the effect is natural looking," says Leland Hirsch, color director at the Nubest Salon in Manhasset, NY, and new-product consultant for Clairol. "Brightening should bring out the complete palette of color gradations in your hair—not cover up or drastically change it." To help you figure out the brightening techniques that will work best for you, read the chart at right. Then turn the page to find out which shades will be most flattering to your hair color, eye color and complexion. You're in for the brightest looks going!

coloring technique	how it works	good for / bad for...
HIGHLIGHTING	Beautiful, bright sunny touches are added to hair with a lightener. Fade-out time: 2 months. Try: Clairol Frost 'n Tip, Revlon Frost & Glow or L'Oréal Brush-On Highlight.	Good for brunettes and most blondes. Not recommended for brunettes and some redheads—contrast would look blaring.
SEMIPERMANENT COLOR	Hair is brightened all over with a nonperoxide color. Fade-out time: 3–4 weeks. Try: Clairol Loving Care, Clairol Color Renewal System or L'Oréal Young Blonde.	Good for all hair colors.
PERMANENT COLOR	Hair is tinted all over with a peroxide-based formula. Fade-out time: 4–6 weeks. Try: L'Oréal Préférence, Clairol Clairesse, Revlon Colorsilk.	Good for blondes, and brunettes and brownettes with creamy or ruddy skin. Not recommended for redheads, brunettes and brownettes with sallow or olive skin because color will fade to brassy reddish-orange tones.

ERIC ROMAN

Coloring can be tricky and though you can get great color at home, consider going to a pro the first few times you color your hair. You can take advantage of his or her professional experience, new special-effects techniques and colors available only at salons. Vivid examples, here: an array of vegetable dyes from Jazzing by Clairol and...

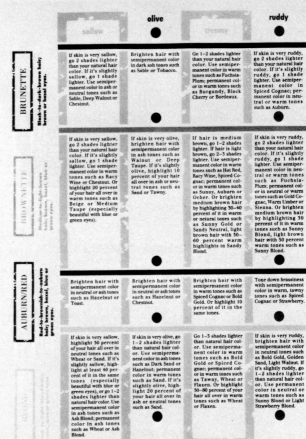

	sallow	olive	creamy	ruddy
BRUNETTE Black-to-dark-brown hair; brown or hazel eyes.	If skin is very sallow, go 2 shades lighter than your natural hair color. If it's slightly sallow, go 1 shade lighter. Use semipermanent color in ash or neutral tones such as Sable, Deep Walnut or Chestnut.	Brighten hair with semipermanent color in dark ash tones such as Sable or Tobacco.	Go 1–2 shades lighter than your natural hair color. Use semipermanent color in warm tones such as Fuchsia-Plum; permanent color in warm tones such as Burgundy, Black Cherry or Bordeaux.	If skin is very ruddy, go 2 shades lighter than your natural hair color. If it's slightly ruddy, go 1 shade lighter. Use semipermanent color in Spiced Cognac; permanent color in neutral or warm tones such as Auburn.
BROWNETTE Medium-to-light-brown hair; brown, hazel, blue or green eyes.	If skin is very sallow, go 2 shades lighter than your natural hair color. If it's slightly sallow, go 1 shade lighter. Use semipermanent color in warm tones such as Racy Wine or Chestnut. Or highlight 20 percent of your hair all over in warm tones such as Beige or Medium Taupe (especially beautiful with blue or green eyes).	If skin is very olive, brighten hair with semipermanent color in ash tones such as Walnut or Deep Taupe. If it's slightly olive, highlight 10 percent of your hair all over in ash or neutral tones such as Sand or Tawny.	If hair is medium brown, go 1–2 shades lighter. If hair is light brown, go 2–3 shades lighter. Use semipermanent color in warm tones such as Hot Red, Racy Wine, Spiced Cognac; permanent color in warm tones such as Sunny, Auburn or Ocher. Or brighten medium brown hair by highlighting 50–40 percent of it in warm or netural tones such as Sunny Gold or Sandy Neutral, light brown hair with 50–60 percent warm highlights in Sandy Blond.	If skin is very ruddy, go 2 shades lighter than your natural hair color. If it's slightly ruddy, go 1 shade lighter. Use semipermanent color in neutral or warm tones such as Fuchsia-Plum; permanent color in neutral or warm tones such as Gold Cognac, Warm Umber or Sienna. Or brighten medium brown hair by highlighting 50 percent of it in warm tones such as Sunny Blond, light brown hair with 50 percent warm tones such as Sunny Blond.
AUBURN/RED Red-to-brownish-to-auburn hair; brown, hazel, blue or green eyes.	Brighten hair with semipermanent color in neutral or ash tones such as Hazelnut or Toast.	Brighten hair with semipermanent color in neutral or ash tones such as Hazelnut or Chestnut.	Brighten hair with semipermanent color in warm tones such as Spiced Cognac or Bold Gold. Or highlight 10 percent of it in the same tones.	Tone down brassiness with semipermanent color in warm, tawny tones such as Spiced Cognac or Strawberry.
BLONDE	If skin is very sallow, highlight 50 percent of your hair all over in neutral tones such as Wheat or Sand. If it's slightly sallow, highlight at least 40 percent of it in the same tones (especially beautiful with blue or green eyes), or go 1–2 shades lighter than natural hair color. Use semipermanent color in ash tones such as Ash Blond; permanent color in ash tones such as Wheat or Ash Blond.	If skin is very olive, go 1–2 shades lighter than natural hair color. Use semipermanent color in ash tones such as Dark Sand or Hazelnut; permanent color in warm tones such as Sand. If it's slightly olive, highlight 20 percent of your hair all over in ash or neutral tones such as Sand.	Go 1–3 shades lighter than natural hair color. Use semipermanent color in warm tones such as Bold Gold or Spiced Cognac; permanent color in warm tones such as Tawny, Wheat or Flaxen. Or highlight 50–80 percent of your hair all over in warm tones such as Wheat or Flaxen.	If skin is very ruddy, brighten hair with semipermanent color in neutral tones such as Bold Gold, Golden Sand, Light Walnut. If it's slightly ruddy, go 1–2 shades lighter than natural hair color. Use permanent color in neutral or warm tones such as Sunny Blond or Light Strawberry Blond.

How bright can your colorist go without making you look artificial? Check out the chart by Leland Hirsch. It takes the haziness out of hair coloring. Find your natural hair color on the left, then look across to your skin tone. P.S.—As the tints and highlighters make your locks luminous, they'll strengthen and condition them, too.

the bright touch

CHRIS BAKER

1004
Joanne Mancino Art Director/Illustrator
Tom Hall Design Director
Long Beach State Univ. Visual Communication
Design Workshop Agency
Long Beach Museum of Art Client
Hermosa Beach CA

1005
Rick St. Vincent Art Director
Edward Leighton Designer
Harry Shilling Copywriter
St. Vincent, Milone & McConnells Inc. Agency
Dorr-Oliver Inc. Client
New York NY

The mark of durability.

If you want to know how old a tree is, look at the rings. And if you want to predict the life span of a piece of pulp mill equipment, check out the manufacturer's nameplate. If you find the name Dorr-Oliver, then you know the equipment has been built to deliver decades of dependable, on line service.

At Dorr-Oliver we build equipment like complete reacausticizing systems, pulp washers and thickeners, screens, savealls and waste treatment products to perform and to last.

We build equipment in our own modern plant, with quality conscious shop people who care. We use the latest computer controlled machine tools and advanced manufacturing technology. So when a Dorr-Oliver quality inspector writes "O.K. to ship" on your work order, you can be sure you're getting the most reliable equipment your money can buy. That's because we know that the quality of what you do depends on the quality of what we do.

Depend on us. Write Bob Adams, pulp and paper industry manager, for our new booklet on how Dorr-Oliver serves your industry. Dorr-Oliver, Stamford, CT 06904.

DORR-OLIVER
A step ahead in process equipment

The standard of service.

At Dorr-Oliver we know how important on time is to your mill. On time delivery of equipment. On time parts supply. Quick response to your questions or needs.

So on time is important to us. We have remodeled our manufacturing plant and equipped it with modern machine tools and systems to make certain we can meet urgent delivery requirements. We've installed a highly effective computer controlled parts supply system that accelerates delivery of critical spare parts. Our field service engineers respond quickly to emergency downtime situations.

You can look to Dorr-Oliver for quality products such as complete reacausticizing systems, pulp washers and thickeners, savealls, pulp screens, and wastewater treatment equipment. Equally important, you can look to us for quality service. That's because we know that the quality of what you do depends on the quality of what we do.

Take some time. Write Bob Adams, pulp and paper industry manager, for a copy of our new booklet on how Dorr-Oliver serves your industry. Dorr-Oliver, Stamford, CT 06904.

DORR-OLIVER
A step ahead in process equipment

1006
Alain Escot, J. Larcher Art Directors
Imprimerie Pantinoise Agency/Client
Larcher Workshop Studio
Cergy. France

the DANGEROUS D ANISH
and other tales of

As I sit down to begin writing this article, I feel a familiar reluctance rising in me. I don't *want* to write. I don't want to have to sit facing this blank sheet of paper while the painful excitement and the heavy dread of writing grapple in my chest. I hate saying good-bye to all the little pleasures that have to be set aside for work: the freedom to browse mindlessly through magazines, the swing of physical activity, the life of the senses, the coziness of my own habitual thoughts. As the moment draws near when I can no longer put off starting, all the denied delights fuse into a single, seductive image, somehow charged and made more potent by the anxiety of approaching work. I don't want to write, I want . . . I want . . .

I want an Entenmann's raspberry Danish twist! No. I want *two*. And if nobody is around to watch me, I will grab a handful of dollars, tiptoe down the stairs, scurry across the street to the deli, buy them (avoiding the cynical eyes of the counterman, who I'm sure *knows* I'm not having ten friends over for coffee and cake), rush upstairs, and . . .

And indulge in my own bizarre secret-eating ritual, unique to me, yet not so different from that of millions of other women eating furtively all across America. I will gouge my fingers into the gutters of raspberry jam. I will pick off and devour the icing, the butter crumbs and the nuts, leaving only the dough, the part that

BY ANNIE GOTTLIEB

(cont'd on p.256)

E CRET **EATING**

Having a craving for cookies? Suffering a Big Mac attack? Undergoing a cheesecake crisis? You're not the only one. All over America, women are snacking on the sly—and feeling guilty about it

1007
Paula Greif Art Director
Wynn Dan Designer
MADEMOISELLE, Conde Nast Client
New York NY

1008
Fritz Haase Art Director/Designer
Atelier Haase + Knels Agency
Druckerei Asendorf Production
BDG Bremen Client
Bremen. West Germany

1009
Jason Calfo Art Director
Doug May Designer
Mary Woods Writer
Carnese Inc. Design Firm
World Typeface Center Inc. Client
New York NY

Vorbildliche Schriftgestaltung aus den USA des Type Directors Club of New York · Überseemuseum Bremen · 9.–30. März 1984

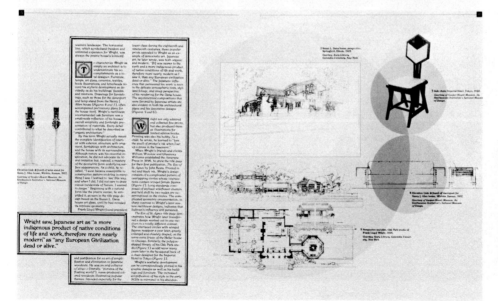

1010
Marshall Harmon Art Director
Lucille Tenazas Designer
Harmon Kemp Inc. Agency
Lee Daniels Printing Production
International Paper Company Client
New York NY

1011
Johann Hoekstra Art Director/Designer
Eugene Hardy Copywriter
Grey-Phillips, Bunton, Mundel & Blake Agency
Liberty Life Client
Johannesburg, RSA

Springhill Reports:

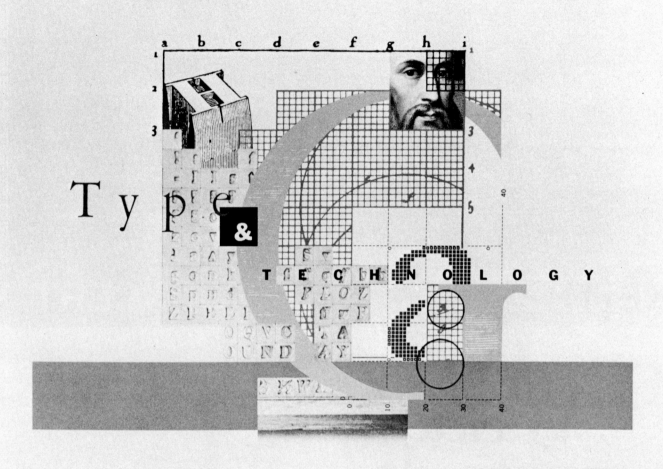

Type & TECHNOLOGY

KEITH JARRETT IN CONCERT

What not to do in bed.

You can read.

You can rest.

You can sleep.

You can make phone calls.

You can eat breakfast.

You can watch television.

You can listen to music.

You can exercise.

You can snore.

You can even eat crackers—
provided you're alone.

And yes, you can snuggle.

But don't ever light up a cigarette
when you're in bed.

Because if you doze off just once,
all your dreams can go up in smoke.

R.J. Reynolds Tobacco Company

1012

Rolf Laub, Peat Jariya Art Directors
Peat Jariya Illustrator
University of Houston Client
Houston TX

1013

Paul Blade Art Director
Jack Silverman Copywriter
Leber Katz Partners Advertising Agency
R.J. Reynolds Tobacco Co. Client
New York NY

1014

Edwin Torres Art Director/Designer
Moshe Brakha Photographer
Jeff Weiss Copywriter
PROpaganda Production
ISLAND Magazine Client
New York NY

1015

Louise Kollenbaum Art Director
Dian-Aziza Ooka Designer
Mackenzie & Harris Typesetting
MOTHER JONES Magazine Client
San Francisco CA

1016

Michael Rosen, Ann O'Daniel Art Directors
John E. Hankwitz Photography
Joe Sraeel Copywriter
Hammond Farrell Inc. Agency
ASEA Industrial Systems Client
New York NY

Q'UESTCE QUE SAY LA, what time is it hollywood?

Q: WHAT'S NEW NEW?

A: HOLLYWOOD COWBOYS. (I MEAN CADILLAC COWBOYS)

Caring Sharing Relating
THE *man/woman* TREND *of* TODAY

JILL (not her real name, which is Alison) is 33. With her high cheekbones, friendly smile and good posture, she could easily be taken for a new-products-marketing group head, or perhaps a planning-and-development research coordinator. Surprisingly, though, she is an administrative policy liaison, working at a large Chicago corporation. • A few weeks ago, Jill met Kevin (Michael, actually), 41. People who meet Kevin feel instantly drawn toward him, and Jill was no exception. With his lean, spare body and easygoing manner, Kevin has the look of a telephone lineman who fools you by not looking anything like a telephone lineman and instead resembling a shale derivatives consultant. He is a bassoonist. • The two met at the Jade Palate, a fashionable Chinese restaurant on the North Side. "He overheard me ordering the Five Happiness Special Sea Biscuits," Jill remembers, "and he leaned over and said, 'Not without a side of gamma globulin, you don't.' Well, I'm not normally that impulsive about things, but I switched to the Chicken With Flavor Taste right away. A week later, we were living together. • "At first, it was incredibly intense," she continues. "We had both 'been with' people before—Kevin had been married, in fact—but neither of us had felt so close to anybody. Other men would listen to my life story, but Kevin actually optioned it. I had sometimes had a hard time in relationships before, and at first I had a lot of trouble letting myself be comfortable with being vulnerable—vulnerable to what, I'm not sure, maybe just to being comfortable. And I wondered if being open to being vulnerable to being trusted to be comfortable being honest still lets you be free, or if you have to close off some of the closeness in order to have the selfness as well as the otherness. I felt that we were moving out of a place that was 'we' into a place that was 'us'; from 'each other' into 'one another.' And I guess I didn't know if I was ready for that." • Kevin, too, remembers the early days of the relationship as exhilarating and special. "With Jill," he says, "I felt that I was discovering all kinds of intimate places inside myself. My pancreas, for example, is shaped like a little booth at a cocktail lounge, and of course it's pretty dark in there." • Soon, though, Jill began to feel that "something was missing. I was discovering that I wanted a deeper kind of commitment," she says. "More than that, I found myself wanting all kinds of things that my parents had wanted, things I thought I would never want.

• *by* **CHARLIE HAAS** • *Illustration by Mary K. Brown*

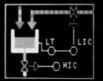

soft
sell

1017
Alan Bottger Art Director/Designer
Mark Cohen Photographer
Linda Chadsey Copywriter
Wm Joseph Bologna Int'l Agency
Key Parmaceuticals, Inc. Client
New York NY

1018
Janet Nebel Art Director/Designer
Susie Fitzhugh Photographer
The Woods Group, Inc. Agency
Johns Hopkins Hospital Client
Baltimore MD

WHEN I GROW UP
I'LL CARRY A STICK
AND BE
VERY DIGNIFIED
I'LL HAVE A WATCH
THAT WILL REALLY TICK
MY HOUSE WILL BE TALL
AND BUILT OF
BRICK AND NO ONE
WILL GUESS
THAT IT'S JUST
A TRICK
AND I'M REALLY
MYSELF INSIDE

RADIO

Pura: Other Other Cooking Oils

MVO: If if you look look on the back of the pack pack of some solid cooking cooking oils you'll notice notice that other things things are added added like animal animal oil oil...So they're not not pure vegetable oil oil like they used to be be...

If you look on a Pura pack you'll see only one ingredient...100% pure vegetable oil...There's nothing else added.

So don't be confused confused about added ingredients ingredients ingredients in other solid cooking cooking oils...

Insist on Pura solid vegetable oil.

110% pure vegetable oil...

with no added extras extras.

1020

Steve Ward Copywriter
Ayer Barker Ltd. Agency
Molinaire Sound Studio Studio
Steve Ward Production
Pura Lard—Brittania Client
London, England

I.G.I.

SFX: Music up and under

FV: Michael?...

MV: Yes, dear.

FV: Michael, I know it's too late now, but I do so wish you'd listened to my father and insisted your broker insure you with IGI. You'd have been paid out weeks ago, you know. Why, only yesterday at the club, Daddy was saying that when it comes to the payout, IGI don't go into reverse.

MV: Pity it wasn't Daddy's Porsche you backed over the cliff.

MVO: For all your insurance...your car, your, business, your home, your life...IGI. We don't hassle, we pay.

1021

Les Sharpe Creative Director
Wynn Crane Copywriter
Preller Sharpe Rice Agency
Audio arts Studio
I.G.I. Client
Johannesburg, RSA

Friendship Cottage Cheese #1: "Sidesaddle"

SFX: Driving noises, car shifting gears, horns, traffic, etc.

MOTHER: So, Miss Career Nut, did you get a raise?

DAUGHTER: No, Ma. *Men* get raises. *Women* get roses.

MOTHER: Well, a rose...is a rose...is never a raise I always say.

DAUGHTER: Oh I give up. I feel like eating an entire strawberry cheesecake.

MOTHER: You will not! Instead, we'll go right home, we'll get out the blender, and put a big container of Friendship Cottage Cheese in it. Fresh, soothing, not-so-fattening.

DAUGHTER: Ma, watch out for that car!

(SFX: Screeching tires)

MOTHER: Then...we'll add a pint of strawberries and a teaspoon of vanilla to the Friendship Cottage Cheese.

DAUGHTER: If we live that long.

MOTHER: Then...we'll put the pretty pink blended stuff in the freezer...

DAUGHTER: Sounds like strawberry cheesecake ice cream!

MOTHER: Yeah, but it's *much* kinder to your thighs. (SFX: Screech, crash!!) Agh! Men drivers!

DAUGHTER: Men...women...Life doesn't make sense, Ma!

MOTHER: Toots...if life made sense, *men* would ride side saddle.

ANNCR: Friendship Cottage Cheese. When you know what good is.

Friendship Cottage Cheese #2: "Carlos"

SFX: Kitchen noises, tea kettle whistling, water running, etc.

DAUGHTER: Hey Ma...you know I've really grown to *like* Friendship Cottage Cheese.

MOTHER: See...Friendship is good anytime. And it's not just what you eat for a week after you eat a whole chocolate cake for lunch. In fact, Friendship is *better* than chocolate cake.

DAUGHTER: It is? What gave you *that* idea?

MOTHER: Therapy.

DAUGHTER: (Pause) *You* were in therapy? Why?

MOTHER: Well...I couldn't decide whether to marry your father. Or Carlos.

DAUGHTER: (Pause) Car-los?

MOTHER: Oh could he cha-cha! What a dreamboat! But you see, Carlos was like chocolate cake. For ecstasy, you pay. *What a bum.*

DAUGHTER: And Daddy?

MOTHER: Oh Daaddy...Well Daaddy is like Friendship Cottage Cheese. Always sweet. Always fresh. Doesn't make me break out. *What a doll.*

ANNCR: Friendship Cottage Cheese. When you know what good is.

MOTHER: I wonder if Carlos is in the phone book?

DAUGHTER: Ma!

Friendship Cottage Cheese #3: "Sushi"

SFX: Japanese music and people in background

MOTHER: ...So this is a Japanese sushi bar. What are those pretty canapés?

DAUGHTER: That's sushi, Ma. Taste.

MOTHER: Raw fish? I'd rather clean the oven.

DAUGHTER: C'mon, Ma...

MOTHER: I'll have some Friendship Cottage Cheese, thank you. Fresh. Sweet. Cooked.

DAUGHTER: The Japanese don't know from Friendship Cottage Cheese, Ma.

MOTHER: What! So maybe you should open a Friendship Bar in Tokyo...

DAUGHTER: Ma...

MOTHER: For lunch, you could serve them Friendship Low-Fat with chopped vegetables. For dinner, you know honey, you could go Friendship California Style. You could put fruit, nuts, raisins...

DAUGHTER: Ma...people are staring!

MOTHER: (whispers) For breakfast, you could serve them Friendship Pineapple Cottage Cheese in a bowl, nice, and cut up a banana on top!

DAUGHTER: Oh, Ma...just like you did for me when I was a baby...

MOTHER: That's right. You know, when you were a baby the only food you'd eat was Friendship Cottage Cheese. Everything else, you'd spit across the room.

ANNCR: Friendship Cottage Cheese. When you know what good is.

1022

Dianne Fiumara, Jane Hrubec Art Directors
Jane Hrubec Copywriter
Louise Lasser, Arlene Sorkin Talent
Ogilvy & Mather Partners Agency
Mary Miranda Producer
Friendship Cottage Cheese Client
New York NY

Ryan Homes
"Changes"

MUSIC: Instrumental theme

BOB: The changes are subtle, at first. You get up earlier. You're an expert on lawns and interior decoration. What's happening? (PAUSE) You've bought *a house.* It's *your* house. Now you can invite people to come by *the house.* Saturdays, you work around *the house.*

A house is a sanctuary, and a worthy investment. It's also *yours.*

Ryan's been helping people like you find their way home for 36 years. Right not there are over 15 Ryan Homes communities around Atlanta...homes that are attractive, energy efficient and start in the 40's. And we have our own mortgage company.

We can help you get your own home. Look for our ad in Sunday's paper, then come see us. Just follow our directions, because we know the way home.

SING OUT: "Ryan knows the way home, Ryan knows the way home."

1023

Mark Johnson Copywriter/Producer
Jack Turner, Oliver Wells Composers
Garret/Lewis/Johnson Agency
Doppler, Atlanta Production
Ryan Homes Client
Atlanta GA

1984 Capri
"Picture This"

SFX: Music begins with "standard" rock...

1st ANNCR: Picture this for a second.

SFX: Music starts to evolve into something more unique.

1st ANNCR: Approximately two and a half feet in front of your car radio, a different song is being played.

SFX: Music is now a blending of original music & SFX.

1st ANNCR: The song of a turbocharger,

SFX: Musical whirrr...

1st ANNCR: spinning at over 100,000 RPM's. In harmony, Bosch Multi-Port

SFX: Musical "squiring" effect

1st ANNCR: Electronic

SFX: Add electronic SFX.

1st ANNCR: Fuel Injection. Total Effect? The rush of Power:

SFX: Music and SFX build.

1st ANNCR: 145 High Tech Horsepower that can push you right back in your seat.
If this sounds good to you, this may sound even better.

SFX: Sudden silence

1st ANNCR: This engine comes in a car that's sticker-priced under 10,500 dollars.
Repeat...
Under 10,500 dollars.
The car? The 2.3 litre, 5-speed Mercury Capri Turbo RS.

SFX: Music swells as Doppler effect begins: Car accelerating from afar, passing by, receding into distance

1st ANNCR: Finally, a performance car that's in tune with your desires is also in tune with your budget.

SFX: Hushed wind noise & music to fade

2nd ANNCR: Horsepower rating as measured by SAE J-1349. Sticker price excludes title, taxes and destination charges.

1984 Capri
"Last Time"

SFX: Music begins with "standard rock" (but different rock from comm'l #1)

1st ANNCR: When was the last time you turned off your car radio

SFX: Music starts to go away

1st ANNCR: just so you could listen to the throb of a robust engine and the singing of high performance tires?

SFX: Silence as the question sinks in

1st ANNCR: That long, huh?

SFX: Capri theme begins to come up

1st ANNCR: Well, now, there's a car that's actually worth listening to.

SFX: Turbo SFX merge with music

1st ANNCR: The new Mercury Carpri Turbo RS

SFX: Turbo SFX merge with music

1st ANNCR: Propelled by an AiResearch Turbocharger that spins at over 100,000 RPM's

SFX: Whoosh SFX inside intake manifold

1st ANNCR: ...and is fed by
Bosch Multi-Port

SFX: Musical Squirt SFX

1st ANNCR: Electronic Fuel Injection

SFX: Musical Squirt SFX

1st ANNCR: ...The Capri puts out 145 decidedly healthy horse power from just 2.3 litres. If that sounds pretty good to you, this may sound even better.

SFX: Sudden silence

1st ANNCR: The sticker price is under 10,500 dollars! Repeat...

SFX: Tape rewinds

1st ANNCR: The sticker price is under 10,500 dollars!

SFX: Doppler SFX

1st ANNCR: The Mercury Capri Turbo RS. A more enlightened approach to performance.
Even with the radio on.

2nd ANNCR: Horse power rating as measured by SAE J-1349. Sticker price excludes title, taxes and destination charges.

1984 Capri
"Turn Off Your Radio"

SFX: Music begins with "standard rock" (but different rock from comm'ls #1 and #2)

1st ANNCR: Turn off your car radio for 5 seconds and listen to the sound of your engine.

SFX: A few seconds of dead silence

1st ANNCR: Not exactly thrilling, is it? *Now,* listen to this.

SFX: Turbo wail, pistons drumming, then our unique Capri theme music blends with appropriate SFX.

1st ANNCR: This engine is fed by

SFX: Appropriate SFX

1st ANNCR: Bosch Multi-Port Electronic Fuel Injection. It's propelled by an AiResearch turbocharger that spins at over 100,000 RPM's.

SFX: Whoosh SFX inside intake manifold

SFX: Powerful musical SFX

1st ANNCR: And stuffs 145 horse power into just 2.3 litres. Sound pretty good? It *is.* Especially if you consider that this engine comes in a car which you can actually afford.

SFX: Car SFX and music back up

1st ANNCR: The car?
The new Mercury Capri Turbo RS. The sticker price? Under 10,500 dollars!
The 1984 Mercury Capri Turbo RS. A more enlightened approach for you. And a much-needed rest for your radio.

2nd ANNCR: Horse power rating as measured by SAE J-1349. Sticker price excludes title, taxes and destination charges.

1024

Josh Carlisle Copywriter
Justin Mobray, Hunter Murtaugh Music
Studio 55 Recording Studion, Howard Schwartz Recording Studios
HEA Productions, Inc. Production
Lincoln-Mercury Client
New York NY

Mickey Gilley for Dr Pepper

ANNOUNCER: For Dr Pepper, here's Mickey Gilley

MICKEY GILLEY: In a world where people do their best to try and be like all the rest, it's such a joy to see true originality, and if you take your time and hold the line soon you're gonna see.

BACKGROUND VOCALS: It's wait-in there for you, and all you gotta do is...

MICKEY GILLEY: Hold out for the out of the ordinary. Hold out for Dr Pepper, don't be sold out! It's a taste that's extraordinary, there's no doubt it's Dr Pepper. (Repeat.)

Irene Cara for Dr Pepper

ANNOUNCER: For Dr Pepper, here's Irene Cara.

IRENE CARA: In a world where people do their best to try and be like all the rest, it's such a joy to see true originality, and if you take your time and hold the line soon you're gonna see.

BACKGROUND VOCALS: It's wait-in there for you, and all you gotta do is...

IRENE CARA: Hold out for the out of the ordinary. Hold out for Dr Pepper, don't be sold out! It's a taste that's extraordinary, you know there's no doubt it's Dr Pepper. (Repeat and fade.)

Full Vocal for Dr Pepper

VOCAL: In a world where people do their best
to try and be like all the rest,
it's such a joy to see true originality,
and if you take your time and hold the line
soon you're gonna see.

It's wait-in there for you,
and all you gotta do is...

Hold out for the out of the ordinary. Hold out for Dr Pepper, don't be sold out! It's a taste that's extraordinary, there's no doubt it's Dr Pepper. (Repeat and fade.)

1025

Bill Appelman Copywriter
Hunter Murtaugh Music Producer
Young & Rubicam, Inc. Agency
Cherokee Recording, Automated Sound Studios
House of David, Crushing Enterprises, Inc. Production
Dr. Pepper Client
New York NY

Ribena #1
"Shakespeare"

AUDIO: (Class room noises under)

TEACHER: (English accent) Good day, class. Today we shall discuss some of the major contributions England has made to Western Civilization. Think of it—parliamentary democracy, Isaac Newton, Ribena, Shakes...
  Yes, Harris?

STUDENT: Ribena, sir?

TEACHER: Oh, tut, tut, Harris. I am disappointed. Ribena is an absolutely extraordinary fruit drink, made from the juice of fresh English black currants. It is quite possibly the finest beverage known to man.

STUDENT: Yes, sir, but can one really compare Ribena with Shakespeare and Newton and the Magna Carta...

TEACHER: One most certainly can. Was Sir Isaac Newton enriched with vitamin C?

STUDENT: Well, no, but...

TEACHER: Oh course he wasn't. Was Shakespeare concentrated? Could you add water to Shakespeare and make 5 times as much Shakespeare?

STUDENT: No, but,...(clutching at straws) but Ribena didn't help to colonize North America.

TEACHER: Ah, no...no, Harris, it didn't. It shall simply have to settle for helping to civilize it.

ANNCR: Ribena. Quite possibly the world's most civilized fruit drink.

Ribena #2
"Dickens"

AUDIO: (Classroom noises under)

TEACHER: (English accent) Alright class, as you recall, we've been discussing England's major contributions to the Western world and...(exasperated) Again, Harris?

HARRIS: Yes, sir.
  I believe we may still be a touch confused about how Ribena fits in. We know it's made from the juice of fresh English black currants and that it tastes very good, but to compare Ribena with the great Charles Dickens and the Industrial Revolution and...

TEACHER: Harris, can you imagine what the Industrial Revolution tasted like?

HARRIS: Ah, ...no, sir.

TEACHER: Can you imagine that it would compare to the refreshing black currant taste of Ribena?

HARRIS: I suppose not, sir. But *Dickens*?

TEACHER: Vitamin C, Harris.

HARRIS: Excuse me, sir?

TEACHER: Vitamin C. If you had read your Dickens somewhat more closely, you'd have found that his work displays a woeful lack of vitamin C.

HARRIS: Yes, sir. I suppose you're right, sir.

TEACHER: Oh, well. There's no need to belabour the obvious, Harris.

ANNCR: Ribena. Quite possibly the world's most civilized fruit drink.

Ribena #3
"Steam Engine"

AUDIO: (Class room noises under)

TEACHER: (English accent) Alright, class, let's continue with our discussion of how Ribena fits in with England's other contributions to civilization. Harris. Now that you've actually tasted Ribena, perhaps you'd honour us with some of your more profound thoughts on the subject.

HARRIS: Well, it's really good.

TEACHER: Another thoughtful analysis, eh Harris? But how does it compare to other things England is known for? The invention of the steam engine, for instance. Is a steam engine enriched with vitamin C?

HARRIS: Ah, no sir.

TEACHER: Ah. Well, has a steam engine ever approximated the extraordinary black currant taste of Ribena, then?

HARRIS: No, sir.

TEACHER: Well *there* you have it, Harris. The greatest example ever of England's technological might, and it doesn't hold a candle to Ribena.

HARRIS: But is that fair sir? Ribena couldn't take you across the country.

TEACHER: Harris, if you've already *got* Ribena, why would you need to go across the country?

ANNCR: Ribena. Quite possibly the world's most civilized fruit drink.

1026

Stephin Denvir Copywriter
Daina Liepa Production
Scali, McCabe, Sloves Agency
Bovril Canada, Inc. Client
Toronto, Canada

SYSTEL #1
"Marie"

MANAGER: Uh, Marie.

SECRETARY: Yes, Mr. Morrow.

MANAGER: The boss wants to see my recommendation on the new word processing system.

SECRETARY: It's being typed.

MANAGER: Typed, good. Uh, who's typing it, Marie?

SECRETARY: The SYSTEL.

MANAGER: The SYSTEL. Marie, you didn't buy a word processor without consulting me first, did you?

SECRETARY: A word processor requires a printer, Mr. Morrow.

MANAGER: Good! Well, I don't see a printer. Uh, but your electronic typewriter is going like blazes. And there is a little white box on...

SECRETARY: That's the SYSTEL!

MANAGER: It kind of looks like a word processor to me, Marie.

SECRETARY: It's different.

MANAGER: Uh. Good. What's the difference?

SECRETARY: The SYSTEL costs $4,000 *less*.

MANAGER: Marie, does the SYSTEL do word substitution?

SECRETARY: Uh huh!

MANAGER: Oh! Where's my recommendation that has the name of that other word processing system, could you sub...

SECRETARY: Substitute SYSTEL?

MANAGER: Yes.

SECRETARY: I already did!

MANAGER: Good. Fine. Good.

SECRETARY: Good decision, Mr. Morrow.

MANAGER: Do I have any more appointments this month?

SECRETARY: Not a one.

MANAGER: No. Good!

ANNOUNCER: Now you don't need a whole word processing system to do word processing. All you need is your electronic typewriter and SYSTEL.

  In this area, you can see the SYSTEL demonstrated at the following dealers:

SYSTEL #2
"Computer Cosmos"

SALESMAN: Hi there! Welcome to Computer Cosmos, your computer headquarters.

CUSTOMER: Hi there! I'm interested in a word processor.

SALESMAN: You name it, we got it.

CUSTOMER: SYSTEL.

SALESMAN: We don't have that one. Look, the first thing you're going to need is a word processor keyboard.

CUSTOMER: Not with SYSTEL. I can just use my electronic typewriter as a keyboard.

SALESMAN: The next thing you're going to need is a printer...

CUSTOMER: I don't need a printer with SYSTEL, I can just use my electronic typewriter. Tell you what...

SALESMAN: I've got a package deal here. I've got the printer, I've got the keyboard, I've got the CRT or the disk drive. Everything you need.

CUSTOMER: All I need is SYSTEL and my electronic typewriter. I've got to go now, bye!

SALESMAN: I'm even going to throw in word processing software.

CUSTOMER: SYSTEL comes with its own software. I've got to go, I'm double parked!

SALESMAN: I'm going to give you this desk here, all this stuff sits on. This big desk.

CUSTOMER: I don't need a big desk with SYSTEL. It's very compact. Well, nice meeting you.

SALESMAN: Hey, how about a computer coloring book...

CUSTOMER: Take care!

SALESMAN: Free crayons...

CUSTOMER: Good Bye!

SALESMAN: Balloons...

CUSTOMER: So long!

ANNOUNCER: Now you don't need a whole word processing system to do word processing. All you need is your electronic typewriter and SYSTEL.

1027

Chuck Lebo, John Crawford Copywriters
Chuck Lebo Agency Producer
Tycer-Fultz-Bellack Agency
John Crawford Producer
John Crawford, Radio Production Company
SYSTEL Computers, Inc. Client
Palo Alto CA

Mini Bonbel/Mini Babyel
"Arnold's Mother"

ARNOLD'S MOTHER: My son Arnold said he didn't want peanut butter and jelly for lunch anymore.

  So I said, "I'll give you a little round laughing cow in a red net bag."

  He said his teacher didn't allow animals.

  I said, "Tell her it's cheese."

  He said, "She'll know it's not cheese when it starts to moo."

  I said, "It doesn't moo, it just sits on a cracker."

  He said, "Even if it's quiet, she hates anything with four legs."

  I said, "Hold up the bag and tell her that's what your mother gave you for lunch."

  He said, "If my teacher sees that my mother gave me a laughing cow in a red net bag for lunch, she'll send me to a foster home."

I said, "Laughing Cow is cheese, Arnold. Five delicious bite-size cheeses freshly wrapped in wax with an easy open zip. Mild Mini Bonbel and nippy Mini Babybel. Semi-soft, delicious and natural. So they're good for you, Arnold."

He said, "You talked me into it, Ma."

So today Arnold went to school with the little round laughing cow in a red net bag. And tonight I have to pick him up at the foster home.

ANNCR: Mini Bonbel and Mini Babybel. Delectable cheeses by The Laughing Cow. They'll put a smile in your stomach. From Fromageries Bel. In your dairy case.

1028
Joy Golden Copywriter
Dottie Wilson Agency Producer
TBWA Agency Agency
12 East Recording Studio
Fromageries Bel, Inc. Client
New York NY

Telecom
"Bazaar"

SFX: Bazaar ambience—Crowd noise, hustle, bustle, snake charmer, etc., under.

PCHMN 1 (HUCKSTER): Yo, phones here! Got buttons, got a bell. You'll love it. Hey buddy... Yo, business phones, right here.

ANNCR: These days, everyone's selling business telephones. And everyone has a different pitch.

PCHMN 2 (COMPUTER VOICE): This state-of-the-art digital PBX integrates voice and data trans-missions, while offering parallel and serial interfaces for total office automation...

ANNCR: Who can you believe?

PCHMN 3 (SNOBBISH): Our system can grow to handle users equal to the population of Australia.

MUSIC: Up, under following:

ANNCR: Fortunately, there's Southwestern Bell Telecom. A new company with new ideas. But an old friend when it comes to telephones. We've shopped the market for you. And selected the best systems. From ITT, Northern Telecom, NEC, and others. We find out what your business needs, and recommend the system that fits. At a price that fits your budget. And we'll back it with the kind of service you've always counted on. So don't try to sort through this market by yourself.

PCHMN 1: Yo, it slices. It dices. It'll even call for carry-out...

ANNCR: Call 1-800-DIAL-SWB. Southwestern Bell Telecom. New ideas from the people who started it all.

MUSIC LOGO: Buttons Out.

1029
Mike Fickes Copywriter
Tim Butler Engineer
D'Arcy MacManus Masius, St. Louis Agency
Chicago Recording Company Studio
Dave Henke Production
Southwestern Bell Telecom Client
St. Louis MO

"Out of Shape"

CHORUS: Out of shape: Flabby, flabby, flabby flabby, flab
Overweight: Flabby, flabby, flabby flabby, flab
Getting soft, flabby, flabby, flabby, flabby, flab

PRIS: (simultaneously)Summer is fast approaching...

CHORUS: Butterball: Flabby, flabby, flabby, flabby, flab

And that means swimming suits and skimpy outfits...

CHORUS: Flab, flab, flab, flab, flab, flab, flab
Bad, bad, bad, bad, bad, bad, bad
(Under) Doo, do, do do, do do do do do do do do

PRIS: It's time to lose just a dab of that flab. We'll help you this Saturday from 1 to 3 p.m. at Muncie Mall, so that you can...

CHORUS: Get in shape: lookin' good now, startin' lookin' good

PRIS: Our physical fitness extravaganza...

CHORUS: Not too late: lookin' good now, lookin' mighty good

PRIS: With exercise demonstrations

CHORUS: Feelin' fit now, feelin' mighty fit

PRIS: Saturday from 1 to 3 p.m. at Muncie Mall.

CHORUS: Feelin' trim now, lookin' mighty trim...

1030
Randall L. Rohn Copywriter/Agency Producer
Simon Marketing Agency
Tapemasters, Inc. Studio
Mike Matheson, Priscilla Lindsay Talent
Muncie Mall Client
Indianapolis IN

Bohus for Chicago City Treasurer
"Don't Vote for Chris Bohus"

ANNCR: *Don't vote for Chris Bohus for Chicago City Treasurer.* Sure he's the *only* qualified candidate. A Certified Public Accountant...an experienced financial analyst. But who needs a financial expert like Chris Bohus to fill the Treasurer's job when you could have a politician instead? After all, it's *only* money...just millions really. And who could spend your money better than a politician? Who could explain where your money *went* better than a politician? And what could a smart C.P.A. like Chrish Bohus *possibly* know about your money that a smart politician hasn't already figured out? A politician is a natural for City Treasurer. Qualifications? Who needs those? Everybody knows it's *who* you know. And an accountant like Christ Bohus wouldn't even know which old crony gets what. So keep the financial expert *out* of the City Treasurer's Office. Don't vote for Christ Bohus on April 12th. You'll sleep a lot better knowing that a *politician* is handling *your* money.

BOHUS: Paid for by the Chris Bohus for Treasurer Campaign Fund.

1031
Stephanie Ross, Robert Qually Copywriters/Producers
Qually & Company, Inc. Agency
Harlan Hogan Voice-Over
Paul Libman Music Production
Chris Bohus Client
Chicago IL

Cincinnati Suburban Press
"Bruno Wants a Steak"

SFX: Ring.

WOMAN: (Thru filter) Cincinnati Suburban Press Classified. Can I help you?

MAN: (Whispering) I would like to sell a very unusual parrot.

WOMAN: A very unusual...

MAN: Parrot. Yes, he weighs five hundred pounds, and he eats raw meat.

WOMAN: Could you speak up, sir...

MAN: I'm afraid he'll hear me.

BRUNO: Bruno wanna steak!

MAN: Coming Bruno.

WOMAN: Well sir, your ad will appear in our family of 19 Cincinnati Suburban Press newspapers, reaching over 240,000 homes.

MAN: Oh good...good.

WOMAN: ...And at a very low cost.

BRUNO: Bruno wanna steak now!

MAN: Yes Bruno...nice birdie.

WOMAN: And how would you like the ad to read, sir?

MAN: One very large parrot...

BRUNO: Awk!

MAN: ...Well mannered, must sell.

BRUNO: Hey, who're you talkin' to?

MAN: Nobody.

BRUNO: Give me that phone. Who's this?

WOMAN: Cincinnati Suburban Press Classified.

BRUNO: I'm the parrot. I wanna place an ad.

WOMAN: Parrot?!

BRUNO: Used human for sale!

WOMAN: Used hum...?

BRUNO: House broken!

WOMAN: House br...?

BRUNO: Does tricks too. Listen to this, awk...Hey Howard, go mow the lawn, take out the trash Howard. Bring my slippers, roll over, awk.

ANNCR: Everything sells faster in Suburban Classified. Cincinnati Suburban Press.

JINGLE: Your Good News Neighbor.

ANNCR: To place a classified ad in our family of community newspapers, just call 528-6444.

1032
Horwitz, Mann & Bukvic Advertising, Inc. Agency
Cincinnati Suburban Press Client
Cincinnati OH

L.B. Foster
"Pipe"

ANNCR: How L.B. Foster Company can take the (SFX: BLEEP BLEEP) out of your life.

CONTRACTOR: I'll tell you about the worst BLEEP BLEEP day I ever had. I'm in the trailer waiting for eight miles of pipe to be delivered. You can't build a pipe line without pipe. When it finally gets here two days late, it isn't coated. Do you believe the BLEEP BLEEP nerve of those BLEEP BLEEP...

ANNCR: For more than eighty years, L.B. Foster has sold pipe, piling and rail. Maybe what makes us special is that we deliver orders not only *when* you need them, but *how* you need them. Because that's just as important.

CONTRACTOR: So the refinery calls and says, "Hi, Joe. How's the old job coming? Gonna meet the deadline, old buddy?" Right then, the truck driver walks in and asks me where he can put the pipe. And I tell him BLEEP BLEEP BLEEP BLEEP...

ANNCR: Whether you're laying an oil, gas or water line. Save yourself a headache. L.B. Foster can meet all you pipe needs, including fusion bonded coating.

CONTRACTOR: Then I called L.B. Foster. Next time, I'll call them first.

ANNCR: For pipe, piling, rail and value-added services, call L.B. Foster Company. We'll take the BLEEP BLEEP out of your life.

TAG: There's a Foster sales office right here in (Pittsburgh)...

1033
Ben Feiler Copywriter
Jane Arkus Creative Director
Marsteller, Inc. Agency
Jon Cohill Production
L.B. Foster Client
Pittsburgh PA

INDEX